French and Provençal Lexicography

Essays presented to honor

Alexander Herman Schutz

French and Provençal Lexicography

Edited by
Urban T. Holmes
and
Kenneth R. Scholberg

Ohio State University Press

Copyright © 1964 by the Ohio State University Press
All Rights Reserved
Library of Congress Catalogue Card Number: 64–17108

Foreword

WITH this volume the friends of Alexander Herman Schutz, the administration of the Ohio State University, the Ohio State University Press, and his colleagues in the Department of Romance Languages of the Ohio State University, express their gratitude for the many years of stimulating and affectionate association they have shared with him. Some of those whom he has known best are not represented in these pages because of other commitments, but all join in wishing him many more happy and fruitful years. Those who have known him well have never found him wanting.

The articles presented are arranged, roughly, in three categories which emphasize the field of research that have concerned him most: Old French lexicography, Provençal lexicography, and Renaissance French lexicography. The fields of General Romance linguistics and stylistics, in which he has also been interested, are also included.

URBAN T. HOLMES

KENNETH R. SCHOLBERG

Contents

Alexander Herman Schutz
   Urban T. Holmes   3

Part I: General and Old French Studies

Lexicography and Stylistics
   Helmut Hatzfeld   13

The *Pucelle* Is Not for Burning
   Eleanor Webster Bulatkin   30

Les Gloses Françaises dans le Pentateuque de Raschi
   Raphael Levy   56

The Affective and Expressive Values of Verb-Complement Compounds in Romance
   Frederick Koenig   81

Pleine Sa Hanste in the *Chanson de Roland*
   Julian Harris   100

Carestia
   Henry and Renée Kahane   118

Part II: Old Provençal

Quelques Observations sur le Texte des *Vidas* and des *Razos* dans les Chansonniers Provençaux AB et IK
   Jean Boutière   125

The Name of the Troubadour Dalfin d'Alvernhe
   Stanley C. Aston   140

Three Little Problems of Old Provençal Syntax
   Kurt Lewent   164

Flamenca Gleanings
    Edward B. Ham   183

The Lady from Plazensa
    Frank M. Chambers   196

The Vocabulary of the New Testament in Provençal
    Robert White Linker   210

Part III: Renaissance French

Flux et Reflux du Vocabulaire Français au
XVIe Siècle
    Raymond Lebègue   219

Archaism in Ronsard's Theory of a Poetic Vocabulary
    Isidore Silver   227

Montaigne's Later Latin Borrowings
    William L. Wiley   246

The Coins in Rabelais
    Robert Harden   257

Bibliography of Alexander Herman Schutz
    Kenneth R. Scholberg   275

Abbreviations Used in the Text and Footnotes

FEW	W. von Wartburg, *Französisches etymologisches Wörterbuch* (Bonn, 1928——)
P.C.	Pillet-Carstens, *Bibliographie der Troubadours* (Halle, 1933)
REW	Wilhelm Meyer-Lübke, *Romanisches etymologisches Wörterbuch* (3 ed.; Heidelberg, 1935)
RLR	*Revue des langues romanes*
Tobler-Lommatzsch	Adolf Tobler and Erhard Lommatzsch, *Altfranzösisches Wörterbuch* (Berlin: Weidman, 1925–63)
ZRPh	*Zeitschrift für romanische Philologie*

French and Provençal Lexicography

―――――――――*Urban T. Holmes*―――――――――

Alexander Herman Schutz

MY ASSOCIATION with Alex Schutz has been so close over the past forty years that it would be difficult for me to write about him in an impersonal way. Those who have observed our attachment to each other during the years will understand this very well.

Alexander Herman Schutz was born in Chicago on March 27, 1894. His father, a merchant, had migrated to this country from East Prussia; and although he always remained a small businessman, he had a fine mind and spoke many languages. For years he wrote his son a weekly card in Hebrew, which he used well and wittily; and I can remember many a passage which Alex read to me. His mother, a native of Rumania, was a charming person who spoke French to her son almost constantly. It is not difficult to understand that their son chose to become a philologist. Another talent of his which was thoroughly developed was music. During his early teaching career, Alex continued to be a very good violinist.

Alex's principal education was in the Chicago public schools. He obtained his Ph.B. degree from the University of Chicago in 1915, and after this he was obliged to seek a teaching position. He went to the University of Mississippi for two years as an instructor in French. At the outbreak of World War I, however, he was drafted and served in France with the Army Engineer Corps (Railroad Division).

Those were trying times for almost everyone; but Alex has a droll sense of humor and his stories of those war years have always been most entertaining. Since he spoke French beautifully, he was in constant employment as an interpreter, meeting people of all kinds. Some of these individuals appear in a French reading book which he wrote many years later. His division was not assigned to active combat, but he came very close to it on one occasion when German shock troops broke through the American front lines. With the war over, he was given a year of graduate study at the University of Montpellier where his chief mentor and frequent companion was Professor Millardet. It was this association which influenced him greatly in the direction of Provençal.

Back in America, he received his master's degree from the University of Chicago in 1920, where his principal teacher was Professor T. A. Jenkins. He remained in the graduate school without interruption until he was granted the Ph.D. in August, 1922. Another influence from the war years, which he had spent among people in the French provinces, may be seen in his choice of a dissertation topic. It was rather unusual for that time: "The Peasant Vocabulary of George Sand." He had acquired an interest in the later development of the French language.

In those days most of the students who were working toward the doctorate in romance languages at the University of Chicago had a study room in the library building which was officially designated as W32. Each occupant had a small writing space with a drawer for papers and a shelf for books.

There was a flat roof just outside the window which seemed to them admirably suited for an "open air café." For years Alex remained a loyal alumnus of that room, and the stories which centered around W32 warmed the hearts of those of us who had never studied there. I knew the room only from several visits in later years.

Professor Karl Pietsch of the University of Chicago faculty has a special place in the memory of his students. His devotion to Old Spanish syntax and the inimitable accent with which he dictated titles of books and articles in his course in Romance bibliography made a deep impression on those who took his course. I have said that the Pietsch accent was inimitable, but Alex Schutz could reproduce it beautifully, always in respectful admiration.

Alex's closest friends among his fellow students at Chicago were Louis H. Allen, of Toronto, and William S. Hendrix, who was on leave from the Ohio State University. These three "pundits" received their doctorates at the same commencement. Their picture was taken formally together, in cap and gown. Fellow students referred to the photograph as the "Three Wise Men." Robert Valentine Merrill was another warm friend who continued to play a part in Alex's life.

His first job after receiving the doctorate was at the Iowa State Teachers' College at Cedar Falls, where the head of department was George A. Underwood, who became a warm admirer. He recognized the younger man's great potentialities and advised him to take a post at a large university as soon as he could. It was then that Alex went to the University of Missouri in the fall of 1923, and it was there that we met and our friendship began. I had been fortunate enough to acquire the rank of assistant professor. Schutz has never had a trace of jealousy in his makeup during his whole life; but he did want a promotion very much. I can hear him now saying: "Holmes, I am not in the profession until I am an assistant professor." We made great plans together. We organized all sorts of philological courses, which, very obligingly, the department at the University of Missouri allowed us to introduce. We dreamed of a journal (which, just as we wished it, came into existence some thirty-seven years later as *Romance Notes*, at the University of North Carolina).

My association with him, in those early years, meant much for my professional competency; I only hope that I benefited Alex Schutz as much as he did me. We came from different environments, from the University of Chicago and from Harvard University, but each had something to give the other. During the summer of 1925, we were together in Chicago when I received my call to the University of North Carolina. My acceptance broke forever our daily association, but it was the beginning of a long and fruitful relationship by correspondence. Alex returned that September to Columbia, Missouri; he was promoted and took over all the philological courses in the department, including Old French. During the next two years, his warmest friends were Professor Hermann B. Almstedt, head of the German Department, and Professor W. J. Burner, who taught Spanish. Both men were considerably older than Alex. Burner was a homespun wit whose nasal drawl still rings in my ears: "Well, boys, it'll all be the same a hundred years from now." Burner's attachment to Alex can be seen in the fact that he followed him to Ohio State, where Burner received his doctorate in 1930 when he was fifty-two years old.

Louis Allen, who died in the early 1930's, taught at Ohio

State in the summer of 1926. He agreed with Professor Hendrix that the post in French philology at that institution could be very well filled by their old friend Alex Schutz. Alex went there in September, 1927. He married Deborah Libauer, of Baltimore, in 1929—a marriage which has been most happy during these thirty-five years. I saw Schutz and his bride in Paris during the summer of 1930. Some of his best stories date from that time, particularly those that concern visits the three of us made to the Flea Market. Alex often describes me getting on the Metro with a medieval battle axe which I had bought at the Flea Market resting on my shoulder.

His career began to develop fully in Columbus. He was made an associate professor in 1933, a full professor in 1938. Recently, he served as director of graduate studies in his department. Immediately after his call to Columbus, he became very active in research. At first, he wanted to prepare an edition of the poems of the troubadour, the Dalfin d'Alvernhe. This was in 1928. The plan was blocked, however, when he learned that someone else had undertaken the same project, so he turned to Daude de Pradas, with results that can be seen in his bibliography. I collaborated with him on a history of the French language and on a source book on this same subject. It was not easy to get these into print, for we had an original approach that was not appreciated by everyone.

Alex continued in Provençal and the history of the French language, and he served two terms on the editorial committee of the Modern Language Association as adviser in these subjects. He has always enjoyed the *Gargantua* and the *Pantagruel* of Rabelais, for his own humor is based on a delight in the Rabelaisian incongruities. The fact that most of his teaching has been confined to the medieval period is the only reason that he has not devoted much time to Renaissance research. After World War II, he had some thought of investigating the possible influence of the troubadour *chansonniers* on the poets of the Pléiade group, and he obtained a Fulbright research grant in 1952 for this investigation. The trail led to no tangible results, however; and on the suggestion of the late Professor Gustave Cohen, he studied instead the inventories of the sixteenth-century printers in Paris.

His association with the critical bibliographies of French literature, edited by D. C. Cabeen, has been noteworthy. This undertaking began with a section on Provençal literature, which comprised the first volume, on which he collaborated. Following the death of his old friend Robert Valentine Merrill, however, he took over the editorship of the volume on the sixteenth century (Volume II), and prepared the sections on the history of the French language for several others.

Alexander Schutz's reputation as a research scholar rests on very secure foundations. He has lectured at Cambridge University in England and has received honors from the Provençalists in France. He may be said to have succeeded the late Professor W. P. Shepard, of Hamilton College, as the leading Provençalist in the United States. His mind has always been exceedingly active and fertile. There were times when he was discouraged by the lack of appreciation on the part of others. The road was sometimes hard for young medievalists in the 1930's. Perhaps this was a result of the Great Depression. To some in high positions, it looked as though medieval studies might be something that could be overlooked for a while.

Beginning in the 1930's, Alex's headquarters during vacation periods shifted to Baltimore, where my family and I visited him frequently. During World War II, when I was stationed in Washington, D. C., he was a fairly frequent visitor to our apartment. Just prior to the entry into the war of the United States, he spent part of a summer in Chapel Hill at the Casa Brasileira, which was maintained for rapid training of teachers of Portuguese. From this date, he gave instruction in that language at Ohio State, especially during the war period.

Robert, Alex's first child, was born in 1932; Leonard, his second, in 1938. They are doing so well in their careers as chemist and doctor that we must mention them at this point. We wish only that their Grandfather Schutz could see them now.

Alex Schutz has always been a marvelous teacher. He was at his height as both teacher and scholar in the 1950's. It was my privilege to visit with him and his family almost every year. Those whom I met in his house were his students and his colleagues, and they became my friends also. He and I no longer dreamed as much as we used to. The older scholars whom we tried so hard to please in the 1920's and 30's had passed away. We ourselves were now the senior men.

In 1949, I tried to persuade Alex to drive with us to the meeting of the Modern Language Association in Palo Alto, California. He could not accompany us, however, for he had been obliged to take some radium treatments. In 1957, though, our two families were together again in France, at La Motte en la Richardais (Brittany), and later in Paris. We wanted to drive together to Lisbon, but our little brown Austin could not hold five adults (Leonard was with his parents at the time), so the Holmes's drove to Lisbon and the Schutz's went there by train. It was the first trip to Portugal that any of us had ever made, and it was marred only by the theft of the Austin, for one day. Alex and I have always had a peculiar way of walking together through city streets. I have tended to stride a bit ahead while he follows, both of us talking at a fast clip. The inhabitants of Lisbon must have wondered at us, especially on such occasions as the time I stood talking with a bare-headed Scots Highlander in kilts while Alex watched the puzzled faces of those who passed by.

In the fall of 1957, Alex returned to France for a Provençal congress at Aix-en-Provence. The hotel keeper with whom he stayed in Paris told me a year later that she thought he looked quite ill. This was the beginning of the trouble from which he has been suffering ever since. At Christmas, 1959, when the Modern Language Association met in Chicago, Alex and I stood together once more in the hotel lobby, greeting our old and new friends. He has not attended another meeting. The Modern Language Association has not been the same for me—even though I now follow the custom of describing everything to him by letter.

This story of Alex Schutz and our friendship must not end upon a sad note. Although his presence in the classroom will be missed by students, he is still working with his friends and colleagues. I am mindful of a distant cousin who addressed these words to Julia Ward Howe:

> "To be seventy years young is sometimes far more cheerful and hopeful than to be forty years old."—
> OLIVER WENDELL HOLMES.

―――――――――――――*Part I*―――――――――――――

General and Old French Studies

———————*Helmut Hatzfeld*———————

Lexicography and Stylistics

WHEN Urban T. Holmes invited me to contribute to this volume in Dr. Schutz's honor, he wrote me: "The theme of the book will be *Lexicography* but we are interpreting the term broadly and would like to include stylistics." Since, as a stylistician, I read any sentence as a palimpsest, I believed to find beneath the lines the following thought: "You know that we would like to have only strict lexicologists as contributors according to the sound principle Ἀγεωμέτρης μὴ εἰσίτω but since you cannot do such a thing, write something about stylistics; what's the difference?" This was a challenge and, in order to save face, I thought it would be a good thing to write about a combination of specialties as far as vocabulary is concerned: their separation, mutual penetration, and methodological similarities and disparities. I wished to do this all the more since this problem has been for me, not only a theoretical one, but one that has created difficulties from my earliest scholarly efforts to some rather recent dissertations which I have had to direct. Thus, what I want to submit to your pertinent judgment will be a *macédoine*, as the French say, of problems, discussions, criticisms, and experiences. My attempt has, beyond these personal considerations, a certain actuality, since the Russians, as I learn from the latest number of the *Revue de linguistique romane*, have created chairs "de lexicologie et de stylistique."[1] In our western romance-language camp, the sociologically minded lexicologists would prefer to sever the link between lexicography and stylistics. Therefore, Greimas and Matoré only expect that "la lexicologie entretiendra avec la stylistique des rapports courtois, mais distants."[2] Other western lexicologists, like Julio Casares who has no less than four chapters on our problem,[3] and G. von Proschwitz, are for closer relations between the two disciplines because: "Bien des fois la création d'un mot nouveau dépend uniquement de considérations de style."[4]

The point stressed by Von Proschwitz may be considered the most evident among the many relationships between lexicography and stylistics, the point that a stylistic word or meaning creation finally becomes a lexical necessity. Lexicography, the definition and description of the various meanings of the word which are of compulsory acceptance for everybody, makes the entry of an individual word or semanteme only possible when the word starts spreading from an "occasional" application to a "usual" one, according to the terminology of Hermann Paul.[5] At that moment the word becomes free of context and enters a "casier de cases isolées."[6]

The specific conditions under which a stylistically created word or its personal semantic interpretation has escaped into the lexicon by semantic necessity are difficult to assess. We generally can observe the process only diachronically: e.g., abstracts such as *alliance, ménage, abstinence, faveur, justice,* and *miséricorde* have become as concrete as *ring, married couple, ecclesiastical law, silk ribbon, judge,* and *dagger*[7] had become earlier; yet "idealistic" explanations out of the "spirit" of an epoch remain unsatisfactory. Albert Douglas Menut,[8] searching for genuine and pseudo-doublets, found that the lexicalization process of a stylistically created learned doublet is slow, hard, and rare. Whether it is due to the humanistic endeavor of Oresme or to an attempt at satirizing pedantism on the part of Rabelais, its lexical acceptance only depends on semantic necessity. To understand this general concept of necessity, it will be well to recur to the precision which Walter von Wartburg gave to Gilliéron's rough concept of unbearable homonymy. At the moment, Von Wartburg explains, when the Gascons were forced to replace *gal* ("rooster"), because it had become homonymous with *gat* ("cat"), by something else, they would not have been able just to "invent" a word *bigey* ("vicaire") for this purpose. A witty mind had compared the cock among the hens to the "vicaire qui a la charge des pieuses et dévotes femmes du village" long before the appearance of this unbearable homonymy made another word mandatory. The individual metaphor chosen by the community at that moment, *faute de mieux*, then lost its wit and affectivity and became a neutral term for general usage.[9]

New words and meanings crying for lexical admission in general not only find the drawers of the lexicographer closed but are still held back in the stylistic domain by syntactical fetters. Closeness to concrete expressions, linkage to exclamations, blends with the indefinite article, make abstracts temporarily concrete; but severed from such contexts, they simply fall back into their abstractness. Thus the lexicon cannot deduce a usual meaning from Lorca's concretizations: "¡Qué *pena* tan intensa la fachada sin cristales . . . qué *amargura* la casona deshabitada!"[10] Since the connection of Spanish female proper names with the mysteries and shrines of Mary (Asunción, Concepción, Anunciación, Dolores, Rosario, Reliquia, Gloria, Pilar, Monserrat) have already prepared speech habits of a strong abstract-concrete twilight, so that a lover may call the beloved one *alboroto, arrebato, encanto, espasmo, locura, tortura, obcecación,* one would think that such expressions were ready for usual concrete lexical meanings. But this is not the case. They remain in an area of affectivity and, even in contact with those very proper names and clearcut concrete concepts, particularly accompanied by very concrete adjectives, they cannot escape from their stylistic context and from their condition as *Augenblicksbildungen (Beinhauer),* e.g., "¡Oye, estupefacción *morenita—Soledad,* mi gloria bendita—encanto, cielo, paraíso!" [11] Olaf Deutschmann lists one single example of an abstract exclamation having become a popular designation of quantity. The usual critical astounded outcry "¡qué barbaridad!" has led to the expression *una barbaridad de* with the lexical meaning of "many": *una barbaridad de libros.*[12]

Ferdinand de Saussure had already seen that syntagmatic relations in contradistinction to associative relations are not helpful in creating lexical meanings.[13] The radical change of the positive meaning of *pas, point, personne, rien* to negative meanings on a lexical level because of syntactic "contagion," as Darmstetter called this change, is extremely rare. An associative relationship, on the other hand, may entitle great language makers to impose upon the lexicon meanings occasionally given by them to a special word. A case in point is Victor Hugo's successful semantic change of *fauve* from "yellowish red" to "wild," both qualities referring at first to game.

Modern lexicographers, semanticists, and stylisticians are

agreed on the necessity of looking at words not in isolation but within their word area, their linguistic field. The word area of the lexicographer and that of the stylistician are, however, very different. The lexicographer's wordfield has to be looked for within the language, that of the stylistician within individual speeches. The lexicographer's wordfield makes sense only within a diachronic situation, even if he chooses a limited historic layer of words. If this layer is not contrasted with another layer as to shifted meanings and word substitutions, the field primarily analyzed makes no sense, at least not in the concept of Jost Trier, founder of the *Wortfeld-Theorie*. To him, the relationship between the "feudal" field of knowledge, wisdom, and shrewdness of around 1100 A.D. makes sense only if opposed to the "mystical" field of wisdom, art, and knowledge of around 1300 A.D.[14] Kurt Baldinger has established the notional wordfield with its synchronic and diachronic dimensions as the *conditio sine qua non* for any scientific lexicography.[15] A lexical wordfield is supposed to reveal, at least as a by-product, usual meanings which are unknown to, or ignored by, the traditional dictionaries. A student of mine, Sr. M. Lucy Tinsley, produced such meanings, e.g., for *dévotion* and *esprit* in her wordfield study on spirituality,[16] which has been acknowledged by Vidos [17] as particularly valid among the few wordfield studies existing in the Romance sector because of its diachronical, wide range.

A fence-straddler between lexicography and stylistics is that type of onomatological study which reveals the ideology of an author and, at the same time, the ideology of an epoch on the basis of the meanings distilled from an important word. A case in point is the recent study by Henri Vernay, *Les Divers sens du mot "Raison" autour de l'œuvre de Marguerite d'An-*

goulême, reine de Navarre, 1492–1549 (Heidelberg; 1962). Another study concerns an adjectival "champ morpho-sémantique," namely Otto Ducháček's *Le Champ conceptuel de la beauté en français moderne* (Universitas Brunensis, 1960). The field presents a kaleidoscope of *beau, bon, joli, gentil, noble, gracieux, esthétique, chic, coquet.*

The wordfield study of the stylistician, as already mentioned, makes sense only within the *parole* of a text. His wordfield concerns concepts dependent on a literary, often fictional, frame of information. It is strictly synchronic. If comparative fields are introduced, they have only the purpose of bringing out nuances of meaning with uttermost precision. These nuances are primarily not destined to enter the lexicon but to deepen the understanding of the text. Another student of mine, Sr. Gonzaga L'Heureux, has, with the aid of stylistic wordfields, grasped mystical language; and through it, the spiritual progress and growth of the Ursuline mystic, Venerable Mother Marie de l'Incarnation, O.S.U.[18] The originality of her research consists in the discovery that the same word assumes different connotations and new meanings in the new configurations of constantly higher levels of spiritual life. Are such "technical" meanings fit to enter the dictionary? There is, of course, a difference between words of engineering, pharmacology, and chemistry and words of degrees of piety. Therefore such a connoisseur of these matters as J. Dagens actually believes mystical terms should be included in the dictionary, all the more so because the liberal lexicographers of the nineteenth century did not know them or avoided them purposely.[19]

The adepts of the stylistic wordfield do not operate with the lexicographer's *Feldkern* but with *mots-thèmes* and *mots-*

clefs, which spring from the subject matter of a work and the attitude of its author. Pierre Guiraud, who does not know, however, that Leo Spitzer with his *Motiv-und-Wortforschung* has already paved the way, has combined the motive-word principle with the statistic principle of frequency. He tries to find in any text the highest recurrence of ordinary words (*mots-thème*) and the frequency of *écarts* from ordinary basic vocabulary (*mots-clefs*). Guiraud makes the worst mistake a stylistician (*vs*. lexicographer) can make: he severs the words from their context, forgetting that the vocabulary he analyzes is, in the final analysis, a contextual vocabulary; and he is not entirely clear in purpose when, by frequency count, he singles out from Corneille's language a specific group of words like *mérite, estime, devoir, vertu, générosité, gloire, pouvoir, honneur, coeur* ("courage").[20] They certainly do not represent an area. Guiraud is more articulate in his wordfield studies of the symbolists. Here, he defines the *mot-poétique*, which is not eligible for the dictionary: "La valeur poétique d'un mot est une association complexe, où le sens . . . est bien moins opérant que d'autres qualités."[21] This brings up the real contextual vocabulary problem which Ullmann calls "semantics of 'la parole.' "[22] Guiraud pays only lip-service to quality and value within his structural type of linguistics.

Much more refined is the study of wordfields in Pascal by Dom Michel Jungo.[23] He constructs, for instance, a field of *vanité* which contains words like *affectation, grimace, air, bigotterie, pédant, brave, se piquer, enfler, faire montre*. This field is, of course, valid only for Pascal's own ideology and preoccupations, not as a field of general associations which should enter a "dictionnaire d'idées." Now, from Pascal's *langage* and his esthetic-moral wordfields—considering his irony, spirituality, biblicism, Augustinianism, Jansenism—Jungo constructs five vocabularies: general; systematic (word-families in the sense of modern dictionaries [Corominas]); analogical (grouping in the sense of Hallig and Von Wartburg); statistic; and lexicological (semantisms worthy of entering the lexicon, e.g., *s'abêtir, divertissement*).

If the stylistician remains in his own domain and does not ape, but explores, lexicographical methods, then he can open new dimensions of a word, as Gérald Antoine has done with Baudelaire's key word *gouffre*.[24] He develops Baudelaire's bipolar symbolism according to which *gouffre* means Hell as well as Heaven, torment as well as bliss, and so, as M. Antoine states, do its poetically symbolic synonyms *ciel, mer, chevelure*.

A borderline of lexicography and stylistics might also be drawn between phraseological fixity and verbal mobility within unstable word clusters, phrases, and clauses, just as there is between frozen and living metaphors. The lexicon absorbs all those word-compounds whose elements are not understandable if separated, coined expressions with nuances for which the French language has so many terms: *cliché, dicton, locution courante, formule consacrée, idiotisme, expression proverbiale, tour, tournure*. The lexicographer shares with the stylistician the problem of how much of this phraseological material belongs to the lexicon; and he builds, with the latter, surplus-material dictionaries which are far removed from the basic *Wörterbuch*. These are called stylistic and paremiological dictionaries, *Satzlexica, Le Mot dans la phrase*, etc.[25] In the Spanish sector, the dictionaries of *modismos* and *refranes* play an enormous role. One actually cannot do without the *Gran Diccionario de refranes*, by José María Sbarbi, or the *Re-*

franero español, by Sainz de Robles. Spanish, along this line, cannot be compared with French or Italian, since "l'espagnol est une langue dont le vocabulaire et chaque mot *a priori* ont un sens large." [26] The role of the lexicographer when confronted with phraseological material is always a diachronical and explanatory one, the same as it is for the "cultural" words, e.g., *estribo* ("stirrup," or "step of a coach"). Why has the phrase "El abad canta donde yanta?" preserved its archaic meaning since the Middle Ages? Why has "Avoir du foin dans ses bottes?" had the same meaning since the sixteenth century? The stylistician will be interested in such frozen locutions only in the stage of their creation, or when affective, stilted, ironical usage within particular social or literary contexts might defrost these archaic expressions. He watches also whether a creative application instils new force into elements of such compounds, which as a whole have been petrified while their single elements are still in flux. Archaism remains, in general, the hallmark of lexical locution.[27]

The now generalized idea of a thesaurus *vs.* lexicon, based on the principle of the collocation of words, has made considerable inroads in stylistics in France also because the thesaurus lists, in addition to fixed idiotisms and clichés, all possible variations and constructions. A verb, for instance, like *passer* would appear, according to the so-called *projet Dubois*, as case zero (*les jours passent*), together with ten syntactically conditioned and unconditioned modifications and expansions.[28] This is, however, not as new as it looks, since Caro and Cuervo had already conceived of a *Diccionario de construcción y regimen de la lengua castellana* which is presently being published in Colombia.

Nothing is more hated by the lexicographer and more loved

by the stylistician than polysemic ambiguity. What equivalent should a lexicographer choose for "translating" the locution, "Je suis la cinquième roue au carrosse," when according to different situations and environments, it may mean: "I am out of work," "I am bored," "Nobody cares for me," "I am a liability to everyone," "They are fed up with me"? [29] Actually, he will have to empty the locution of its wealth of psychological nuances by the pale rendering "to be superfluous," with some possible interpretative hint of affective, conversational, vulgar usage. But the stylistician studying Mallarmé's sonnet of the white swan, handicapped in his movements by the frozen lake, is urged to ponder the many possible meanings of the expression "des vols qui n'ont pas fui": a child that dies in innocence; a woman who preserves her virginity at the cost of motherhood; a poet who keeps his great vision in the stage of thought and never betrays it by writing it down; a painter, a "Raphael without hands," who keeps the concept of ideal beauty from contamination by line and color.

The same problem of handling ambiguity concerns the problem of synonyms. The lexicographer, concerned with conceptual synonyms to be defined and elucidated by antonyms, will be glad if he feels able to make a list of shaded quasi-synonyms within the language. The stylistician will hunt for synonyms which express emotions and, more vaguely still, mixed feelings, and will also include in his synonymic lists of special texts metaphors, metonymies, epithets, and appositions—all of which help to interpret the more psychological than logical synonyms and their, from an aesthetic viewpoint, kaleidoscopic arrangements within a text.

There are cases in which the tasks of the lexicographer and the stylistician fall closely together. The lexicologist, not the syntactician, has to deal with word formation also. He has to consign to the dictionary words with distinguishable suffixes, be they augmentative or diminutive, and words with original suffixes which have become meaningless, or formal, endings. He has to explain through these actual, or virtual, suffixes the original meaning. From a synchronic viewpoint, there may be at issue a quite normal word, a neologism, an archaism, or a technicism; but diachronically, there is the etymological problem. A classical example is the French word *soleil*. The great Meyer-Lübke once caused hilarity among his colleagues when, as a stylistician-lexicographer, he tried to explain the etymon of this gigantic heavenly body, *soliculus*, by "little" sun instead of treating it as a word of endearment, or a formal substitute, as he finally did in his *REW*. J. Corominas accounts for the probable shift of "goodly" to "beautiful" in the diminutive *bonito* (from *bueno*) as a normal process in an area of a καλὸς κ'ἀγαθός-concept which almost repeats the vulgar Latin *bellus* from *bonulus* from *bonus*. In languages with very lively suffixes, such as Italian, Spanish, and Portuguese, the lexicographer has been able, as far as suffixes are concerned, even on a synchronic level, to grade word meanings according to notional, emotional, temperamental, evaluative, courteous, effusive, and affective meanings. This has been made clear by Amado Alonso in his telling studies on "Semiología y estilística." [30]

There exists also a curious circuit from special lexicon, to style, to the general lexicon. Saint-John Perse, because of the number of his readers since he won the Nobel Prize, will be able to bring the obsolete, rare, exotic, technical connotations of his vocabulary into general lexicon consciousness. Giacomo Devoto describes this problem as far as popular terms and dialectisms are concerned. They can be (says Devoto) if overdone, a misuse; but if used with moderation, they become an artistic fact, an isolated and concrete realization of an expressive exigency; although they are not yet an element of general linguistic tradition, they may become so later.[31] A case in point is the use of medical terms for the characterization of Charles in *Madame Bovary* as short of brains, and for depicting the boasting pharmacist Homais as proud of his alleged culture. The material is so overwhelming that a bulky dissertation has been written on it.[32] In Old French, as Halina Lewicka has shown, a use of a suffix for comic intent might bring the word into the dictionary as a neologism; conversely, an ending taken from a dictionary under the necessity of finding a rhyme may create a new learned substitute with solemn-comical implications: "Jamais je n'eus intention / De faire omicid*ation*."[33] In modern times, one may even follow closely the way by which the realists launch their popularisms into the general lexicon. Flaubert uses italics for words that are not yet *comme il faut*. Balzac justifies them by hinting at their use by vulgar persons.[34] Their possible diffusion[35] or short life[36] decides whether they belong to a dictionary or to a glossary only.

A dubious lexicographer is the maker of a glossary.[37] His stress on style, degree of intensity, and domain of application are points which, as Weissgerber proposes, ought also to be taken over by the lexicographer. According to Bruno Migliorini, "Vocabulari dedicati a un singolo autore raccolgono le parole in cui egli se scosta dall' uso generale."[38] Thus the maker of a glossary decides mainly on the *écarts* of a vocabulary; he becomes a lexicographer when he is dedicated to complete "dizionari metodici d'autori," as they exist in Italy for Carducci, Pascoli, and D'Annunzio, and in France for the "Grands Ecrivains." The complete glossaries often give the lexicographer a new *terminus a quo* or *ad quem* for the history of a word. Thus Marcel Cressot, in his V*ocabulaire des quinze joies de mariage*, found that *robe* which in the fourteenth century mainly designated the *habit d'homme* had in the fifteenth a regression of meaning to *vêtement de femme*.[39] The same Cressot makes a point of the surreptitious intrusion of Huysman's *Augenblicksbildungen* into the French general lexicon: *érotiser, humanitairerie, corédemptrice, intémérabilité (sans souillure)*.[40] On the reason for this possibility, a word will be said in the next paragraph.

Compromise between lexicography and stylistics is demonstrated by the stylistic dictionary in which, together with the most important words, the current epithets are given. The "outils grammaticaux" are listed together with all their possible constructions; and, finally, an exhaustive list of meanings (not only selected examples) is established for the polysemic "mots-vedettes."[41] On the theoretical level, the question has been raised whether a dictionary has only to contain groups of signs called *vocables* or units of meaning, "unités lexicales," which enter the dictionary as *lexides* on their own and by the same right as the vocables.[42] Along the line of successful suffixation, a suffix may actually be "une pédale de la langue et du style," and progressive dictionaries will accept neologisms derived from suffixation which conservative dictionaries reject.[43] From a systematic viewpoint, one could say that in a certain historical moment the associative, situational, sociological, referential context of a word coincides with the operational, functional, syntactic, literary context of the word.

And here Cressot's study on Huysmans may be mentioned again. Huysmans was able to be so creative lexicologically only because the bohemians, on the one hand, and the clergy and educated Catholics, on the other, read the neologisms in the novels of Huysmans as a kind of *déjà vu* experience in their own language. Here also lies the justification, if any, for Georges Matoré's inclusion of the prose works of Gautier on the same level with catalogues, advertisements, special lexicons, and whatnot, when he assesses Le Vocabulaire et la société sous Louis Philippe by "champs notionnels" and "mots temoins." [44] His enterprise, more sociological than linguistic, leaves only a very small margin for stylistics, perhaps in his distinction between "néologismes littéraires-plaisants" and "néologismes proprement dits." [45]

Confronted with the newest quantitative-mathematical and deterministic lexicography, the stylistician has to bow out. At least Pierre Guiraud gives him this advice: "La langue est entraînée dans le déterminisme statistique suivant ses lois propres. . . . La méthode la plus simple consiste à comparer le vocabulaire d'un texte avec une liste de fréquence. . . . Les spéculations sur la valeur stylistique . . . sont . . . dangereuses." [46] A stylistician cannot accept this "conception bien connue qui établit une hiérarchie des sciences selon le degré plus ou moins élevé de leur mathématisation." [47] Since the linguisticians have tried to supplant the linguists, the lexicologians are looking for other fellow travelers from the field of cybernetics, communication, and logistics. Their ideal has become high-speed computation of lexico-statistical indices with the aid of IBM electronic data-processing machines.[48] In a lexicological system without the stress on meaning and syntactical context—which makes a shamble out of any mentalistic and humanistic tradition—there is no room for the "esprit de finesse." The stylistician cannot do without this, however. Can the lexicographer? I do not think that a machine would be the right instrument to handle and compute such favorite words of the troubadors as *pretz, valor, joy,* and *joven.*

1. M. A. Borodina, V. B. Chemietillo, and V. G. Gak, "Bibliographie des études lexicales en U.R.S.S. (1945–1959)," *Revue de Linguistique Romane,* XXVI (1962), 183, 184–223.

2. M. Greimas and G. Matoré, "La Méthode en lexicologie," *Romanische Forschungen,* LXII (1950), 208.

3. Julio Casares, *Introducción à la lexicografía moderna* (Madrid, 1950), pp. 102–64.

4. Gunnar von Proschwitz, *Introduction à l'étude du vocabulaire de Beaumarchais* ("Romanica Gothoburgensia," V [Stockholm, 1956; Paris, 1956]), p. xi.

5. Hermann Paul, *Principles of the History of Language* (London, 1891), chap. iv, pp. 65–67.

6. Robert Godel, *Les Sources manuscrites du cours de linguistique générale de Ferdinand de Saussure* (Genève, 1957), p. 145.

7. Helmut Hatzfeld, "Über die Objektivierung subjektiver Begriffe im Mittelfranzösischen: Ein Beitrag zur Bedeutungslehre" (Ph.D. dissertation, Munich, 1915), *passim.*

8. A. D. Menut, "The Semantics of Doublets Studied in Old and Middle French" (Ph.D. dissertation, Columbia University, 1922), p. 129.

9. Walther von Wartburg, *Problèmes et méthodes de la linguistique* (Paris, 1946), pp. 124–26.

10. Olaf Deutschmann, "Abstrakt-konkrete Ausdrucksformen im Spanischen," *Festgabe für Rudolf Grossmann* (Hamburg, 1962), p. 358.

11. *Ibid.,* pp. 364–65.

12. Olaf Deutschmann, "Untersuchungen zum volkstümlichen Ausdruck der Mengevorstellung im Romanischen," *Romanistisches Jahrbuch,* IV (1951), 260 ff.

13. Ferdinand de Saussure, *Course in General Linguistics,* ed. Charles Bally and Albert Sechehaye (New York, 1959), p. 122.

14. Jost Trier, *Der deutsche Wortschatz im Sinnbezirk des Verstandes: Die Geschichte eines sprachlichen Feldes* (Heidelberg, 1931). A close imita-

tion in the French field: H. Bechtoldt, "Der französische Wortschatz im Sinnbezirk des Verstandes," *Romanische Forschungen*, XLIX (1935), 21–180.

15. Kurt Baldinger, "Grundsätzliches zur Gestaltung des wissenschaftlichen Wörterbuchs," *Deutsche Akademie der Wissenschaften zu Berlin*, 1954–1956.

16. Sister Lucy Tinsley, S.N.D., "The French Expressions for Spirituality and Devotion: A Semantic Study" (Ph.D. disseration, Catholic University, Washington, D. C., 1953).

17. B. E. Vidos, *Manuale di linguistica romanza* (Firenze, 1959), p. 71.

18. Mother Aloysius de Gonzaga L'Heureux, O.S.U., "The Mystical Vocabulary of Venerable Mère Marie de l'Incarnation and Its Problems" (Ph.D. dissertation, Catholic University, Washington, D. C., 1956).

19. J. Dagens, "Observations sur l'histoire du vocabulaire religieux au XVIe et au XVIIe siècles," *Coloques internationaux sur lexicologie et lexicographie françaises et romanes, Strasbourg, 12–16 novembre 1957* (1960), pp. 195–98.

20. Pierre Guiraud, *Index du vocabulaire du théâtre classique. Corneille: Cinna, Le Cid, Horace, Polyeucte* (Paris, 1955–57).

21. Pierre Guiraud, *Index des mots d'Alcools de G. Apollinaire* (*Index du vocabulaire du symbolisme*, I [Paris, 1953]).

22. Stephen Ullmann, *Semantics: An Introduction to the Science of Meaning* (New York, 1962), p. 151.

23. Dom Michel Jungo, *Le Vocabulaire de Pascal* (Paris, 1950).

24. Gerald Antoine, "Pour une nouvelle exploration 'stylistique' du gouffre baudelairien," *Le Français moderne*, XXX (1962), 81–98.

25. See L. Kukenheim, *Esquisse historique de la linguistique française* (Leijden, 1962), pp. 148–67.

26. Pierre Kohler, "Le Sens large du vocabulaire espagnol," *Romania*, LXXV (1954), 498–511.

27. Pierre Guiraud, *Les Locutions françaises* (Paris, 1961), p. 7.

28. J. Dubois, "Esquisse d'un dictionnaire structural," *Etudes de linguistique appliquée*, I (1962), 47.

29. Walter Müller, *Französische Idiomatik* (Heidelberg, 1961), p. v.

30. Amado Alonso, "Noción, emoción, acción y fantasía en los diminutivos," in *Estudios lingüísticos: Temas españoles* (Madrid, 1951), pp. 195–229.

31. Giacomo Devoto, *Nuovi studi di stilistica* (Firenze, 1962), p. 229.

32. J. Annweiler, "Die stilistische Funktion der medizinischen und naturwissenschaftlichen Ausdrücke in Flauberts *Madame Bovary*" (Ph.D. dissertation, Heidelberg, 1934).

33. Halina Lewicka, *La Dérivation* (*La Languc et le style du théâtre comique français des* XVe—XVIe *siècles*, I [Paris, 1960]), p. 353.

34. Robert Dagneaud, *Les Eléments populairs dans le lexique de la 'Comédie humaine' d'Honoré de Balzac* (Paris, 1956), p. 269.

35. G. Matoré, "Le Néologisme: Naissance et diffusion," *Le Français moderne*, XX (1952), 87–92.

36. Michael Riffaterre, "La Durée de la valeur stylistique du néologisme," *Romanic Review*, XLIV (1953), 282–89.

37. Mario Pei and Frank Gaynor, *Dictionary of Linguistics* (London, 1960), p. 83.

38. Bruno Migliorini, *Che cos'è un vocabolario?* (Firenze, 1921), p. 123.

39. Marcel Cressot, *Vocabulaire des quinze joies de mariage* (Paris, 1939), Introduction.

40. Marcel Cressot, *La Phrase et le vocabulaire de J. K. Huysmans: Contribution à l'histoire de la langue française pendant le dernier quart du XIX*ᵉ *siècle* (Paris, 1938), pp. 184, 235, 267, 458.

41. *Dictionnaire Quillet de la langue française* . . . , rédigé sous la direction de Raoul Mortier (Paris, 1961), p. ix.

42. Eric Buyssens, *Les Langages et le discours: Essai de linguistique fonctionnelle dans le cadre de la sémiologie* (Bruxelles, 1943).

43. Alexis François, *La Désinence "ance" dans le vocabulaire français, une "pédale" de la langue et du style* (Genève, 1950).

44. Georges Matoré, *Le Vocabulaire et la société sous Louis-Philippe* (Paris, 1957).

45. *Ibid.*, p. 369.

46. Pierre Guiraud, *Problèmes et méthodes de la statistique linguistique* (Paris, 1960), pp. 21, 10.

47. A. J. Greimas, "La Linguistique statique et la linguistique structurale," *Le Français moderne*, XXX (1962), 241–54.

48. John B. Carroll and Isidore Dyen, "High Speed Computation of Lexico-Statistical Indices," *Language*, XXXVIII (1962), 274–78.

The *Pucelle* Is Not for Burning

AGAIN it is Ernst Curtius who points the way! In the Excursus IV on "Jest and Earnest in Medieval Literature," he raises the question as to whether there can be jest in hagiographic context, and he cites examples from the passions of St. Lawrence and St. Eulalie as they are related in the *Peristephanon* of Prudentius.[1] It is the purpose of this study to explore the problem further by examining a metaphoric expression in the Old French *Cantilène de Sainte Eulalie* against the background of hagiographic conventions, and an incidental result of the analysis will be the suggestion of yet another solution for the controversial word *pulcella*.

The line of martyrological traditions of which the Old French *Eulalie* is a product can be traced in the monumental researches of the erudite Bollandist, Hippolyte Delehaye, who has made a contribution of inestimable value for literary studies in his definitions of the hagiographic genres.[2] Reduced to its barest essentials, the ordering which Delehaye proposes would classify the literature of the passions of the Christian martyrs under two main headings: the *historic passions* and the *artificial, or epic, passions*. The historic passions are assigned two subcategories: eye-witness accounts of the martyrdom itself and panegyric eulogies in high rhetorical style pronounced by the fathers of the early post-Constantinian period of the state church. The artificial passions are of a later period and comprise recitals in which the sparse facts of the historic event are augmented by fictitious elaborations. They were composed, for the most part, by anonymous authors and begin to make their appearance in that epoch of intellectual decadence which accompanied the decline of the empire after the fourth century.[3]

Contemporaneous records of the acts of the Christian martyrs are rare, and evidence that martyrdom occurred is usually provided only by the date of the anniversary observed by a small community of mourners who gathered at the place of interment to commemorate the event, often using the tomb as an altar. The dates and locations were recorded much later in martyrological calendars, where a few bare facts of the *passio* might also be recounted. However, some recitals of the acts of the martyrs which were written immediately after the event have come down to us in the form of encyclical letters, recorded verbal testimony, and, at times, in a little book. Delehaye shows that such records manifest realism of detail and a rich variety of material which falls into no special traditional pattern, and he points out that such characteristics argue strongly for authenticity.[4]

When Christianity became a state religion, the timid rites of commemoration of the period of persecution blossomed into joyous celebrations of the anniversary at which the presiding bishops eulogized the martyr in panegyrics in the best tradition of sophistic epidictic. The model of the oration was elaborate. After a preamble containing appropriate expressions of humility and modesty, the speaker would treat: (1) the country, town, or race to which redounded the honor of having produced the martyr; (2) his family; (3) his birth, especially if accompanied by some miraculous sign; (4) his natural qualities; (5) his education; (6) his childhood; (7) his manner of life and occupations; (8) his acts; (9) his fortune; and, lastly, (10) comparisons.

To the credit of the antique good taste which still prevailed, the speaker would gracefully pass over any of the *topoi* (race, birth, family, education, etc.) on which he had no information, but, as could be expected, the virtues of the martyr were expounded in elaborate hyperbole, as were also the cruelty of his torturers and the horror of his *passio*. Outstanding among the martyr's virtues were his eagerness for martyrdom and the superhuman courage—even joy—which he manifested under torture: he would walk on burning coals as if they were roses, he would throw himself into the fire as if it were cool water.

The stoic fortitude of the martyr was set in further relief by extensive and detailed descriptions of the tortures inflicted on him and by ennumerations of the instruments. Amplification of the horror was accomplished by long lists of the tortures which the judge or executioner customarily employed, but the panegyric did not indulge in the excess of having one individual undergo all the tortures in the list, as did the later accounts in the artificial or epic passions.

Another device of the panegyric was the apostrophe of the martyr, who harangued the executioner in impeccable rhetoric on theological matters, demanding imperiously that all the tortures be brought on quickly, for he was avid for his martyrdom.[5]

In his concluding comments on the hagiographic panegyric,

Delehaye remarks that "l'élément fourni par l'histoire y occupe l'arrière-plan" (*Genres*, p. 232), and he implies that the demands of epidictic rhetoric have already somewhat distorted fact and begun to forge the rigid *topoi* of what will later become the conventional martyr, subjected to a traditional "persécution déchaînée par des monstres de cruauté qui versent le sang à torrents" (*Genres*, p. 233).

Even before that waning of the golden age of Latin Christian eloquence concomitant with the decline of the general level of culture of the disintegrating empire, there began to appear a corpus of mainly anonymous literature which, it would seem, derives from the antique panegyric, but which also embodies some new characteristics. In this literature, the historic facts of martyrdom are so richly ornamented as to become veritable tissues of fiction, and the forms of the stereotyped *topoi* become so rigidly conventionalized as to confer on the composition the quality of a product of assembly-line manufacture (*Genres*, p. 237). From such "artificial" or "epic" passions is derived the hagiographic form of the Latin and vernacular lives of the saints and martyrs which survives in the Middle Ages.[6]

The Old French sequence relating the passion of Saint Eulalie stands as our earliest (882–890 A.D.) monument of belletristic literature in the Romance vernacular. A re-reading of the text, provided here for convenience of reference, will serve to recall the naïve simplicity of a story whose charm has not dimmed through a millenium.

   Buona pulcella fut Eulalia,
    bel auret corps, bellezour anima.

Voldrent la veintre li deo inimi,
voldrent la faire dïaule servir.
5   Elle non eskoltet les mals conselliers,
qu'elle deo raneiet, chi maent sus en ciel.
Ne por or ned argent ne paramenz,
por manatce regiel ne preiement.
Nïule cose non la pouret omque pleier,
10 la polle sempre non amast lo deo menestier.
E poro fut presentede Maximiien,
chi rex eret a cels dis soure pagiens.
Il li enortet, dont lei nonque chielt,
qued elle fuiet lo nom christiien.
15 Ell' ent adunet lo suon element
melz sostendreiet les empedementz,
Qu'elle perdesse sa virginitet:
poro s furet morte a grand honestet.
Enz enl fou la getterent, com arde tost.
20 elle colpes non auret, poro no s coist.
A czo no s voldret concreidre le rex pagiens:
ad une spede li roveret tolir lo chief.
La domnizelle celle kose non contredist
volt lo seule lazsier, si ruovet Krist.
25 In figure de colomb volat a ciel,
tuit oram, que por nos degnet preier,
Qued auuisset de nos Christus mercit,
post la mort et a lui nos laist venir
    Par souue clementia.[7]

"Eulalie was a good little girl. She had a beautiful body, a more beautiful soul. The enemies of God wanted to conquer her, they wanted to make her serve the devil. She does not listen to the evil councils that she deny God. . . . " and so forth. The facts of the unadorned narrative are recounted without connectives—declined, one might almost say—as the essential facts of the life of Christ are enumerated as articles of belief in the Credo. Yet, when viewed in the light of Delehaye's exposition of the stereotypes of hagiographic tradition, almost every statement could, if it were desired, be traced to a conventional *topos* of the mainly fictitious epic passion.

In his edition of the *Peristephanon*, Lavarenne states that it is Prudentius (*ca.* 400) who provides us with the earliest document on Eulalie, naming the city of her birth as Emerita (Mérida) in southwestern Spain and informing us that she was martyred at the instigation of Maximian.[8] Laverenne (p. 53) cannot accept the mention of Maximian as definitive indication of an approximate date for her passion, however, because, since the persecution unleashed in 304 by Maximian and Diocletian was generally considered the most violent of all, it was a convention to attribute all martyrdoms of uncertain date to the reign of these emperors. The hieronymian martyrology lists Eulalie's celebration under the tenth, eleventh, and twelfth of December, but Delehaye (*Culte*, p. 363) deduces that the tenth should be the proper day, since that is the date which appears in both the Carthaginian and the Mozarabic calendars.

Delehaye remarks (*Genres*, p. 312) that in the writings of the Cappadocian fathers and of St. John Chrysostomos, and especially in the *Peristephanon* of the Spanish writer Prudentius, are to be found perhaps the earliest works which served as models for the anonymous, artificial, or epic, type of *passio*. He signals out particularly the hymns to St. Vincent (V), St. Eulalie (III), St. Lawrence (II), and St. Roman (X) as compositions which typify the genre. Thus, the events of the extensive narrative which Prudentius relates concerning

Eulalie's childhood, her dialogue with the persecutors, and so forth, are to be interpreted in the main as stereotyped *topoi*, clustered around a small nucleus of fact. But however small the kernel of historical truth may be, there can be little doubt that it was Prudentius who delineated the major outlines of Eulalie's literary portrait for the Middle Ages.

Of especial interest to the purpose of this study are the manner of her death and the events immediately preceding it. In a thirty-line apostrophe to the judge (lines 66–95), Prudentius has Eulalie call Maximian every nasty name in the book, accusing him of feeding on innocent blood and gluttonously coveting the bodies of the pious as he tears their sober flesh. The judge then threatens her with torture and death by either the sword, or wild beasts, or burning, unless she consents to touch the salt and incense of the altar. For reply she spits in his face, breaks the holy idols, and tramples on the sacred flour.[9] Two executioners then tear her chest and flanks with iron claws, while she counts her wounds and announces to Christ that His victories and name are written on her in the purple of blood. The executioner then holds burning torches to her sides and chest; her sweet-smelling hair slides over her body to preserve her modesty. The flame flies to her face and embraces her head, and she drinks in the fire. Suddenly a dove, whiter than snow, is seen to come from her mouth and fly off to the stars: it is the soul of Eulalie—white as milk, swift, and innocent. It cries out in triumph in heaven. The judge and the executioner see the miracle and, fearing their crime, flee from the place. Then winter covers her body with snow as if with a shroud.

It is evident that, in the Old French version of Eulalie's passion, the narrative of Prudentius is greatly condensed and also somewhat changed. It is now the emperor, Maximian himself, who acts as her judge (line 13: "*Il* li enortet"), and the content of the long dialogue with the judge is reduced to a few brief statements of the essential facts; the spitting episode is suppressed. The method of torture is also changed: no mention is made of tearing the flesh with iron claws, and, although fire is used, the actual death comes by decapitation. The snow is not mentioned.

The motif of death by the sword seems to have been introduced into the story at least before the date of the martyrology of the Venerable Bede (672–735 A.D.), where an entry for December 10 by Bede himself reads:

> Natale S Eulaliae virginis in Barcelona civitate Hispaniae, sub Daciano praeside, quae cum esset tredecim annorum, post plurima tormenta, *decollata est*, et resilient ab ea capite, columba de ejus exire visa est.[10]

It is not known how this motif became a part of the legend, but two possibilities are suggested. The first (and, in my view, less likely) source could be a misunderstanding of the praetor's threat to punish the maiden by means of torture, *either* to cut off her head with a sword, *or* to tear her limbs by beasts; *or*, her form exposed to torches, her relatives the while tearfully grieving, to reduce her to ashes (lines 116–20: "aut gladio ferire caput, / aut laniabere membra feris, / aut, facibus data fumificis, / flebiliterque ululanda tuis, / in cineres resoluta flues").

It has occurred to me that a more probable explanation would lie in contamination with the passion of the virgin St. Agnes (*Peristephenon*, XIV), whose story in many ways resembles that of Eulalie, and who stands beside her in the company of the martyred virgins.[11] The Prudentius passage concerning the death of St. Agnes (lines 85–93) reads as follows:

> Sic fata Christum vertice cernuo
> supplex adorat, vulnus ut imminens
> cervix subiret prona paratius.
> Ast ille tantam spem peragit manu,
> uno sub ictu nam caput amputat;
> sensum doloris mors cita praevenit.
>   Exutus inde spiritus emicat
> liberque in auras exilit; angeli
> saepsere euntem tramite candido.

Thus Prudentius has Agnes bend her neck in prayer, the better to receive the blow. Then the hand of the executioner fulfils all her hope: with one stroke he cuts off her head and quick death prevents the sense of pain. Her soul flies from her body and freely bounds in the air; angels surround it on its shining route.

Also of import to this study is a subtle difference between the way the French and Latin versions of the passion of Eulalie describe the miracle of the dove. In the Latin text, after the dove issues from the martyr's mouth and flies off to heaven, it is specifically stated that "this was the soul of Eulalie, milky white, swift, and innocent" (lines 164, 165: "spiritus hic erat Eulaliae / lacteolus, celer, innocuus."[12] The French version, however, does not mention the soul at this point, and seems to say simply that Eulalie herself flies to heaven in the figure of a dove (line 25: "In figure de colomb volat a ciel). One would naturally suppose that *anima* (cf. line

2) is implied as the subject of *volat*, but this may really have not been the intent. We are reminded that, in the vernacular version, Maximian and his praetor are condensed into one person. May there not also be a similar, but much more ambivalent, telescoping here, indicating a lack of desire to distinguish between the maiden and her soul?

Although figuration of the soul leaving the body as a dove flying to heaven impresses us today as the most banal of commonplaces, this was probably not the case in the early Christian period. One looks first to Biblical texts for authorization for the *topos*, but to my knowledge the figuration is not found in its complete form in the Bible, although it is suggested, as for example in Psalm 55:5-6, where David laments:

> Fearfulness and trembling are come upon me and horror hath overwhelmed me.
> Oh that I had wings of a dove, for then would I fly away and be at rest.

and again in Psalm 74:19:

> O deliver not the soul of thy turtle dove [David] unto the multitude of the wicked: forget not the congregation of thy poor forever.

The descent of the Spirit of God in the form of a dove on Jesus at the time of his baptism (Matt. 3:16, Mark 1:10, Luke 3:22, John 1:32) also suggests the *topos*, since the Spirit would be expected to leave the earthly form at the moment of death, but no specific mention is made of the dove when Christ gives up the Ghost at the crucifixion.[13] It is also worthy of note that, in the fourteen hymns of the passions in the *Peristephanon*, Prudentius reserves the dove exclusively for Eulalie's soul. (It will be recalled that no figure is provided for the departing spirit of St. Agnes.)

In its connotations of purity, innocence, and fidelity in love (Eulalie was a bride of Christ),[14] the figure is so suitable for the little Spanish maiden that it is really not difficult to conceive that popular imagination would, as the vernacular passion of Eulalie seems to have done, confound the maid with the miraculous sign that identifies her as a saint. It is thus implied that Eulalie, within her beautiful body, *is* a more beautiful dove (cf. line 2: "bel auret corps, bellezour anima"), and that death releases her, the dove, from her prison.[15] In this way the attribute of the martyr is confounded with the martyr herself.

That the imagination of the Middle Ages especially liked to dwell on the attributes of saints is demonstrated by the profusion of iconographic symbols manifested in the medieval period of Western Christendom in comparison with the relative scarcity of them in the art of Byzantium and the period of early Christianity. Delehaye discusses the fact that, in the iconography of Christian antiquity, characteristic emblems were only occasionally associated with the images of saints, as in the case of St. Peter with his key and St. Lawrence with his grill.[16] He mentions specifically (*Méthode*, p. 129) that, in the procession of virgins in the Sant' Apollinare Nuovo (St. Eulalie was among them), only St. Agnes is distinguished by her symbol—all the rest have to be recognized by reading the inscription. He maintains, however, that it was in the West during the Middle Ages that the predilection for the figuration of personal characteristics expanded.

Delehaye then enumerates the sources from which the medieval artists derive their characterizing emblems. That one of these sources was the name of the saint suggests a sort of mystic identification of the name of the thing symbolized with the symbol. The lamb, for example, which accompanies St. Agnes from the time of her earliest representations is, of course, a translation of her name. St. Christopher ("bearer of Christ") carries Christ on his shoulders; in Switzerland, St. Maurice is represented as a Moorish warrior; and the Baltic St. Brandan carries a taper in his hand, the word *branden* being associated with the name Brandan by folk etymology. This kind of thinking is, of course, typical of that etymologizing period which believed that the higher spiritual meaning of the thing could be explained through its name. Metaphor becomes more than a figure of speech: it becomes reality, just as the enumerations of antique hyperbole became facts.[17]

Thus it can be seen that, although the vernacular text only implies the fusion by which the dove of St. Eulalie *is* Eulalie, the mystic identification is complete in the case of St. Agnes: Agnes *is* the lamb, a figure which, I might add, is comparable with the dove in such respects as whiteness, purity, innocence, association with Jesus, and so forth. It would, therefore, seem logical to propose that a state of mind in which the name of the person is merged with the word for the symbolic attribute of the person would be conducive to the production of fields of semantically related terms for the person, which have as their center the word for the symbol.

Thus, it could have been the idea of the dove which determined the choice of the word *polle* ("chicken") as a metaphoric term for Eulalie in line 10. This metaphor is clearly an innovation of the vernacular version and does not appear in the *Peristephanon*, where she is called *virgo* eight times, *martyr* three times, *femina* twice, and *pusiola, puella,* and *puellula* once.

The word *polle* comes directly from the Latin *pŭllus, pŭlla*, which had the primary meaning "young animal," especially "chicken." It is attested in the familiar letters of Cicero with reference to doves, and it has, since Classic Latin, been used as a term of endearment for a young human being. At first a word of rustic language, it was usual in Plautus and Ennius, and, with the exception of Roumanian, is universal in Romance.[18] A semantic sequence, *dove* : *young dove* : *young chicken*, is thus established that entrains a concomitant shift in connotations from those of *colomb* ("Holy Spirit" "soul" "innocence" "candor" "purity") to those of *polle* ("young dove" "youth in general" "endearing qualities"). We have now arrived at Eulalie the human being before martydom, a nice little girl, a dear young thing, caressingly called a "young chicken" by a speaking population which always opted for the affective word and rustic, concrete expression.

What then of *pulcella* in line 1? Was this word felt to be related to *polle* and thus connected with the semantic sequence, "dove" : "chicken"? The problem devolves on the question as to whether the word *pulcella* would be understood by a ninth-century speaker of Old French as related to *polle* "chicken," and therefore associated with the semantic area "birds or fowl." In other words, could *polle* be understood to have as a diminutive *pulcella* through addition of the suffix *-cĕlla* or *-ĕlla*? The suffixes *-cĕllu -a*, and *-ĕllu -a* offer no difficulty. Both were viable at that period, and, it would seem, quite productive in names for birds. Thus starting with *avicellu*>*aucellu*>OF *oisel*>MF *oiseau* (REW 827), there may be mentioned CL *tŭrtŭrīlla*>*tŭrtŭrĕlla*>F *tourterelle* (REW 9010); **hīrundella* (<*hīrundo*)>*hirondelle* (REW 4146); as well as *passereau, moineau, corbeau,* and also *paonneau* ("young peacock") and *pigeonneau* ("young pigeon"), where the sense of the diminutive suffix is still understood today. *Agneau* and *dominizella* might also be mentioned, since these words function within the context of the general stylistic pattern: *agneau,* the attribute of St. Agnes, and *dominizella,* another vernacular term for Eulalie.

But would it be possible for a ninth-century speaker to equate phonemically the nexus / -*ŭl* / (<*ūl*) with / -*oll* / (<*ŭll*) through some awareness that they could be alternated? In other words, were derivatives from Latin words having the two forms—long vowel plus single consonant and short vowel plus double consonant—still felt to be related? *Cūpa*>*cuve* (REW 2401) and *cŭppa*>*coupe* (REW 2409) tell us nothing in this case since *cuve* and *coupe* have different meanings, the former "large barrel or drum for storing wine," and the latter, "cup or drinking vessel." However the derivatives of *camēlus* and *camĕllus* survived in France as true doublets, since the Old French forms *chamoil* and *chamel* (>MF *chameau*) both have the meaning "camel." [19] But in this example the doublet alternation occurs in the tonic syllable. Is there an example for the countertonic?

By far the most convincing analogy is offered in another derivative from *pŭllu,* where *pŭllu* plus the diminutive ending -*cīnu* (<-*cēnu*)>*pŭllīcīnus,* which produces MF *poussin* ("a newly hatched chicken"). But the variant forms, OF *pulcin,* attested in the Cambridge Psalter of 1120, and *pucin,* in the *Ysengrinus,* in the meaning "petit d'un oiseau quelconque," [20] point to a proto-Gallo-Roman doublet *pūlicīnus* : *pŭllicīnus*.²¹ It might be mentioned also that the Cassel Glosses show "pulli, honir, pulcins, honchli," ²² which would seem to support an argument in favor of the viability of a doublet when one form is in the simplex and the alternate in the derivative. To put the matter another way, the speaker was aware in this case that *pulcin* ("little chicken") was a diminutive of *polle* ("chicken").

So it would seem that, given the ambience, *polle* : *pulcin*, the speaker could relate *polle* to *pulcella* by sensing that, if a *-cīnus* diminutive of *polle* can be *pulcin*, then a *-cĕlla* diminutive can be *pulcella*. Therefore, it can be posited that the evidence available on the synchronic plane can support the assumption that *pulcella* of line 1 in the *Eulalie* can be included in the semantic chain "dove" : "chicken" and that *pulcella* could have the meaning "little chick," as a caressing term of endearment for a young girl.

The earliest (*ca*. 511 A.D.) attestation of the word *pucelle* occurs in the Merovingian Salic Law as *pulicella*. Here *pulicella* is equated with *ancilla* ("servant"), and would seem to connote a sort of junior rank ("ancilla . . . si pulicella fuerit" vs. "vero ancilla cellaria").²³ The word is also attested in the *Lex romana utinensis*, 89, 24, and the *Leges alamannorum*, 82, 2, as *pullicla*.²⁴ There are numerous Romance cognates of this word, and the meaning seems to be universally "maiden," "young girl," with "virgin" connoted. The various forms suggest a vowel shift $ŭ <> ū$ in proto-Romance as well as $l > n$ and $l > r$ dissimilation.²⁵ The forms in the Gallo-Roman area all seem to have derived from the prototype in $ū$.

Since the time of Diez (258), **pŭllicĕlla* has been proposed as the etymon of *pucelle,* and Meyer-Lübke suggests a contamination with *pūtus* to account for a ŭ>ū shift.[26] The *FEW* favors Meyer-Lübke's proposal, but Spitzer (p. 101) points out that *pūtus* is a Virgilian hapax and maintains that the evidence for its productivity in Gallo-Roman is questionable. Wallensköld has proposed an etymon in **puellicella,* but it must be objected that *puer* and *puella* have been unproductive in Romance, and that his argument for shift *ue>u* needs more support than the analogy of a verb form like *fuerat* (>*furet, Eulalie,* 18).[27]

Leo Spitzer brings new evidence to the support of the much ridiculed idea which Foerster (*ZRPh*, 16, 254) advanced for a derivation from **pūlĭcĕlla* (<*pūlex*) in the sense "little flea." This etymon would be phonologically impeccable for the derivatives manifesting a *ūl* prototype, found mainly in the Gallo-Roman area, and Spitzer proposes a contamination with *dominicella* to account for the forms manifesting *o* and *n*. (Von Wartburg offers the objection in the *FEW* that "die formen mit *o* keineswegs immer auch *n* haben.") Spitzer offers a mass of material in support of a semantic evolution which I take the liberty of summarizing: "little flea" (>"self-effacing servant">"self-effacing Christian")>"servant">"servant of Christ">"noble Eulalie," and he sets up as the ambience of the development a formula of Christian humility such as is found in St. Jerome, "ego pulex et Christianorum minimus," and which derives ultimately from a "climat de politesse orientale exagérée."

Somehow I cannot quite hear St. Jerome's austere pronouncement, "Oh flea that I am and the least of Christians," echoing in the Merovingian scullery. Spitzer also seemed to sense an incongruity, but then suggests that, since the early

Christians are presumed to have chosen for themselves pejorative proper names such as Sterculus, Babosa, Tineosus, Vespula, Porcella (were these *really* self-imposed?), it could be imagined that the servant in the kitchen, through Christian humility, would call herself "ego pulicella," "moi petite puce," and that her masters would accept her self-imposed designation and then speak of her as a "pulicella." He then shows that the semantic transition "servant">"young girl">"noble young girl" can be supported by many analogies.

Spitzer maintains further that *pulcella* "est sur le même niveau de style que la *domnizelle*," both words presumably implying nobility—the one of the Christian order, the other of the social—while *polle*, as a familiar expression of endearment, is on an entirely different plane. He does not discuss *colomb*.

I have the feeling that, perhaps for fear of casting aspersions on the *pucelle d'Orléans*, entirely too much anxiety has been expressed generally over the connotations of nobility in the word *pulcella* of the *Eulalie*. Eulalie's exalted state is guaranteed by the designation *la domnizelle* in line 23, and this, together with the fact of her martyrdom, should be sufficient to confer on the word *pucelle* enough social status for the needs of any saint who comes after her. If the word *pucelle* was not noble before it was used in the *Eulalie*, Eulalie made it so. I submit, therefore, that the semantic chain that I have proposed—*colomb* : *polle* : *pulcella* (or "soul/dove" : "young girl/chicken" : "maid/endearing young chick")—establishes an integrated affective metaphor in the ambience of birds, and that it was meant to oppose the connotations of social order implied in *domnizelle*.

It seems to me that there is really no need to assume contaminating words to explain the Romance derivations.

They can be made without difficulty simply from a pair of doublets, *pūlicella* : *pŭllicella*, the former accounting for the forms in *u*, the latter for the forms in *o*. The analogy of- would answer the question as to whether a *ūl*<>*ŭll* alter- fered in *pulcin, pucin* vs. *poussin*<*pūlicinus* vs. *pŭllicinus* nation in the countertonic provides doublets in Romance. Fi- nally, the forms manifesting *n* and *r* (*puncella*, etc., and *puršela*) can be explained as simple dissimilation by analogy with the coexisting Vulgar Latin forms *cultellus* and *cuntellus* (REW 2381), a possibility which Spitzer considered, but re- jected in favor of his semantic solution. Thus, *cultellus*> *cuntellus* (*l - l*>*n - l*) and *cultellus*>Venetian *kortello* (*l - l*>*r - l*).

The semantic cluster "dove" : "chicken" : "little chick," which has been established as an integrated group of meta- phoric terms for Eulalie, functions in conjunction with an- other, rather strange, semantic cluster in a way that produces a very startling image. It is stated in line 13 that the little chicken Eulalie does not become excited (literally "get heated up") at the exhortations of Maximian:

> Il li enortet, dont lei nonque *chielt*.

Later, in lines 19 and 20, we are told that "they threw her into the fire in order that she burn to toast" and that "she had no sins, for that reason she did not cook":

> Ens enl fou la getterent, com arde *tost*.
> elle colpes non auret, poro no s *coist*.

Finally, they had to cut her head off with a sword.

The word *chielt* is derived from *calere*, which literally signified "to become warm or heated" and already in Classic Latin had acquired the figurative meaning "to become excited." However, the word *coist* derives from *coquere*, which means simply "to cook" in both Latin and the Romance derivatives. The word *tost* from *tostum*, the past participle of *torrere* ("to burn"), gives us MF *tôt* ("quickly") (cf., "se laisser griller"), but also produced an Old French verb *toster* ("to grill"), whence English *toast*. Since *tost* is in assonance with *coist*, it would seem that here both words were intended as cooking terms. The idea implied thus becomes: "Eulalie did not cook," or, when Eulalie is supplanted by her cluster of metaphoric equivalents—"dove" : "chicken" : "chick"—"the chicken did not cook!"

It has already been shown that the vernacular text differs from the Prudentius hymn in the manner of Eulalie's torture and death. In the *Peristephanon*, she is torn with iron claws and then burned; in the French text they try to burn her, but since she had no sin, they could not, and so they cut off her head. The lack of success of the torturers in their first attempt to destroy Eulalie by fire is a thoroughly traditional *topos*, which seems to have had its origin in the *amplificatio* of the early panegyrics, where the atrocious cruelty of the pagan judge was characterized hyperbolically by a long list of the tortures he *customarily* employed. In the epic passions, however, the hyperbole was taken literally, and it is not unusual to find one poor martyr enduring all the tortures in the list, one after another. The cumulation of horror on the head of one individual was made to seem reasonable by presenting the sequence of torture either as a demonstration of the saint's fortitude, or as a manifestation of the inefficacy of the power of evil over the power of good. In the latter case, which is, of course, that of the Old French *Eulalie*, a miracle occurs which confers on the martyr complete insensibility, so that the executioners cannot destroy him until God wills that his soul be released. Frequently the executioners get so tired that they have to stop for a rest.

Delehaye summarizes the sequence of tortures of numerous martyrs. One example, that of St. Christine (*Genres*, p. 285), will more than suffice:

> Elle est frappée à coups de pieds par quatre hommes, jusqu'á ce qu'ils soient à bout de forces; chargée de chaînes et d'un carcan, suspendue, raclée, déchirée, attachée à la roue au-dessus d'un grand feu alimenté par de l'huile, précipitée à la mer une meule au cou, jetée dans un poêle remplie de matières enflammées, enfermée durant cinq jours dans une fournaise ardente, exposée aux morsures des serpents. On lui coupe les seins, puis la langue; des pointes sont enfoncées dans tous ses membres. Elle périt par le glaive.

The martyr always endures his tortures courageously and frequently asks for more with appropriate Christian fervor. It is not unusual for him to express joy, as in the passion of St. Vincent (*Peristephanon*, V), where it is said that, when they tore him with iron claws, the soldier of God would laugh (line 117: "ridebat haec miles Dei"), and that, when the executioners were exhausted, St. Vincent was that much more happy (line 125: "ast ille tanto laetior"). Joy makes him agile, and he hastens to get to his [next] torture before his judges do (lines 211 and 212: "ipso que pernix gaudio / poenae ministros praevenit"). When boiling fat is poured on him, he remains immobile as if he feels no pain (lines 233, 234: "Haec inter inmotus manet, / tanquam dolorum nesciens").

At times the martyr will joke. Delehaye (*Genres*, p. 289), citing from the *Passio SS Timothei et Maurae* in the *Acta Sanctorum*, relates that St. Maura, when plunged in boiling water, jokingly tells the governor that he is making her take an unfortunately cold bath. The governor, trying the water, learns at his own expense that his orders have been well executed. Ernst Curtius discusses at length the passage, now a classic of gruesome humor, from the passion of St. Lawrence (*Peristephanon*, II, lines 401–8), where the martyr, as he is burned on a grill, says:

> "Converte partem corporis
> satis crematam iugiter
> et fac periclum, quid tuus
> Vulcanus ardens ergerit."
>   Prae fectus inverti iubet:
> Tunc ille: "Coctum est, devora,
> et experimentum cape,
> sit crudum an assum suavius."

("Turn over on the other side that part of my body which has been sufficiently exposed, and test the result obtained by the heat of your fire." The judge gives the order to turn him over. Then St. Lawrence says: "Eat, and see if it is nicer raw or roasted.")

It was quite usual to portray the pagan judges and executioners as monsters avid to eat the bodies and drink the blood of their victims, and animal sacrifice was also mentioned as one of their social customs. (The passages cited here were taken at random from the *Peristephan.*) In the passion of Emeterius and Chelidonius (I, lines 97, 98), the pagans are described as demons who, like wolves, eat the entrails of those whom they catch ("daemones, / qui lupino capta ritu devorant praecordia"). In the passion of St. Vincent (V, lines 98–100), the judge calls out, "Give me quickly some executioners, those Plutos of the accused who feed on the cut-up flesh" ("raptimque licotres date, / illos reorum Plutones / pastos resectis carnibus"). St. Vincent tells the executioner (lines 151–52), "Put your hands in [my wounds] and drink the scalding streams of my blood" ("manus et ipse intersere / rivosque feruentes bibe").

In the passion of St. Eulalia itself (III, lines 28–30), Prudentius speaks of the persecution as ordering Christians to burn incense and to offer over the fire of the altars to death-bringing gods the liver of an animal "christicolas que cruenta jubet / tura cremare, iecur pecudis / mortiferis deis"). In her tirade to the judge (lines 87–88), she says that Maximian feeds on innocent blood, lusting gluttonously for the bodies of the pious accused ("sanguine pascitur innocuo, / corporibusque piis inhians").

Thus the Christians accused the pagans of eating the bodies and drinking the blood of the martyrs who, in the *passio* of their death, reinacted the *passio* of Christ.

If, before, the idea that Eulalie did not cook seemed horrible, I should imagine that, in the awareness of the tradition from which the idea stems, it would now seem mild indeed—as a matter of fact, even gently humorous: The chicken didn't cook—what a nasty trick to play on the executioner! How ridiculous he must have felt—how frustrated! And how the Christians laughed at his disappointment! And how silly he was in the eyes of his pagan friends, too! This, I think, is what Freud would call "tendential wit": a joke directed against an agressor which is designed to make him appear ridiculous before an audience, so that laughter is prejudiced in favor of the person making the joke. In the English translation of Freud's essay "Wit and Its Relation to the Unconscious," the editor, Brill, inserts the following story to demonstrate the role that wit plays in hostile aggression:

> Wendell Phillips, according to a recent biography by Dr. Lorenzo Sears, was on one occasion lecturing in Ohio, and while on a railroad journey going to keep one of his appointments met in the car a number of clergymen returning from some sort of convention. One of the ministers, feeling called upon to approach Mr. Phillips, asked him, "Are you Mr. Phillips?" "I am, sir." "Are you trying to free the niggers?" "Yes, sir; I am an abolitionist." "Well, why do you preach your doctrines up here? Why don't you go over into Kentucky?" "Excuse me, are you a preacher?" "I am, sir." "Are you trying to save souls from hell?" "Yes, sir, that's my business." "Well, why don't you go there?"

Brill remarks that "the assailant hurried into the smoker amid a roar of unsanctified laughter," and notes that Phillips not only belittled the aggressive clergyman and turned him into ridicule, but by his clever retort "fascinated the other clergymen, and thus brought them to his side." [28]

In the *Eulalie*, the powers of good play a trick on the powers of evil to make evil seem ridiculous. As a result, the audience is won over to the cause of good through the laughter released by the witty substitution implied in the metaphor "the chicken did not cook" for "Eulalie did not burn." This, then, is why God, through his good in Eulalie, acts as the Joker in his Divine Comedy of the epoch when tragedy could not be.

An illustration from another epoch is to the point. My husband tells me that, during the troubled times in Russia after the October revolution of 1917, a little song, which originated in the cabarets of Odessa, had great popularity. The tune is that of a cheerful folk melody, and he remembers one verse of which the translation runs: "A little chick, a skinny chick, the chicky wants to live. They chased it, and arrested it, and ordered it to be shot!"

The wit, of course, lies in the ridiculous contrast evoked by the image of a firing squad of twenty-four men aiming at one scrawny little chicken. But the chicken symbolizes the average citizen ensnared in the horror of political persecution, and the humor is the ironic humor of tragedy. Thus, in modern times the chicken *does* cook, so to speak, for, since tragedy is again possible and since comedy now can only be human, divine intervention no longer plays jokes on the forces of evil.

1. *European Literature and the Latin Middle Ages*, trans. Willard R. Trask (New York, 1953), pp. 405–35.

2. Hippolyte Delehaye, S. I., *Les Passions des martyrs et les genres littéraires* (Bruxelles, 1921); *Les Origines du culte des martyrs* (Bruxelles, 1933); *Cinq leçons sur la méthode hagiographique* (Bruxelles, 1934). For convenience of reference these works will be abbreviated: *Genres, Culte,* and *Méthode.*

3. *Genres,* Introduction, pp. 1–10.

4. *Genres,* chap. i, "Les Passions historiques," pp. 11–182.

5. *Genres,* chap. ii, "Les Panégyriques," pp. 183–235.

6. *Genres,* chap. iii, "Les Passions épiques," pp. 236–315.

7. Karl Bartsch, *Chrestomathie de l'ancien français,* ed. Leo Wiese (Leipzig, 1927), p. 4.

8. Prudence, *Le Livre des couronnes (Peristephanon liber): Dittochaeon: Epilogue,* tr. M. Lavarenne, with Latin text (Paris, 1951), p. 51.

9. Curtius, p. 427, would seem to classify the unladylike spitting incident as a *topos* of humor in hagiography.

10. Venerable Bede, *The Complete Works*, ed. J. A. Giles (*Historical Tracts*, Vol. IV [London, 1843]), p. 164. Also in the Bede calendar under the date February 12, left empty by Bede and filled in by Florus in the ninth century, there appears the entry: "Barcilona Eulaliae virgines et martyris" (p. 35). Lavarenne (p. 53) explains the discrepancy as to the place of birth as due to the probable existence in Barcelona of a church erected in honor of Eulalie of Mérida, which gave rise to a belief in a local saint of this name.

11. In *Culte*, p. 327, Delehaye mentions Eulalie and Agnes in the procession of Saint Martin in Caelo Aureo in Rome (now Sant' Apollinare Nuovo), and (p. 342) he calls attention to a basilica founded in Biterrae (Béziers) in 455 by the priest Othis "in honorem sanctorum martyrum Vincenti, Agnetis, et Eulaliae."

12. The vastly inferior Latin sequence which immediately precedes the Old French version in the ninth-century MS 143, fol. 141, of the Bibliothéque de Valenciennes, uses the exact wording of Prudentius: "spiritus . . . innocuus." See Foerster and Koschwitz, *Altfranzösisches Übungsbuch* (Heilbronn, 1884), p. 147.

13. Cf. also mention of the dove as a sacrificial animal and sin offering in Genesis 15:9 and Leviticus 12:6 and 14:22.

14. Cf. Songs of Solomon, 2:14, 5:2, *et passim*.

15. Compare the parallel syntax but completely different tone of Prudentius' opening lines 1 and 2: "Germine nobilis Eulalia, / mortis et indole nobilior" ("Eulalie, noble by lineage and by manner of death more noble"), where the vernacular "body" is to the Latin "lineage" as the "soul" is to the "manner of death."

16. *Méthode*, Chap. V, "Les Saints dans l'art," pp. 117–46.

17. It is not implied that the profused flowering of the etymological emblem in the Middle Ages did not have its roots in an earlier period. One thinks, of course, of the fish used by the Christians of the catacombs as a symbol for Christ because the Greek initials IXΘ standing for Iησοῦς Χριστὸς Θεός could be read as an abbreviated form for the word IXΘ[ύς] ("fish"). The symbol served as a secret sign in this period of persecution.

18. Cf. REW 6828 and FEW, s.v.; also A. Ernout and A. Meillet, *Dictionnaire étymologique de la langue latine: Histoire des mots* (4th ed.; Paris, 1960), s.v. *pullus, -i*: "petit d'un animal (cf. poulain, poutre); spécialement 'poulet'. . . . Dans la langue érotique: puer, que obscene ab aliquo amabatur, eius a quo amatus esset pullus discebatur, P.F. 285, 3. . . . D'abord terme de la langue rustique; ancien (Plt., Enn.,), usuel. Panroman, sauf roumain"; and also *Harper's Latin Dictionary*, s.v. 1. pullus: "columbini, Cic. Fam. 9, 18."

19. C. H. Grandgent, *An Introduction to Vulgar Latin* (New York, 1962), pp. 69, 70.

20. FEW, s.v. *pŭllĭcēnus*.

21. Jules Ronjat, *RLR*, LVII, 541, makes the following comment on Meyer-Lübke's articles 6819 **pŭllicĕlla* and 6820 *pŭllicēnus* in the 1911–14 edition of the *REW*: "Explication incomplète. M. Grammont a depuis longtemps (M SL, VIII, 320) fait remarquer que fr. *pucelle*, prov. *piuzela* à côté de *poussin* postulent **pŭl-* à côté de *pŭll-* comme *cūpa cŭppa* etc. Cf. 6852 *pūpa *pŭppa*."

22. Bartsch, p. 1, lines 16 and 17.

23. Leo Spitzer, "Pucelle," *Romania*, LXXII (1951), 100–107. On this point Spitzer cites I. Pauli, *"Enfant," "Garçon," "Fille" dans les langues romanes* (Lund, 1919), a work which was not available to me.

24. *Archiv für lateinische Lexikographie and Grammatik*, III (1886), 500.

25. REW 6819: " **pŭllicĕlla* 'Mädchen'. Amail. *polçella, ponçella*, obw. *puršela*, valenc. *poncella*; serbokr. *pùncjela*. . . . +pūtus 6890: frz. *pucelle* (>ait. *pulcella*), prov. *piuzela* (>apg. *pucella*), akat. *puncella* (>asp. *puncella*)."

26. *Germanisch-Romanische Monatschrift*, I, 635.

27. *Mélanges de philologie et d'histoire offerts à M. Antoine Thomas* (Paris, 1927), pp. 489–92.

28. *The Basic Writings of Sigmund Freud*, trans. and ed. Dr. A. A. Brill (New York, 1938), pp. 698, 699.

—Raphael Levy—

Les Gloses Françaises dans le Pentateuque de Raschi

LES LINGUISTES qui cherchent à approfondir l'historique du vocabulaire français s'aperçoivent d'emblée qu'on a conservé seulement quelque quinze cents vers écrits avant l'an 1100. Les Juifs de la France septentrionale parlèrent la langue d'oïl tout comme les autres habitants depuis le milieu du onzième siècle, sinon auparavant, jusqu'à l'expulsion générale à la fin du quatorzième siècle. Toutefois on constate une différence stylistique due à la nécessité qu'eurent les Juifs de vivre à l'écart des Catholiques. Ceux-ci composèrent une production littéraire qui est caractérisée par une homogénéité fort pieuse, savante et poétique. En revanche, les Juifs formèrent un lexique de la langue française plutôt usuel, artisanal et terre-à-terre.

Il serait oiseux de répéter qu'au moyen âge les documents se rapportant à la culture judaïque étaient écrits en caractères hébreux. Cependant — chose curieuse — même les écrits français des Juifs devaient être rédigés de cette façon. La plupart de ces textes étaient destinés à expliciter les commentaires de la Bible et du Talmud. Autrement dit, ceux de ces ouvrages rabbiniques qu'on a conservés jusqu'ici sont panachés de mots français transcrits en caractères hébreux.

À Troyes — un siècle avant Chrestien de Troyes — vivait

Raschi, nom qui n'est rien d'autre qu'un acrostiche du nom plein Rabbin Schelomo ben Isaac. Il avait l'habitude de parsemer ses commentaires de vocables français pour éclairer les lemmes hébreux qu'il estimait difficiles. C'est au sein même du texte hébreu, dont ces gloses font partie intégrante, qu'il faut aller les chercher. C'est ce que nous nous attacherons à faire dans ce relevé des termes judéo-français qui sont éparpillés dans le commentaire biblique de Raschi.

Grâce à la collaboration de quatre hébraïsants célèbres, à savoir, Abraham ben Isaiah, Benjamin Sharfman, Harry Orlinsky, Morris Charner, les lecteurs de langue anglaise sont maintenant à même de lire une traduction excellente accompagnant le texte hébreu d'une édition qui a paru à Brooklyn en 1950 sous le titre: "The Pentateuch and Rashi's Commentary." Les éditeurs ont précisé leur but dans la préface:

> This work is intended primarily as a linear English translation of Rashi, the commentator par excellence of the Hebrew Bible. It is hoped that this translation will help make Rashi's interpretation, which derives in large measure from the Talmud and Midrash, more accessible to all who would desire to study it. . . . This edition of Rashi with a linear translation will enable the student to acquire a considerable amount of grammar and vocabulary from the pen of one of the founders of Hebrew grammar and exegesis.

Quant aux matériaux qui auraient permis aux quatre érudits de contribuer efficacement à l'historique de la langue française, ils n'en soufflent mot. En s'évertuant à rendre complète cette édition, ils ont reproduit les gloses tant bien que mal. Je les ai relevées toutes dans les cinq volumes d'environ deux mille pages à la Library of Congress. Le bibliothécaire Lawrence Marwick a bien voulu les mettre à ma disposition. Pour résoudre les problèmes d'ordre linguistique, j'ai eu recours fréquemment à trois oeuvres: F. Godefroy, *Dictionnaire de l'ancienne langue française* . . . , dix tomes (Paris, 1880 –1902); A. Darmesteter, "Les Gloses françaises de Raschi dans la Bible" (Paris, 1909), tirage à part des tomes LIII–LVI de la *Revue des études juives*; Raphael Levy, *Contribution à la lexicographie française selon d'anciens textes d'origine juive* (Syracuse, 1960). Le lecteur bienveillant, qui désire se renseigner sur les gloses raschianiques du Talmud, peut consulter A. Darmesteter et D. S. Blondheim, "Les Gloses françaises dans les commentaires talmudiques de Raschi" dans la *Bibliothèque de l'École des hautes études*, tome CCLIV (1929).

L'exposé qui suit donne d'abord une copie de chaque glose judéo-française et de son interprétation anglaise telles qu'elles se trouvent dans l'édition de 1950, puis une liste alphabétique des gloses bibliques de Raschi avec mainte altération.

Genèse

estordison	I 2	astonishment, amazement
acoveter	I 2	hover over
herbaries	I 11	grass
mouvoir	I 24	creeping things
coin	I 27	image
lame	III 24	blade
naistre	IV 18	giving birth by the woman

engendrer	IV 18	the act of begetting offspring by the man
macheube	IV 23	wounding
appareiller	XI 3	get ready
enseigner	XIV 14	train
desenfants	XV 2	childless, lacking children
emisser	XIX 17	escape, slip away
torche	XIX 28	a pillar of smoke
eprouver	XX 16	clarification
fendre	XXII 3	split
donner	XXIII 13	
centenaria	XXIII 16	large shekalim
approuvet	XXIV 14	
humer	XXIV 17	sip
encresser	XXV 21	entreat, be importunate
floche	XXV 25	a garment of wool filled with hair
ouvraine	XXVI 14	work
nuisement	XXVI 21	enmity
compas	XXIX 17	form
septaine	XXIX 28	a period of seven days
herbergerie	XXX 20	dwelling
pointure	XXX 32	dotted with small points, speckled

rouge	XXX 32	red
tremble	XXX 37	poplar
coudre	XXX 37	almond-tree
chastenier	XXX 37	plane-tree
faissie	XXXI 10	grizzled
bast	XXXI 34	saddle of camel
eprouver	XXXI 37	judge
appaisement	XXXIII 10	appeasement
saluer	XXXIII 11	salute, greet
enfantees	XXXIII 13	giving suck, raise their sucklings
paileriz	XXXVII 2	evil report
detourner	XXXVIII 16	turn aside
pistor	XL 1	baker
witis	XL 10	long branches
spanier	XL 10	bud
oublies	XL 16	bread nibblings
marais	XLI 2	bulrush
tenves	XLI 3	lean
tuyau	XLI 5	stalk
sains	XLI 5	rank
hales	XLI 6	blasted
bise	XLI 6	east wind
sains	XLI 7	rank
fosse	XLI 14	pit
entendre	XLI 15	understand

flouet	XLI 19	lean of flesh
garnison	XLI 40	sustain
dejeuner	XLIII 16	dine at noon
maderin	XLIV 2	goblet
maisniede	XLV 2	house
salver	XLVII 7	greet, ask after one's welfare
cordie	XLVIII 7	an amount of one's plowing
essarter	XLIX 6	hough
coriere	XLIX 11	long branch
marche	XLIX 13	border district
trace	XLIX 19	footstep
emolis	XLIX 26	the utmost bound

Exode

junc	II 3	bulrush
rosel	II 3	reed
balbus	IV 10	slow of speech
estouble	V 7	straw
tuiles	V 7	bricks
retrait	V 8	withdrawn
predicar	VII 1	prophesy
etang	VII 19	pool
pedulier	VIII 2	lice

grenouillerie	VIII 2	frogs
vanter	VIII 5	boast
pedulier	VIII 13	lice
inciter	VIII 17	incite
joinchiez	IX 8	handfuls
oulvis	IX 8	soot from drying coals burned in a furnace
caucher	IX 17	tread down
verdure	X 15	green leafage
terziane	X 22	three days
septaine	X 22	seven days
plante	X 26	hoof
lintel	XII 7	lintel
pascua	XII 11	Passover
septaine	XII 15	seven days
serrer	XIV 3	entangle
si por faillance de non fossés?	XIV 11	because no graves?
estordison	XIV 24	be discomfited
plomb	XV 10	lead
decomplaisant	XV 24	murmured
foisson	XVI 5	twice as much
gelide	XVI 14	hoar frost
tenuis	XVI 14	thin
destemperer	XVI 21	become tepid

coriandre	XVI 31	coriander
flestre	XVIII 18	wear away
emportement	XX 5	zealousness
echelons	XX 23	steps
navrure	XXI 25	wound
tache	XXI 25	stripe
betture	XXI 25	striking
chardons	XXII 5	thorns
contrarier	XXII 20	wrong
apaisement	XXV 2	good will
escrin	XXV 10	ark
soulderiz	XXV 18	work of welders
batediz	XXV 18	beaten work
soulderiz	XXV 31	work of welders
batediz	XXV 31	beaten work
maderins	XXV 31	cups
pommeaux	XXV 31	knobs
nieller	XXV 33	model like vessels of silver
tenailles	XXV 38	tongs
fougere	XXV 38	snuff dish
faisse	XXVI 1	sashes of silk
lacels	XXVI 4	loops
fermel	XXVI 6	clasps
estantius	XXVI 15	standing up
esparres	XXVI 26	bars

a discendrer	XXVII 3	remove its ashes
vedil	XXVII 3	shovel
crochets	XXVII 3	flesh-hooks
crible	XXVII 4	a grating
pals	XXVII 10	poles
gonds	XXVII 10	hooks
serventrie	XXVIII 3	ministering
pourceint	XXVIII 4	apron
castons	XXVIII 4	settings
cofea	XXVIII 4	mitre
coudeaux	XXVIII 7	elbows
emcensiers	XXVIII 14	iron balls filled with incense
discernement	XXVIII 15	judgment
asommel	XXVIII 22	border
gant	XXVIII 41	glove
revestir	XXVIII 41	instal
tele	XXIX 13	fat, membrane
abris	XXIX 13	lobe
tendrons	XXIX 20	cartilage of ear
venteller	XXIX 27	wave-offering
luces	XXX 7	lamps
gomme	XXX 34	stacte
theriaque	XXX 34	balsam
lacies	XXXI 10	woven with a needle

decharger	XXXII 3	break off
niel	XXXII 4	engrave
entalier	XXXII 16	graven
luces	XXXV 14	lamps
mireors	XXXVIII 8	mirrors
estendre	XXXIX 3	beat

Lévitique

feuchere	I 9	an offering made by fire
flancs	III 4	loins
lombles	III 4	fat beneath loins
abris	III 4	lobe
foailles	IV 35	an offering made by fire
escourement	VI 21	it shall be scoured
plante	XI 3	hoof
moucherons	XI 11	gnats
espervier	XI 16	hawk
chouettes	XI 17	owl
hibou	XI 17	bird
chauvesouris	XI 18	horned owl
talpa	XI 18	bat
cigogne	XI 19	stork

heron	XI 19	heron
herupe	XI 19	hoopoe whose crest is double
longuste	XI 21	insect
moustille	XI 29	weasel
bot	XI 29	green lizard
herisson	XI 30	gecko
lizard	XI 30	lizard
limace	XI 30	sand-lizard
talpa	XI 30	chameleon
escarbot	XI 42	beetle
centipedes	XI 42	centipede
taie	XIII 2	spots
sainement	XIII 10	quick raw flesh
retrecissement	XIII 23	scar
retrecir	XIII 23	wrinkle
sainement	XIII 24	quick raw flesh
orpale	XIII 37	golden
rouge	XIII 39	tetter
grenon	XIII 45	upper lip
point	XIII 51	a pricking leprosy
tendron	XIV 14	tip of ear
rogner	XIV 41	scrape
arçon	XV 9	saddle
alves	XV 9	saddle

Les Gloses Françaises dans le Pentateuque de Raschi   67

apaisement	XIX 5	that ye may be accepted
espiement	XIX 16	spying
mistre	XIX 19	a garment of felt cloths spun and woven together
flestre	XIX 19	withered
pourpoint	XIX 28	imprints of marks
sourcils	XXI 20	eyebrows
toil	XXI 20	membrane of the eye
prunelle	XXI 20	black of the eye
apaisement	XXII 19	accepted
verrue	XXII 22	wart
septaine	XXIII 8	week
grenailles	XXIII 14	fresh ears
cheville	XXVI 13	peg
anpoules	XXVI 16	a swollen thing whose swelling subsided

Nombres

en son aise	II 17	which is near to him, wherever his hand stretches out

luces	IV 9	lamps
vedil	IV 14	shovel
disant	VI 23	saying
batediz	VIII 4	beaten work
concombres	XI 5	cucumbers
boudekes	XI 5	melons
porels	XI 5	leeks
coriandre	XI 7	coriander
crystal	XI 7	bdellium
esbanoyer	XI 8	go about without toil
enportement	XI 29	be jealous, to envy
parlerie	XIV 36	report
engres	XIV 44	presumptuous
tourteau	XV 20	cake
faisant	XV 35	doing
allant	XV 35	going
tendus	XVII 3	beaten thin
etendre	XVII 4	beat out
murmures	XVII 25	murmuring
encure del tour	XXI 4	because of the affliction of the way
perche	XXI 8	pole
malderas	XXIII 27	curse
destent	XXIV 17	passes by like an arrow

forer	XXIV 17	break down, pick out
emportement	XXV 11	vengeance
isles	XXXIV 6	islands
apendiz	XXXIV 7	cells, chamber of the gate

Deutéronome

oyant	I 16	hearing
emportement	IV 24	jealous
moulant	IX 21	grinding
detournoure	XIII 6	perversion
inciter	XIII 7	entice, incite
affichee	XIII 7	cleave
steinbock	XIV 5	wild goat
plante	XIV 6	hoof
chauve-souris	XIV 16	horned owl
herupe	XIV 18	hoopoe
espalte	XVIII 3	joint of the knee, sole of the forefoot
gardant	XXVII 1	keep
mal du feu	XXVIII 22	fever
astrandement	XXVIII 22	fiery heat
hale	XXVIII 22	blasting, east wind

chaume	XXVIII 22	wheat withers and turns to mildew
estordison	XXVIII 28	astonishment
estordison	XXVIII 37	astonishment
entendre	XXVIII 49	understand
et pourvendrez vous	XXVIII 68	ye shall sell yourselves
benoir soi	XXIX 18	he will bless himself
emportement	XXIX 19	jealousy
herbaries	XXXII 2	tender grass
entortille	XXXII 5	crooked
vinos	XXXII 14	foaming wine, excellent in taste
nouriture	XXXII 30	he brought up
delivrer	XXXII 30	deliver
maintenue	XXXII 36	officer who controls the people
anforcede	XXXII 36	strengthened
splendeur	XXXII 41	glitter
justicia	XXXII 41	retribution
tes pourparlers	XXXIII 3	thy words
askorant	XXXIII 25	will cause to flow

Glossaire du Pentateuque

acoveter (Gen. I 2), planer sur, être étendu sur.
afiché (Deut. XIII 7), attaché, fixé, planté.

aisardement (Deut. XXVIII 22), inflammation, dessèchement.
aise (No. II 17), proximité matérielle.
alant (No. XV 35), allant.
alve (Lév. XV 9), la ventrière de la selle.
anfanter (Gen. XXXIII 13), enfanter.
anpole (Lév. XXVI 16), ampoule sous le derme.
antandre (Gen. XLI 15; Deut. XXVIII 49), comprendre.
antortilié (Deut. XXXII 5), tortueux.
apaiement (Gen. XXXIII 10; Ex. XXV 2; Lév. XIX 5; Lév. XXII 19), apaisement.
aparélier (Gen. XI 3), se préparer.
apendiç (No. XXXIV 7), appentis.
aprover (Gen. XXIV 14), prouver.
arçon (Lév. XV 9), l'arçon de la selle.
ascorre (Deut. XXXIII 25), affluer.
assomail (Gen. XLIX 26; Ex. XXVIII 22), limite, sommet.
balbe (Ex. IV 10), bègue.
bast (Gen. XXXI 34), bât.
batediç (Ex. XXV 18; Ex. XXV 31; No. VIII 4), métal battu.
batedure (Ex. XXI 25), battage.
bendire (Deut. XXIX 18), bénir.
bize (Gen. XLI 6), vent d'est, bise.
blos (Gen. XLI 19), dénué, décharné.
bodeke (No. XI 5), pastèque.
bot (Lév. XI 29), crapaud.
caruede (Gen. XLVIII 7), terre labourée en un jour.

ceguyne (Lév. XI 19), cigogne.

cenpiés (Lév. XI 42), scolopendre.

centenier (Gen. XXIII 16), poids de cent pièces divisionnaires.

chalcier (Ex. IX 17), fouler aux pieds.

chalve-soriç (Lév. XI 18; Deut. XIV 16), chauve-souris.

chardon (Ex. XXII 5), chardon.

chastenier (Gen. XXX 37), châtaignier.

chaston (Ex. XXVIII 4), chaton d'une bague.

code (Ex. XXVIII 7), coude.

coife (Ex. XXVIII 4), coiffe.

coin (Gen. I 27), coin pour frapper les monnaies.

cojongle (Lév. XXVI 13), courroies qui lient le joug au front des boeufs.

coldre (Gen. XXX 37), coudrier.

coliandre (Ex. XVI 31; No. XI 7), coriandre.

comcobre (No. XI 5), concombre.

conmovres (Gen. I 24), reptiles, animaux rampants.

conpas (Gen. XXIX 17), cercle.

contrarier (Ex. XXII 20), contrarier, vexer.

corjede (Gen. XLIX 11), lanière.

crible (Ex. XXVII 4), grillage.

cristal (No. XI 7), cristal.

cro (Deut. XXVIII 22), carthame, safran bâtard.

crocin (Ex. XXVII 3), crochet.

çuete (Lév. XI 17), chouette.

delivrer (Deut. XXXII 30), délivrer.

denon (Ex. XIV 11), sans.

deraisnement (Ex. XXVIII 15), plaidoyer, exposé de la plainte.

desansandrer (Ex. XXVII 3), ôter les cendres.

descharjier (Ex. XXXII 3), décharger, débarrasser.

sei descompleindre (Ex. XIV 24), se plaindre.

desenfanté (Gen. XV 2), privé d'enfants.

destendre (No. XXIV 17), détendre.

destenprer (Ex. XVI 21), détremper, mélanger d'un liquide.

destolture (Deut. XIII 6), branches bâtardes de vigne sauvage.

destorner (Gen. XXXVIII 16), se détourner.

disant (No. VI 23), disant.

disner (Gen. XLIII 16), le repas de midi.

doner (Gen. XXIII 13), donner.

é (Deut. XXVIII 68), et.

ebres (Ex. XXIX 13; Lév. III 4), diaphragme.

en (No. II 17), à, dans.

encensier (Ex. XXVIII 14), encensoir.

encreistre (Gen. XXV 21; No. XXI 4), être dégouté.

enforcier (Deut. XXXII 36), dominer, avoir de l'influence.

engrés (No. XIV 44), présomptueux.

enjendrer (Gen. IV 18), engendrer.

enprenement (Ex. XX 5; No. XI 29; No. XXV 11; Deut. IV 24; Deut. XXIX 19), ardeur, jalousie.

entalier (Ex. XXXII 16), graver.

entenvir (No. XVII 4), laminer, aplatir.
enticier (Ex. VIII 17; Deut. XIII 7), exciter.
erbediç (Gen. I 11), sol couvert d'herbe.
esbaneier (No. XI 8), courir çà et là.
escarbot (Lév. XI 42), escarbot.
eschelon (Ex. XX 26), échelon, degré.
escrin (Ex. XXV 10), arche des tables de la loi.
escurement (Lév. VI 21), nettoyage, toilette.
esjareter (Gen. XLIX 6), couper les jarrets.
esmucer (Gen. XIX 17), se cacher, s'échapper.
espaldon (Deut. XVIII 3), paleron, omoplate d'animal.
espars (Ex. XXVI 26), chevron de bois, éparre.
espenir (Gen. XL 10), l'action de se couvrir de fleurs.
espiement (Lév. XIX 16), espionnage.
esprover (Gen. XX 16; Gen. XXXI 37), prouver, démontrer.
estainboc (Deut. XIV 5), bouquetin.
estanc (Ex. VII 19), étang.
estandre (Ex. XXXIX 3), étendre.
estantif (Ex. XXVI 15), dressé, debout.
estoble (Ex. V 7), éteule.
estordison (Gen. I 2; Ex. XIV 24; Deut. XXVIII 28; Deut. XXVIII 37), étourdissement.
estréner (Gen. XIV 14), initier, admettre à la connaissance.
faisant (No. XV 35), faisant.
faliance (Ex. XIV 11), manque.
fendre (Gen. XXII 3), fendre.

fermail (Ex. XXVI 6), agrafe pour fermer le col de la chemise.
féssed (Gen. XXXI 10; Ex. XXVI 1), grivelé, moucheté.
flanche (Lév. III 4), flanc.
flastre (Lév. XIX 20), flasque, sans fermeté.
flastrir (Ex. XVIII 18), flétrir.
flocheyde (Gen. XXV 25), peau corroyée, étoffe velue.
foaile (Lév. IV 35), foyer.
foede (Lév. I 9), combustion, holocauste.
foizon (Ex. XVI 5), foison, abondance.
forjier (No. XXIV 17), percer.
fosse (Gen. XLI 14), fosse.
fossé (Ex. XIV 11), fossé.
gant (Ex. XXVIII 41), gant.
gardant (Deut. XXVII 1), gardant.
garnizon (Gen. XLI 40), armes, arsenal.
gome (Ex. XXX 34), gomme.
gon (Ex. XXVII 10), gond.
grenaille (Lév. XXIII 14), un ensemble de graines.
grenoiliede (Ex. VIII 2), ensemble de grenouilles.
grenon (Lév. XIII 45), favoris, moustache.
hasled (Gen. XLI 6; Deut. XXVIII 22), desséché par la bise.
herberjerie (Gen. XXX 20), auberge, hôtellerie.
hériçon (Lév. XI 30), hérisson.
héron (Lév. XI 19), héron.
herupe (Lév. XI 19; Deut. XIV 18), huppe qui porte une touffe ébouriffée.

humer (Gen. XXIV 17), avaler en aspirant.
ibou (Lév. XI 17), hibou.
isle (No. XXXIV 6), île.
jaloyne (Ex. IX 8), le contenu des deux mains jointes en forme de coupe.
jelede (Ex. XVI 14), givre.
jonc (Ex. II 3), jonc.
justise (Deut. XXXII 41), justice.
lacediç (Ex. XXXI 10), étoffe de lacet.
laçol (Ex. XXVI 4), petits lacs.
lame (Gen. III 24), lame.
langouste (Lév. XI 21), sauterelle.
leizarde (Lév. XI 30), lézard.
limace (Lév. XI 30), limace.
lintier (Ex. XII 7), linteau, jambage d'une porte.
loce (Ex. XXX 7; Ex. XXXV 14; No. IV 9), lampe.
lonble (Lév. III 4), lombe.
lor (No. XXI 4), leur, à eux.
machadure (Gen. IV 23), meurtrissure, lésion traumatique.
maderin (Gen. XLIV 2; Ex. XXV 31), coupe à boire en bois veiné.
maldire (No. XXIII 27), maudire.
malevoi (Deut. XXVIII 22), fièvre chaude.
marche (Gen. XLIX 13), frontière.
maresc (Gen. XLI 2), marais.
méntenedor (Deut. XXXII 36), celui qui maintient.

mesnede (Gen. XLV 2), le personnel d'une maison, la suite d'un seigneur.

miredoir (Ex. XXXVIII 8), miroir.

molant (Deut. IX 21), moulant.

mostoile (Lév. XI 29), belette.

muiseron (Lév. XI 11), moucheron.

murmurediç (No. XVII 25), murmures.

naistre (Gen. IV 18), naître.

navredure (Ex. XXI 25), blessure.

neel (Ex. XXXII 4), nielle en creux où l'on coule un émail noir.

neeler (Ex. XXV 33), orner de nielles gravés.

noreture (Deut. XXXII 20), nourriture, élevage.

nuisement (Gen. XXVI 21), dommage, action de nuire.

oblede (Gen. XL 16), oublie.

olve (Ex. IX 8), cendre de charbons de four.

orable (Lév. XIII 37), susceptible d'être doré.

ostoir (Lév. XI 16), autour, épervier.

ouvrayne (Gen. XXVI 14), ouvrage.

oyant (Deut. I 16), entendant.

pal (Ex. XXVII 10), pieu, poteau.

parlediç (Gen. XXXVII 2; No. XIV 36), bavardage, commérage, calomnie.

paske (Ex. XII 11), pâque.

pedoiliere (Ex. VIII 2; Ex. VIII 13), vermine.

perche (No. XXI 8), perche de bois.

pestor (Gen. XL 1), boulanger.
plante (Ex. X 26; Lév. XI 3; Deut. XIV 6), plante du pied.
plom (Ex. XV 10), plomb.
point (Lév. XIII 51), piqué.
pointure (Gen. XXX 32), piqûre, blessure étroite.
pomel (Ex. XXV 31), pommette qui orne un chandelier.
por (Ex. XIV 11), à cause de.
porceint (Ex. XXVIII 4), ceinture, tablier.
porel (No. XI 5), poireau, porreau.
porparledure (Deut. XXXIII 3), entretien.
porpoint (Lév. XIX 28), piqûre faite avec un instrument tranchant.
porvendre (Deut. XXVIII 68), vendre.
poseydure (Ex. XXV 38), seau pour recueillir la cendre, cendrier.
predejeir (Ex. VII 1), plaideur, interprète.
prounele (Lév. XXI 20), prunelle.
redognier (Lév. XIV 41), rogner.
retraire (Ex. V 8; Lév. XIII 23), retirer, se rétrécir.
retreiement (Lév. XIII 23), rétraction, contraction.
revestir (Ex. XXVIII 41), investir, consacrer.
rosel (Ex. II 3), roseau.
rous (Gen. XXX 32; Lév. XIII 39), roux.
saluder (Gen. XXXIII 11; Gen. XLVII 7), saluer.
sanement (Lév. XIII 10; Lév. XIII 24), santé.
sein (Gen. XLI 5; Gen. XLI 7), sain.

serer (Ex. XIV 3), enfermer.
serjanterie (Ex. XXVIII 3), service des officiants, sacerdoce.
setene (Gen. XXIX 28; Ex. X 22; Ex. XII 15; Lév. XXIII 8), sept jours.
si (Ex. XIV 11), est-ce que?
solder (Ex. XXV 18; Ex. XXV 31), presser ensemble, souder.
son (No. II 17), son.
sorcilos (Lév. XXI 20), chassieux.
splandor (Deut. XXXII 41), éclair.
tache (Ex. XXI 25), une tache.
talpe (Lév. XI 18; Lév. XI 30), taupe, chiroptère.
teie (Lév. XIII 2), une tache blanche, une taie.
teile (Lév. XXI 20), taie opaque sur la cornée, leucome.
teile (Ex. XXIX 13), graisse qui recouvre la panse, tissu adipeux.
tenailes (Ex. XXV 38), tenailles.
tendrum (Ex. XXIX 20; Lév. XIV 14), lobe de l'oreille (d'un animal).
tenve (Gen. XLI 3; Ex. XVI 14; No. XVII 3), mince.
terçaine (Ex. X 22), une triade de jours.
tes (Deut. XXXIII 3), tes.
tivle (Ex. V 7), tuile.
torche (Gen. XIX 28), colonne de fumée.
tortel (No. XV 20), galette cuite sous la cendre.
trace (Gen. XLIX 19), trace.
tranble (Gen. XXX 37), le tremble.

triacle (Ex. XXX 34), thériaque.
tudel (Gen. XLI 5), tuyau, tige.
vadil (Ex. XXVII 3; No. IV 14), pelle à feu.
vanter (Ex. VIII 5), vanter.
vedis (Gen. XL 10), sarment, vrille d'une vigne.
venteler (Ex. XXIX 27), agiter de côté et d'autre.
verdure (Ex. X 15), verdure.
verue (Lév. XXII 22), verrue.
vinos (Deut. XXXII 14), vineux, plein de vin.
vos (Deut. XXVIII 68), vous.

―――――*Frederic Koenig*―――――

The Affective and Expressive Values of Verb-Complement Compounds in Romance

THE TERM "verb-complement" is not an entirely satisfactory descripion of the formation to be dealt with here, but has been adopted as a matter of convenience to avoid a more cumbersome designation. Actually, the second element of these compounds, although most often a complement, may equally well be a vocative or another verb. As examples in which the second element is a complement, one may cite: *crève-coeur, sacabotas, cut-throat, touche-à-tout, tentempié, battinzecca, hug-me-tight, passe-partout, posapiano, pick-up*. Illustrative of forms with the vocative are: *pêche-martin, andaniño, saltamartino, go-devil*. When the second element is a verb, it may be co-ordinated with the first or simply a reduplication: *tourne-vire, vaiven, quitapon* (also *quitaipon*), *coupe-coupe, pegapega, hushhush*.

The precise grammatical nature of the first element is not particularly material to the present study, but I doubt that there are any scholars in the Romance field who do not concede it to be imperative.[1]

This type of composition is very much alive in all the Romance languages, and is more productive in English than is generally realized. The dictionaries of the various languages contain hundreds of examples, but these represent only a fraction of the number actually in use. The verb-complement compound tends to be either popular in nature or confined to the vocabularies of highly specialized groups; often, consequently, it does not find its way into the literary language or even into writing. While the conclusions reached here are based primarily on French, Spanish, and Italian, sufficient sampling was done to indicate that they hold substantially for Portuguese, Provençal, Rhaeto-romance, and English, too.

With the field of investigation so defined, some precision concerning affectivity is in order. Strictly speaking, affectivity means the conveyance or evocation by a speech form of some emotional reaction—approval, disapproval, pleasure, displeasure, pity, surprise, amusement, indignation, etc. Nevertheless, there are some words which have no apparent emotional content—at least, one is unable to pin any particular emotional label on them—but which still produce marked stylistic effect by their incisive character, by their vividness, by the vigor or boldness of their imagery. As samples of verb-complement formations which appear to me to be precisely of this nature, let me cite some words which designate either technical or very prosaic objects: *emporte-pièce, pare-chocs, boute-feu, vide-vite; sacaembocados, saltaregla, cascanueces, cortafrío; battifuoco, cacciavite, cavafango.* A priori, one might indeed expect all verb-complement formations to have this character since their first element generally expresses movement and since they are essentially metonymies in which the thing signified is designated by a function or characteristic action. In any case, we shall not want to ignore expressive quality even though it may not be strictly classifiable as affective.

Affectivity itself is of two orders. We must distinguish between the kind which appears as a constant characteristic of certain speech forms, which is inherent in them, and the kind with which any speech form may be clothed as a result of the situation or special circumstances in which it is used. The first of these may be termed intrinsic affectivity—intrinsic, that is, to the speech form—and the second, extrinsic. Take, for instance, the terms *kitty, cat, feline*. For most people, *kitty* calls forth the same feelings—interest, warmth, tenderness. *Cat*, while neutral for the majority, may affect some individuals pleasantly, others unpleasantly, because of their respective fondness or aversion for the animal. *Feline* used in a scientific environment is neutral, but used in everyday language may provoke mirth because of its inappropriateness. The affectivity of *kitty* is intrinsic; that of the other two words, when they have it, extrinsic. Affectivity achieved through intonation is, of course, extrinsic. While extrinsic affectivity is by no means devoid of interest for the student of stylistics, the nature of our inquiry requires that we be concerned here only with the intrinsic variety.

It is not, however, always easy to determine whether affectivity is intrinsic or extrinsic. What shall be the criterion? Going back to *kitty*, how can we be sure that its affectivity does not stem from the thing designated rather than from the speech form? One way to resolve this problem is to compare the form in question with synonymous expressions.[2] Since *small cat* does not have the connotations of *kitty*, we can rest assured that the latter's affectivity is intrinsic. Another, perhaps still better, index of intrinsic character is the constancy of the affectivity in the speech form under consideration. Most people, even those who do not like cats, are conscious of the affective values of *kitty*.

If we go now a little further with *kitty*, we may note that its affective values are shared by virtually all English diminutive formations in *-y* and its alternative *-ie*. Intrinsic values, then, may be characteristic of particular types of formation. For these values to be associated with a certain type of formation, however, it is not necessary that all representatives of the type possess them. The existence of non-pejorative forms like *vieillard* and *montagnard* does not alter the fact that French formations in *-ard* generally have the depreciatory value found in *fuyard, braillard, dreyfusard*, etc.

A preliminary survey of the whole field of verb-complement compounds, however, yields no immediately apparent regularity of affective content. Some forms are affective, others are merely expressive, still others are not even that. Of those that are affective, the values are not all of the same order: a good many are depreciative, but some are laudative; again, many are ironical or whimsical; and there are still to be found scattered representatives of varied other affective content. At first sight, then, it might seem doubtful that there are any particular affective values intrinsic to the verb-complement pattern. However, since the verb-complement formations comprise a field vastly more extensive than the suffix formations mentioned above, they can be expected to present a more complex problem. Closer analysis and segmentation of the field may result in the emergence of some order.

But before proceeding with our segmentation, let us make some observations on those forms which have no affectivity and little or no expressiveness. We have already remarked that, by reason of their verbal element and metonymic character, the verb-complement compounds can be expected to be at least expressive, if not affective. And most of them are. Further, the failure to be so of a good part of those that are not can be explained. Naturally words whose verbal elements are no longer recognizable could not be expected to retain the expressiveness which would ordinarily result from having such an element. Thus: *cloporte* ("clore"), *bacul* ("battre"), *morpion* ("mordre"), *tocsin* (Pr. *tocasenh* < *tocare* + *signum*).[3] Again, the verbal element—doubtless as a result of the frequency of its appearance in these compounds, coupled with its failure to express physical action or movement—may have ceased to be felt as verbal and have become a mere prefix. The descendants of *portare* and *guardare*, which in all the Romance Languages enter into composition much more frequently than any other verbs, are the principal cases in point. Few of their numerous compounds have either affective or expressive value; and when they do,[4] it must be regarded as accidental and not intrinsic to the formation. That Sp. *porta-* is nothing more than a particle is born out by the fact that *portar* as an independent verb has long been obsolete in the senses which it has in its compounds.[5] We may mention here also the French formations having *para-* as their first element. *Parasol, parapet,* and *paravent* are loan-words. Forms like *parapluie, parafoudre, paratonnerre, parados, parachute* are obviously analogical [6] and tend, consequently, to be less expressive than genuine formations from *parer* like *pare-chocs, pare-boue, pare-étincelles, pare-éclats,* etc.

Although at its inception the verb-complement compound appears to have been epithetic [7] and most of its representatives retain something of this character, its current function is predominantly substantival. In fact, it is only in French that adjective forms appear to any extent, and even there their use is limited. The substantives occur as both proper nouns and common nouns. The common nouns may designate persons, living things, or inanimate objects; they may likewise be abstract. Here, then, is a basis for our segmentation of the field: let us first consider the proper nouns, which constitute the earliest forms on record, and then let us attack the vast mass of common nouns, subdividing them as just indicated.

Among the proper nouns, a high incidence of depreciative and derisive terms becomes immediately apparent. Place names like *Pendleu, Pisseleu, Gasteblé, Crievecuer, Couppegueule, Prends-y-garde, Crievepance, Chantereine, Cantarranas, Rascavielas, Mojabragas, Despeñaperros, Mazagatos*[8] were obviously bestowed in contempt. While some place names are just as obviously laudatory or merely descriptive— e.g., *Tenegaudia, Portegoie, Mirebel, Chantemerle, Salvatierra, Miraflores, Cantalapiedra*[9]—the majority are depreciatory.

In respect to person names, the tendency is even more pronounced. Although many of the verb-complement person names have become family names, they originated as sobriquets and these tend naturally, as Albert Dauzat has remarked,[10] to take an uncomplimentary turn. Much like the Latin cognomena, they call attention to some physical or moral trait of the bearer, and almost invariably one unfavorable to him. Typical are *Torcul, Engoulevent, Besediable, Couvedenier, Brisepot, Papelart, Gaaignenéent, Torne-en-fuie, Foutvielle*. Even apparently neutral or laudatory terms were often applied ironically. Thus, the very common *Boileau* (cf. It. *Bevilacqua*) appears to have been originally an antiphrasis for drunkard.[11] Forms which can be definitely identified as laudatory—e.g., *Taillefer*,[12] *Fierabras*,[13] *Poincheval, Tueleu*—exist, but are rare. When they do occur, they seem to have to do with military or cynegetic prowess. Included here, although not the name of a person, should be the name of Gerer's horse (*Chanson de Roland*, 1380): *Passecerf*. Some verb-complement names appear to be simple descriptions of the occupation of the bearer, but even in these cases it is frequently difficult to rule out at least the possibility of underlying irony. While appellations like *Fillesoie* and *Portelyaue* could hardly have lent themselves to gibing, can we be sure that even so innocent an appearing name as *Abatbois* was a mere equivalent of *bucheron*? *Poinbuef* and *Poinlasne* seem even more suspect, particularly since they are found to be borne by persons not likely to have actually performed such menial tasks nor to have descended from persons who performed them. When we find bearing the sobriquet *Chacelievre* a person otherwise qualified as "miles" and "forestarius,"[14] we may be fairly sure the name was given with jeering intent. Even more obviously is this the case of *Chassepie* and *Pescheveron*. The frequence with which our verb-complement names occur in the works of writers with a sardonic bent is further confirmation, if any more were needed, of their character: they abound in the *fabliaux*, in the animal epics, in Coquillart, and particularly in Rabelais.[15] Obviously, however, in those sobriquets which have survived as family names, the ironic or depreciatory nuance has been largely lost.

Common-noun forms designating persons show the same preponderance of pejoratives that we have found in the proper nouns. Terms like *fesse-mathieu, grippe-sous, lèche-fesses, vaurien, faitard, rêve-creux, coupe-jarret, gobe-Dieux, pisse-*

froid, tâte-au-pot, trouble-fête, aguafiestas, tragaldabas, matasiete, pinchauvas, quitapelillos, pisaverde, lameculos, hazmerreir, sputasenno, spazzacontrade, pelapolli, cacazibetto, spaccamonte, scalzagatto, gabbasanti, baciapile comprise the bulk of these words. The majority of the non-pejorative forms are compounds of *porter, portar, portare* and *garder, guardar, guardare*, which, as we have already noted, are seldom affective under any circumstances. The non-pejoratives remaining after exclusion of the *porte-, porta-* and *garde-, guarda-* compounds are rather rare. As definitely neutral we may cite: *serre-freins, chauffe-cire, serre-file, pique-mine, echapellas, batihoja, cuidaniños, sacamanchas, pisauvas, battiloro, battinzecca, battistrada, tiraloro, filaloro, apriporta, conciatetti, cavamacchie, nettapanni, taglialegna, tagliapietre, guidarmenti*. Some others—*tourne-broche, gagne-pain, ganapán, picamulos, limpiabotas, lavaplatos, lavapiatti, lavascodelle, lustrascarpe*—may not always be strictly pejorative, but often seem to be used with depreciative nuances. It will doubtless have been noticed already that all the non-pejorative formations mentioned describe occupational functions. The same thing is true of virtually all the *porte-, porta-* and *garde-, guarda-* compounds which designate persons.[16] One might, consequently, be led to conclude that verb-complement formations denoting the performer of an occupational task are generally not affective. Actually, this is far from the fact. The plethora of terms like *fesse-cahier, chasse-chiens* ("beadle"),[17] *hale-boulines* ("lubberly seaman"), *gratte-menton, croque-note, croque-morts, pique-puces* ("tailor"), *pousse-cailloux* ("infantryman"), *gâte-sauces, cagatintas* ("office drudge"), *azotaperros* (cf. *chasse-chiens*), *rapabarbas, picapiojos* (cf. *pique-puces*), *matatías* ("pawnbroker"), *tapagujeros* ("clumsy mason"), *pintamonas* ("hack portrait painter"), *sacamuertosymetesillas, sacamuelas, sacapotras, matasanos, medicastronzolo, cavadenti, becamorti, lavaceci, tirapiedi* ("hangman's assistant"), *torcileggi* leaves no doubt that even in the case of words denoting occupational function, there is a decided association of the injurious and the derisory with the verb-complement compound.

Common nouns indicating place or location are few and tend to be pejorative: *brise-cou, casse-cou, casse-gueule, coupe-gorge, pince-cul* ("cheap dance hall," also *pince-fesses*), *claque-dents* ("low dive"), *fourre-tout, spazzavento*. However, Sp. *parteaguas* is neutral, while *vide-bouteilles* and *tourne-bride* are on the good-natured side.

The common or familiar names of many biological—particularly ornithological and botanical—species are verb-complement formations. These words are frequently affective, but the regularity which prevails in the nouns indicating persons is lacking. Depreciation is common, but cannot, in this case, be associated so definitely with the formation. While some words ascribe to the thing signified noxious or ridiculous qualities— e.g., *enfle-boeuf* ("golden carabid"), *gâte-bois* ("wood borer"), *crève-chien* ("black nightshade"), *tue-brebis* ("butterwort"), *fouille-merde* ("dung chafer"), *matahombres* ("blister beetle"), *mataojo* (South American tree which gives off an eye irritating vapor), *detienebuey* ("rest harrow"), *cavalocchio* (kind of wasp)—there are almost as many which connote approval: *dompte-vénin* ("asclepias" or "swallow-wort"), *chasse-bosse* ("loose-strife"), *passe-rage* ("pepperwort"), *casse-lunettes* ("euphrasy"), *passe-fleur* ("anemone"; the name implies that it surpasses the ordinary flower), *passe-pomme* (variety of apple supposed to be superior), *passe-cressane* (variety of pear supposed to be even better than the cressane). But most of these species names seem to have been created with no idea of approval or disapproval; the intent seems rather to have been to produce a vivid or picturesque characterization of the thing signified: *lèche-pattes* ("sloth"), *fouette-queue* ("wagtail"), *torcol* ("wryneck"), *gobe-mouches* ("flycatcher," "gnatsnatcher," "Venus flytrap"), *girasol, rompesacos* ("spiked hardgrass"), *quebrantapiedras, trepatroncos* ("woodpecker"), *saltimpalo* ("stone chat"), *abracciaboschi* ("honeysuckle"), *cazzavela* ("seagull"). Often humor shows itself in the form of exaggeration, whimsicality, or simply coarseness: *engoulevent* ("goatsucker"), *monte-au-ciel* ("fumatory"), *pisse-chien* (variety of mushroom), *pisse-en-lit, pisse-sang* ("chokeweed"), *pousse-pied* (variety of barnacle), *saltamontes* ("grasshopper"), *saltaojos* ("peony"), *picarrelincho* (variety of woodpecker), *cagaaceite* ("missel thrush"), *cagarropa* (a small fly), *tenvergüenza* ("sensitive plant"), *quitameriendas* ("autumn saffron"), *espantalobos* ("bladder senna"), *tentenlaire* ("hummingbird" in Argentina), *ahogaviejas* ("Venus' comb"), *matagallegos* ("milk thistle"), *quitacalzón* ("wasp"), *rompezaragüellos* ("reedgrass"), *pisciacane* ("chokeweed"). Humor is to be found too in certain forms involving a vocative: *bêchelisette* ("vine grub"), *pêche-bernard* ("kingfisher"), *saltaperico* ("grasshopper").

A very large proportion of our formations denote non-living things. They are to be found as technical terms for tools, instruments, devices, machines used in virtually every industry and profession; they designate, as well, a wide variety of homely objects encountered in everyday life. We have already met some examples in our opening paragraphs; to these may be added: *compte-fils, tourne-à-gauche, presse-étoffe* (pressure foot of a sewing machine), *chasse-goupille* (tool used by gunsmiths), *rogne-pied* (farrier's hoof scraper), *serre-fine* (a surgical instrument), *essuie-glace, tire-cartouche, coupe-circuit, presse-étoupes* (packing ring on shafts and piston rods), *tiralíneas* ("drafting pen"), *tientaguja* ("sounding rod"), *abrebocas* ("surgeon's speculum"), *pesalicores, cubreengranaje, alzaválvulas, cortarrenglón* (marginal stop on typewriter), *apagachispas, arrancaclavos, buscahuella* ("spotlight"), *rompeátomas, lisciapiante* ("shoemaker's polisher"), *cavastracci* ("gun worm"), *sbrattaneve, rompighiaccio, curaporti* ("dredge"), *tagliamare* ("cutwater"), *mazzafrusto* ("balista"), *passacorde* ("bodkin"), *foraterra* ("dibble"), *grattacacio, infornapane.*

These words, it can readily be seen from the examples given, generally do not have affectivity proper, but—excepting always the abundant *porte-, porta-* and *garde-, guarda-*compounds—they are usually expressive. Truly affective forms are by no means lacking, however. Humor in the form of hyperbole, irony, and whimsy is to be found, particularly in the words that belong to familiar, rather than technical, speech: *brûle-gueule, tape-cul* ("balance," "light two-wheeled cart," any jolting vehicle), *guide-âne, vide-poches* ("small stand with drawers"), *ahorcaperros* ("slipknot"), *tentemozo* ("prop," "brace"), *excusabaraja* (type of covered basket), *tragaluz* ("skylight"), *tragaperras* ("slot machine"), *tragavino* ("funnel"), *hurtadineros* ("child's bank"), *castraporci* ("knife of poor quality"), *gastigamatti* ("whip"), *saltafossi* ("rattletrap").

In soldier's and sailor's language and in slang, words with these qualities are, as might be expected, more frequent: *secoue-paletôt* ("machine gun"), *monte-à-regret* ("scaffold," "guillotine"), *coupe-vent* ("nose"), *bouche-l'oeil* (gold or silver coin), *coupe-choux* ("broadsword"), *tire-jus* ("handkerchief"), *descuernapadrastros* (kind of cutlass), *sacanabos* (hook for extracting bombs from mortars), *matasoldados* ("mizzen staysail"), *baticulo* (part of top mast rigging). We might include here mention of the use of ordinarily non-affective verb-complement compounds in grotesque metaphors: *cure-dents* and *tournebroche* for *baïonnette*, *abat-jour* for *casque colonial*, *lance-pierres* for *fusil*, *lance-bombes* for *cuisine roulante*, *pousse-pousse* for *chemin de fer à voie étroite*, *torche-cul* for *circulaire*.[18]

Formations designating articles of clothing and personal adornment show a marked tendency towards affectivity, humor of the same type as that just mentioned above still being involved: *claque-oreille* ("floppy brimmed hat"), *cache-nez*, *passe-montagne*, *rase-pet* ("short jacket"), *happelourde* ("fake jewel"), *accroche-coeur* (curl of hair worn on forehead), *cache-misère* (overgarment worn to hide shabby clothing beneath it), *décrochez-moi-ça* ("secondhand hat"), *grattez-moi-dans-le-dos* (kind of corset), *suivez-moi-jeune-homme* (long double ribbon worn trailing behind), *pincez-moi-ça* (ribbon worn in a bow on the back of a dress), *taparrabo* ("loin cloth," "trunks"), *rascamono* ("fancy hair pin"), *tapabocas* (cf. *cache-nez*), *alzacuello* ("stock"; cf. Fr. *hausse-col*), *espantavillanos* ("cheap flashy jewelry"; cf. *happelourde*), *batticulo* ("breeches"), *saltamindosso* ("scant, shabby garment"), *picchiapetto* (jewelled cross worn on bosom), *scopamare* ("sailor cap").

Terms indicating items of food or drink follow the same pattern: *amuse-gueule*, *croque-monsieur*, *vol-au-vent*, *casse-museau* or *cache-museau* (kind of pastry), *abat-faim*, *casse-*

croûte, croquembouche (kind of pastry), *hochepot, tournedos, tire-fiacre* ("horse meat," "tough beef"), *chasse-cousin* ("poor wine"), *chasse-ennuie* ("cup that cheers"), *casse-poitrine* ("rotgut"; also called *tord-boyaux, casse-pattes, arrache-bide*), *pousse-café, saute-barrières* ("wine"; also called *brouille-ménage*), *pousse-au-crime* ("brandy"; also called *remonte-moi-le-moral, traine-par-terre*), *tentempié* ("snack"), *matahambre* (kind of marzipan in Cuba), *aguapié* ("weak wine"), *matarratas* ("rotgut"), *sciaquadenti* ("light meal"), *tornagusto* ("appetizer"), *cacciacristo* ("bad wine").

As abstracts, verb-complement nouns are generally expressive and frequently affective, the affectivity taking various forms, but with humor predominating: *crève-coeur, chasse-ennui, sauve-l'honneur, rabat-joie, trompe-l'oeil, trompe-conscience, passe-droit, tape-à-l'oeil, casse-tête, attrape-parterre* ("ham acting"), *casse-bras* ("setback," "mishap"), *quitapesares, quitamiedo, quitasueño, hurtacuerpo* ("slight," "cold shoulder"), *rapapolvo* ("reprimand"), *soplamocos* ("punch in the nose"), *passagonzalo* ("flick"), *zurrapelo* ("sharp dressing down"), *mazagatos* ("row"), *trabalenguas, trabacuenta, buscapié, trocatinta* (exchange made by error), *batticuore, battisoffia, grattacapo* ("worry"), *cantafavola* ("nonsense"), *cacciaffani* (cf. *chasse-ennui* and *quitapesares*), *rompicapo* (cf. *casse-tête* and *rompecabezas*), *bacciabasso* ("bow," "reverence"), *rompicollo* ("rash undertaking"), *battibecco* ("argument"), *lavacapo* ("rebuke"), *scavezzacollo* ("dangerous fall"), *tornaconto* ("profit"), *giracapo* ("vertigo"), *crepacuore*.

Our compounds are frequently used as names of games and as gaming terms. Virtually all of these are highly expressive, and the majority have an element of humor: *cache-cache, cligne-musette* (same as *cache-cache*), *frappe-main* ("hot cockles"), *tourne-case* (game on the order of backgammon), *attrape-pognon*, *tape-cul* ("seesaw"), *passe-boule* (game in which balls are thrown into a hole representing the open mouth of a figure), *coupe-tête* (same as *saute-mouton*), *passe-dix* (game played with three dice), *coupe-cul* (term used in *lansquenet*), *ganapierde* ("giveaway"), *escondecucas* ("hide and seek"), *tragabolas* (same game as *passe-balles*), *matarrata* (a card game), *scaldamano* ("hot cockles"; also called *beccalaglio*), *salincerbio* ("leap frog"), *scaricalasino* (a game with checkers), *scaricabarili* ("tiptop castle").

Verb-complement forms have been used to designate diseases. Naturally these are pejorative: *trousse-galant* ("cholera morbus"), *pisse-sang* (a disease of cattle), *pasa-campana* (tumor which forms on the hocks of equines), *cacasangue* ("dysentery").

Spanish uses a number of our formations, usually humorously, to describe weather phenomena: *rabiazorras* ("east wind"), *matacabras* ("harsh north wind"), *calabobos* "penetrating drizzle"), *matapolvo* ("light rain"), *descuernacabras* ("severe north wind"). Related, although not abstract, are *calamoco* ("icicle") and *aguapié* ("slush").

Many verb-complement compounds occur in fixed prepositional phrases outside of which they are generally not to be found.[19] All are picturesque and highly expressive: *à brûle-pourpoint, à musse-pot* (or *muche-pot*), *à cloche-pied, à écorche-cul* ("sliding along on one's backside," hence, doing something unwillingly), *à dépêche-compagnon* (with *se battre*, "to the finish"), *à étripe-cheval, à rebrousse-poil, à tue-tête, à tire-larigot, à lèche-doigts, d'arrache-pied, en un tourne-main, en rase-mottes, à la va-comme-je-te-pousse, a rodeabrazo, a tente bonete, a regañadientes, a quemarropa, a macha-*

martillo, a rapaterrón, a volapié, a pasaperro (bookbinding term), *a pasatoro, de hurtamano, a bruciapelo, a crepapanci, a crepapelle, a squarciagola, a squarciasaco* (with *guardare*, "look with an evil eye"), *a straccabraccia, a strippapelle, a tiratira* (with *fare*, "draw lots"), *a strappabecco* ("inconsiderately"), *a scaricabarili* (with *fare*, "foist the blame for something on someone else").

We have already remarked that the use of verb-complement formations as adjectives is confined to French and even there is limited. Adjective forms abound in the works of the Pleiade,[20] but the vogue for them—perhaps as a result of their abuse by Du Bartas—was short-lived. There are a few literary survivals: "la gent trotte-menue" (La Fontaine), "l'animal porte-jupe" (Regnard), "l'oiseau porte-foudre" (Diderot), "l'enfant porte-bandeau" (Béranger). Naturally, words created expressly for poetic effect tend to be not only expressive but likewise affective. Turning to more prosaic language, we find *fainéant* (*les rois fainéants*), *ferre-mule* (*un servant ferre-mule*), and *coupe-choux* (*un frère coupe-choux*), all three pejorative. However, most of the adjectival forms in current use belong to technical or commercial language and are non-affective: *un vaisseau serre-file, un canon porte-amarre, un livre classe-feuilles, du papier tue-mouches, du papier chasse-punaises, une charrue tourne-oreille, une clef tourne-écrous*.[21]

After our survey of the field, I believe the following conclusions to be warranted:

1. Verb-complement compounds are generally expressive and frequently affective.

2. With the whole range of the formation in view, the prevailing affective values—particularly dominant in the proper

nouns and in the common nouns designating persons and places, but cropping up also to greater or lesser degree in the other types—are depreciative and derisory. Outside of the proper-noun, person, and place-name categories, the derision tends to become more good-natured, and frequently weakens to simple chaffing and whimsicality.

3. While other affective values manifest themselves at times, they fail to do so with sufficient regularity to warrant their being associated with the formation.

4. When lacking affectivity proper, as is frequently the case, the verb-complement compounds usually achieve expressiveness through the evocation of vivid and vigorous images. Providing the verbal element does not become obscured through phonetic erosion and does not deteriorate into a mere prefix as in the case of the *porte-, porta-* and *garde-, guarda-* formations, the verb-complement compounds seem to retain their original expressiveness regardless of the time elapsed since their creation and contrary to what happens in the case of most stylistic phenomena.

These conclusions are hardly startling. For the most part, either they might have been predicted or they have been anticipated in the course of previous treatments of other aspects of our formations. This is, however, the first study specifically devoted to a systematic review of the affectivity and expressive qualities of these compounds, and the conclusions, even when merely negative or corroborative of what had already been advanced, do put the matter on a firmer basis.

It was not our purpose here to consider the origin and development of the verb-complement compounds. However, a few words on the subject may not be amiss. The most recent treatment of the matter is to be found in Spitzer's appendage (Rom., LXXIII, 42 ff.) to his discussion of certain metaphoric uses of the imperative. Spitzer engages in some rambling and, on the whole, idle—since they cannot be substantiated—speculations. His arguments are neither particularly perceptive nor convincing. While he is doubtless correct in affirming—after Suchier—that our formations in their earliest appearances were sobriquets, his tracing of their development from that stage is frequently not only open to dispute but highly improbable, and at times not even in accord with known facts. All that it is safe to assume can, I think, be summed up succinctly as follows: At its inception, the formation seems to have been an apostrophe in which the person apostrophized was defied to do something dishonoring or ridiculous. The scornful challenge is a common human device to dissuade someone from doing something the challenger fears or of which he disapproves (cf. Eng. *tattletale*). The step from apostrophe to epithet is easy. The figure was subsequently extended to places and to living things, finally to inanimate things and abstractions. In the beginning, the person, place, or thing was urged to do something to excite contempt or laughter, and it was implied that this action was characteristic. Later, the subject was simply called upon to perform some characteristic action, good or bad. The original character of the formation is, then, best reflected in the person names, least in the names of inanimate objects.

---

1. See H. Suchier in Gröber's *Grundriss der rom. Phil.*, I (1888), 661; Edouard Bourciez, *Eléments de linguistique romane* (4th ed.; Paris, 1946), p. 203; Kr. Nyrop, *Grammaire historique de la langue française* (Paris-

Copenhagen, 1899–1930), III, 273 ff.; Arsène Darmesteter, *Traité de la formation des mots composés* (2d ed.; Paris, 1894), pp. 168 ff.; idem, *De la création actuelle de mots nouveaux dans la langue française* (Paris, 1877), pp. 161 ff.; Louis-Francis Meunier, *Les composés qui contiennent un verbe à un mode personnel en latin, en français, en italien, et en espagnol* (Paris, 1885); Hermann Osthoff, *Das Verbum in der Nominalcomposition* (Jena, 1878), pp. 236 ff.; Leo Spitzer, "Sur quelques emplois métaphoriques de l'impératif," *Romania*, LXXIII (1952), 42 ff.

2. This is, of course, the measure of affectivity proposed by Charles Bally in his various works on stylistics.

3. The phenomenon is virtually nonexistent in Castilian and in Tuscan, because they have been more stable phonetically than French.

4. There are several formations with an element of humor: *porte-maillot* ("bit actor"), *porte-respect* ("firearm"), *porte-fainéant* ("seat for the teamster on the shaft of a dray-cart"), *porte-fafiots* "billfold"), *porte-pipe* ("face"), *garde-fou*, *guardainfantes* (a kind of crinoline used in eighteenth-century Spain and Italy to conceal pregnancy).

5. See my "Notes on Spanish Word Formation," *Modern Language Notes*, LXVIII (1953), 17.

6. See Darmesteter, *Traité*, p. 225, n. 2; and Meunier, pp. 220–21.

7. Cf. Darmesteter, *Traité*, pp. 228–29.

8. Darmesteter (*Traité*, pp. 171 ff. and 206 ff.) and Meunier (pp. 12 ff.) give extensive repertories of these names. See also A. Longnon, *Les Noms de lieu de la France* (Paris, 1920–29), pp. 529, 537 ff.; and my "Notes on Spanish Word Formation," pp. 14–15.

9. Spitzer (*Romania*, LXXIII, 49) considers that all these names had ironic, hence depreciatory, nuances. While this is possible, though not very probable, for *Tenegaudia*, *Portegoie*, and *Chantemerle*, it becomes extremely doubtful in the cases of *Mirebel*, *Salvatierra*, and *Cantalapiedra* and even more so in the cases of *Miramar*, *Miraflores*, etc.

Incidentally, Spitzer misquotes Dauzat on this matter. Dauzat does not say specifically (*Les noms de lieux*, p. 28) that *Chantemerle* and *Chantelauze* are ironical, but that compounds of this type sometimes are.

10. In *Les noms de famille et prénoms de France* (2d ed.; Paris, 1949), p. 181.

11. Dauzat, *Noms de famille*, p. 207.

12. In both *Les Noms de famille*, p. 209, and in *Les Noms de personnes* (Paris, 1925), p. 103, as well as in his *Dictionnaire étymologique des noms de famille et prénoms* (Paris, 1951), Dauzat labels *Taillefer* "surnom professionel," but neglects to say what profession he thinks it describes. Since in its earliest appearances it is used to qualify valiant and noble warriors, and since in the Middle Ages war was the only profession sufficiently characterized by the cleaving of iron for this action to have furnished an epithet, it may be safely assumed that *Taillefer* originated as a term of praise for knights adept

at penetrating enemy armor. A smith, it should be noted, characteristically beats rather than cuts iron. Moreover, I have been able to find no instance of the term's being associated with smiths or, for that matter, with the members of any other trade. Spitzer's supposition (*Romania*, LXXIII, 47) that *Taillefer* was from the beginning used with ironic intent is not only pure supposition but in disaccord with the few facts we possess.

13. While the dictionaries, s. v. *fier-à-bras*, are virtually unanimous in offering *fera bracchia* as the etymon of *Fierabras*, this etymology is completely unacceptable on phonological grounds. See *Modern Language Notes*, LXXI (1956), 356–57.

14. See Meunier, p. 39.

15. See Meunier, pp. 67 ff., and Darmesteter, *Traité*, pp. 209, 215 ff.

16. Miss A. G. Hatcher correctly points out (*Word*, II, 226) that the ordinary speaker of French tends to feel the first element in the *garde-* compounds as a noun, especially when the compound designates a person. She then attempts to account for this on the grounds that in current French, verb-complement compounds have an inevitable depreciatory nuance and that, consequently, if *garde-* were interpreted as a verb, words like *garde-chasse*, *garde-barrière*, etc. would take on a pejorative cast. This explanation is, of course, not only hopelessly naïve, but is untenable on a number of grounds—chief among them, the existence of a fair number of verb-complement compounds whose verbal element is unmistakable and which do not have the slightest pejorative connotation; e.g., *porte-parole*, *serre-file*.

17. The meanings of formations will be indicated in the cases of the less familiar terms whose significations are not readily apparent from their components.

18. For many of the examples cited in this paragraph, I am indebted to Dauzat's *L'Argot de la guerre* (Paris, 1919).

19. Cf. Darmesteter, *Traité*, p. 234.

20. See Meunier, pp. 98 ff.; Darmesteter, *Traité*, pp. 216 ff.

21. See Darmesteter, *De la création*, pp. 163 ff.

Pleine Sa Hanste in the Chanson de Roland

THE EXPRESSION "pleine sa hanste," which occurs eight times in the Oxford version of the *Chanson de Roland* (lines 1204, 1229, 1250, 1273, 1287, 1295, 1498, 1534),[1] has been variously interpreted by scholars of Old French. Godefroy[2] listed *pleine sa hanste* and *pleine sa lance* (s.v. *plein*) as if they were one and the same expression and defined them as "de toute la force de la lance." However, he cited one example of *plaine sa lance* with the meaning "de la longueur d'une lance." Jenkins,[3] in the glossary of his edition of the poem, defined *pleine sa hanste:* "the full length of his spear handle (s.v. *hanste*)," but "*with* [my emphasis] the full length of his shaft (s.v. *plein*)." Foulet[4] defined it: "avec la hanste toute entière; d'un grand coup de lance," adding that "l'idée de complétion s'accompagne d'une idée de vigueur et détermination." Bédier[5] translated it "à pleine hampe" in each of the eight passages—an expression by which he no doubt meant simply "d'un grand coup de lance" (cf. *à pleines voiles, boire à plein verre, à pleine bouche,* etc.).

Bédier made it clear that he did not attach any special significance to the expression when he referred to it as a *vers-refrain*.[6] He declared that Stengel was wrong to insert "pleine sa hanste" at line 1603 [1559] even though it was found in V⁴, T, L, and n.⁷ He wrote: "On résiste à la tentation d'imiter ici Stengel, si l'on observe que d'autres descriptions de combats se passent du vers-refrain Pleine sa hanste . . . : on le cherche en vain après le v. 1266 et après le v. 1893." He seems not to have noted that the expression was missing from the description of not two but twenty-four mounted combats in the *Chanson de Roland* and that actually it was present in only eight. Thus it is clear that he really regarded it as a *vers-refrain* in the *Chanson de Roland*, just as *plaine sa lance* is in the later *chansons de geste*, and that he considered the two expressions identical.

In his article on the word *plein*, however, Littré⁸ cited our expression and, between parentheses, glossed it: "sans briser la lance." Although he offered no proof of this original interpretation, and although none of the commentators or translators of the *Chanson de Roland* has, so far as I know, adopted it, I believe this may well have been the original meaning and the meaning as the author of the *Chanson de Roland* used it. However, constructed on the analogy of such absolute expressions as "saus lur cors," it was probably already archaic in the early twelfth century; and by the end of the century, it was so obsolete that it was misunderstood by the scribes and jongleurs who, after all, were naturally unaware of the fine points of mounted combat in earlier times. Rychner⁹ has pointed out how the second-rate *chansons de geste* were made up largely of set expressions. Our expression, filling the first part of a decasyllabic line as it did and having a fine epic sound, was naturally used over and over by jongleurs who were incapable of inventing new ones. When a six-syllable *cheville* was needed, they merely had to write "toute pleine sa lance."

Constantly used by careless jongleurs, the expression lost its pristine meaning, I think, and even its original form. "Plaine la lance" is a different expression from "pleine sa hanste": *plaine* (from *plana*) is different from *pleine* (from *plena*), *sa* is different from *la*, and a *hanste* is only the wooden shaft of a lance. Godefroy cites many examples of the word *hanste* meaning "spear shaft" but never meaning "spear" and, of course, never written "lance." Even if the two expressions seem eventually to have been used interchangeably with the general meaning "with a full blow of the lance," this does not prove they were identical. Or, to put it differently, the fact that *plaine la lance* came to be used as a rather meaningless *cheville* does not prove what *pleine sa hanste* meant to the author of the *Chanson de Roland*. The fact, for example, that the word *orateur* meant only "orator" in the seventeenth century does not alter the fact that it meant both "orator" and "prose writer" in the sixteenth. Everyone knows that the meaning of a word can change from the specific to the general, from general to specific, from literal to figurative, or even from one meaning to an entirely different one. It is not surprising that an expression made up of three words should develop new meanings—especially when it develops a new form. There is no doubt, of course, that *pleine* [or *plaine*] *sa* [or *la*] *lance* came to have the two meanings given by Godefroy. He provided numbers of examples that prove this; and, besides, every student of the Old French epic has seen the expression used scores of times so loosely that it could mean either.

It is fairly certain that the expression *pleine sa hanste* did not mean "with a full blow of the lance" to the authors of the "other versions" of the *Chanson de Roland*,[10] for in practically all cases, they omitted it. The only one that rendered it with any consistency, V [4], merely wrote "plena a ses asta" in seven of the eight passages, and inserted it in two additional places. We have no way of knowing whether or not the *remanieur* knew what it meant in the original. But the authors of the rest of the other versions and translations made only sporadic gestures towards rendering it: T reads "pleine sa lance" in two of the passages; L, "tant com tint l'aste" once; n, "the length of his spear shaft" three times; e, "with distans" once; w, "in one fall" once; and CV [7]PTL "plena sa (la) lance" once. The author of the Middle High German paraphrase seems to have suppressed it in all eight passages. Now it is well known that scribes and *remanieurs* tend on the one hand to copy automatically whatever is obvious and commonplace and, on the other hand, to omit, correct, or modernize words or expressions that are to them obscure, unusual, or archaic; therefore, it seems reasonable to conclude that the meaning of our expression was neither obvious nor commonplace to the authors of the other versions of the poem. Then what did it mean to the author of the Oxford version of the *Chanson de Roland?*

As the spear could not be readily maneuvered by a person on foot, the expression occurs, of course, only in descriptions of mounted combats—and, as it happens, always at the end of the description of a tilt. To the modern reader, descriptions of mounted combats (there are no less than thirty-two of them in the *Chanson de Roland*, as we remarked above) may seem monotonously similar because we cannot envisage clearly any of the details of a tilt; but to the medieval audience, each detail was clearly understood and the entire description was fascinating. It was far more important (and natural) for them to appreciate the fine points of mounted combat than it is for us to understand the technical expressions used to describe a game of baseball (or cricket), because in addition to being the greatest sport of the Middle Ages, jousting was absolutely fundamental in warfare.

The role of the spear is quite as necessary as that of the sword both in epics and romances—if not more so; and its use is much more varied, colorful, and spectacular. It is true that spears were not given names as swords were, but that is because the life of a spear was inevitably brief. Aside from its use for giving signals of various kinds (and our poet used it thus repeatedly), the variety of ways it could be employed in mounted combat is surprising: now a knight may merely split an opponent's shield with it; now he may cut through both shield and hauberk without injuring his opponent; or he may cut through shield, hauberk, flesh, and bones, cutting through various parts of his anatomy (liver, lungs, backbone, etc.); or he may thrust his spear all the way through his opponent so that the point extends some distance beyond his body. He could even thrust his spear and his gonfanon through the body of his opponent. Most important of all, he could be clever enough to kill his opponent without breaking his spear, or he could be so awkward as to break his spear without wounding his opponent.

In the tournaments of the later Middle Ages, knights sometimes had three or four spears each; but on the field of battle at the end of the eleventh century, a knight had only one spear. To break it was a serious matter; it could be a matter of life and death. Today the expression "to break a lance" has come to mean merely "to have a heated argument." Rabelais protested that even in his time people were using the expression figuratively and inappropriately. When Gymnaste was teaching Gargantua the art of "chevalerie," he taught him to use his spear without breaking it! Rabelais wrote: "Là rompoit non la lance, car c'est la plus grande resverye du monde dire: 'J'ai rompu dix lances en tournoy ou en bataille'—un charpentier le feroit bien—mais louable gloire est d'une lance avoir rompu dix de ses ennemys. De sa lance doncq asserée, verde et roide, rompoit un huys, enfonçoit un harnoys . . . ," etc. (*Gargantua*, Chap. XXIII).

If a knight *did* succeed in thrusting his spear through or well into the body of his enemy, he was then faced with two possibilities: he could leave the spear in the body, or he could try to remove it so he could continue fighting with it. The most skillful knights—such as Roland and Olivier—removed the spear and went on fighting with it. But how did a knight go about retrieving his spear? This brings us to another expression that has a variety of meanings.

In five of the eight cases in which a knight kills his opponent *pleine sa hanste* in the *Chanson de Roland*, the poet tells us in the line immediately preceding (lines 1203, 1249, 1272, 1286, 1540), "[Il] Empeint lo bien." Although *empeindre* has a variety of meanings, I think the author of the poem originally used it as a technical term to describe the maneuver of alternately thrusting and jerking by which a spear was extracted from an opponent's body. He wrote: "Empeint lo bien, fait li brandir lo cors" (line 1203). "Empeint lo bien que mort lo fait brandir" (line 1429). Although this expression is usually translated "enfoncer vigoureusement" (so Foulet, *s.v. empaindre*), it is used in many cases where it could not possibly have that meaning. For example, when Roland is about to blow his horn, the poet tells us: "Rollant ad mis l'olifant a sa buche, / Empeint le ben, par grant vertu le sunet" (lines 1753-54). No one could possibly imagine that Roland "thrust his horn into his mouth vigorously" like an inebriated New Year's Eve reveler! He surely put the horn against his lips carefully—as any skilled bugler would do. Bédier translated correctly—and elegantly, as one would expect: "Il l'embouche bien."

The infinitives *empeindre* (*empaindre*) and *empoindre* and the nouns *empeinte* (*empainte*) and *empointe* were used with such a variety of meanings in the course of the Middle Ages that we can not be absolutely sure what the words meant at a given time and place. But there can be no doubt that getting the spear out of the body of the enemy was a matter of great importance; indeed, poets sometimes mentioned the fact that knights even had to work their *swords* out of the body of their opponents. And in many cases, when a poet says a body falls dead to the ground, it is just after he has said the successful knight did something (*empeint*, for spears; *brandist*, for swords) that could remove the weapon so that the body of the opponent was free to fall to the ground. Repeatedly in the *Chanson de Guillaume*, we read that a knight who has killed a pagan with his spear: "Empeint le bien, si l'ad trebuché mort" (line 440); and "Empeint le bien, par grant vertu l'abat" (line 1125). Likewise, in *Aliscans*, 1464-66, we read: "Parmi le cors mist la lance pleniere. / Ains ke li glous ait guerpi l'estriviere, / Saisit le ber l'espil [espiet] od la baniere." And again, *Aliscans*, lines 5159-60, we read: "Parmi le cors li mist le fust fraisnin, / L'espil traist fors od l'ensengne sanguin." Such details make it clear that the removal of the spear was a very important matter. In *Florimont*, a tilt ends with an awkward maneuver that is just the opposite of the fine technique exhibited by Roland and Olivier: "De l'espié l'empaint en tel guisse / Que tote s'anste frosse et brisse" (lines 6661–62). It is not only force that can break spear shafts; awkwardness can do it.

Let us see precisely how the expression is used in the *Chanson de Roland*. Here is the description of the first mounted combat of Roland—a complete description, step by step, of a tilt carried out by a knight of the greatest conceivable physical skill. (The nephew of Marsile has just made an insulting speech about Charlemagne).

> Quant l'ot Rollant, Deux! si grand doel en out!
> Son cheval brochet, laiset curre a esforz,
> Vait le ferir le quens quanque il pout.
> L'escut li freint e l'osberc li desclot,
> Trenchet le piz, si li briset les os,
> Tute l'eschine li desevret del dos,
> Od sun espiet l'anme li getet fors,
> Empeint le ben, fait li brandir le cors,
> Pleine sa hanste del cheval l'abat mort. (lines 1196–1204)

This is usually translated as follows: "When Roland hears that, God! he has very great grief because of it. He spurs his horse, lets him run full tilt, and goes to strike him [the count does] as hard as he can: he breaks his shield and cuts through his hauberk, he cuts through his chest and breaks his bones, he severs the spine of his back. With his [very] spear, he drives out his soul. He thrusts it well, shakes the body, and with a full blow of his lance, he knocks it down dead from the horse." But I think the last two lines mean: "He thrusts and jerks it skillfully, shakes off the body, and, without breaking his spear shaft, drops it from his horse stone dead. (The verb *abattre* is still used with the meaning "to fell [a tree]," "to bring down," "to drop [a man or an animal]").

After he has described in detail the heroic course of the spear through the shield, the hauberk, and the body of the Saracen, it seems to me impossible that a good poet could then remark lamely that the hero had done it with a full blow of his lance. And if he happened to be so inept once, would he have made the same slip eight times in the poem—in the very places where he was trying to describe most impressively the skill of his greatest heroes?

It is obvious that Roland *did not* break his spear shaft, because after this first blow of the battle, he goes on fighting with his spear. The poet tells us that he kept on fighting with it as long as the spear shaft lasted, but that after fifteen tilts, he has broken and destroyed it (line 1322). Only then did he draw Durendal (line 1324).

Olivier's fighting follows the same pattern as Roland's, except that even after he breaks his spear shaft, he goes on fighting with the butt end of it. He uses it as a club to bring down the pagan named Malun "along with 700 of theirs" (!) and finally shatters the butt end of his spear in killing Turgis and Esturgoz (line 1359). Roland even jokes about his fighting with a *baton* and asks where his sword is. Olivier declares that he is so busy fighting that he hasn't time to draw it! Fighting with swords is never so gay—and varied—as fighting with spears.

The archbishop Turpin likewise kills his first opponent *pleine sa hanste* as do Geriers, Anseis, and Engeliers. Only twice does the poet use the expression in describing the blows of pagans who kill Christians (Climborin killing Engelier, and

Valdabron killing Samsun); and in each of these cases, the mighty pagan is immediately brought down—Climborin by Olivier (line 1552) and Valdabron by Roland (line 1586). Thus, by showing Olivier and Roland killing with their *swords* two highly skilled pagans who, having their spear shafts intact, should be able to keep them at a safe distance, the poet enhances still further the courage and skill of the two Christian knights. At least it is clear, I think, that the poet did not regard the expression as a *vers-refrain*.

In other early texts, there are numerous passages in which *pleine sa hanste* or even *plaine sa lance* is opposed to "sa lance brise" (*froisset, fraint, estruset, escantelet,* etc.) It is interesting to note that in the *Roland,* after the twelve peers have each killed a pagan, a valiant Saracen named Margariz attacks Olivier in fine style but fails to wound him, breaks his spear (line 1317), and runs away! When Roland declares that Olivier is a fine knight for breaking spears (line 2210), he surely must mean for breaking the spears of his opponents—as here. In the decasyllabic version of the *Roman d'Alexandre,* which, according to P. Meyer, is particularly precise in its descriptions and in its use of words, Nicolas breaks his spear in tilting against the hero, but Alexander's shaft is strong and he unhorses Nicolas *plena l'asta* (lines 750, 759, ed. Meyer). In *Aliscans,* Naymer kills Caenon *plaine sa lance,* but *sa lance brise* when he tilts with Aukin. Guiëlin attacks the grotesque Tabur and nearly kills him but his spear shaft breaks (*Willame,* line 3181); then Guillaume comes to the rescue, but although he has killed Corberan *pleine sa hanste,* he breaks his spear in three pieces on the grotesque Tabur (line 3184). (Tabur is finally killed by Reneward with his famous *tinel.*) Little Gui slays two pagans without breaking his spear shaft, but the third one he kills breaks it as he falls: "Quant le gluz chaï, la hanste li estruse" (*Willame*, lines 1825, 1830, 1842). Gui is so small that he is perhaps not strong enough to retrieve the spear before the pagan falls forward on it and breaks it. Earlier in the battle, Guillaume kills sixty opponents with his spear (line 1804), and only when his horse is killed under him does he draw his sword (line 1809).

In *Raoul de Cambrai*, many blows are struck *pleine la lance* but in none of these, nor in any of the hundreds of descriptions of mounted combats in epic and romance I have examined, have I been able to find a single one in which a blow struck *pleine sa hanste* caused the spear shaft to break and only one in which a spear broke when a blow was struck *pleine sa lance*. We shall return to this case in a moment. It is possible that such examples exist; but if our expression had the meaning "de toute la force de la lance" throughout the Middle Ages, we could surely expect poets to say frequently that the spear shaft had broken as a result of such powerful blows.

Chrétien de Troyes, who is always careful to be specific in his descriptions of *any* activity, often shows that he knows the importance of using a spear correctly. When Yvain must fight three knights at once in order to save Lunete's life, he breaks all three of his opponents' spears with his shield (!) and keeps his own intact (*Yvain*, ed. Roques, lines 4476–79). Erec's skill is equally remarkable: the first of the five robbers misses him completely (*Erec*, ed. Roques, line 2859), but Erec kills three of them without breaking his spear. When the other two flee, he pursues them and breaks his spear by stabbing one of them in the back as he flees (line 3046). Chrétien shows specifically how a knight retrieves his spear by twisting it out of the wound: "Au retrere a son cop estors / e cil cheï" (*Erec*, lines

2868–69). In the combat between Erec and Maboagrain, at the first clash they both pierce the other's shield but do not wound each other. Then: "Chascuns au plus tost que il pot / A sa lance sachiée a lui . . ." (lines 5900–1). Chrétien never used *pleine sa hanste* nor even *pleine sa lance* so far as I know. For an expression of distance, he used "tant con hante dure": "Erec, tant con hante li dure / le trebuche a la tere dure" (*Erec*, lines 2135–36). It is curious that, some eighty years earlier, the author of the *Chanson de Roland* used this very expression to mean, literally, "as long as his spear shaft lasted": "Fiert de l'espiet tant cume hanste li duret" (line 1322).

If it is obvious that the spear played a paramount role in mounted combat throughout the Middle Ages, it is equally clear that the author of the *Chanson de Roland* was fully aware of its importance. Repeatedly, when he wanted to evoke the emotion of terror or dread, he would refer specifically to the destruction of spear shafts. In Charlemagne's nightmarish vision before the first battle, Ganelon appeared and jerked his spear from his hands with such force that he shattered it to splinters (lines 720–22). In his terrible dream before his battle with Baligant, he saw spear shafts of ash and of fruit wood burning (line 2537), and again, the shafts of sharp spears breaking (line 2539). When Gautier de l'Hum comes down to Roland for protection at the end of the battle, in order to show that he has fought a good fight, he merely says: "Ma hanste est fraite et percet mun escut" (line 2050). In the general description of the desperate first battle, the poet mentions, in particular, that many spear shafts are bloody and broken (line 1399); and in evoking the atmosphere of the battle with Baligant, he wrote: "Deus! tantes hanstes i ad par mi brisees" (line 3386). Such remarks were repeated so often in the later *chansons de geste* that they no longer seem to us very significant. Thus, if we would like to understand expressions with their original freshness, I think it is necessary to divest our memory of subsequent usage.

Here is the passage in which the Count of Normandy strikes Gormont *pleine sa lance* and yet breaks his spear shaft. It occurs in the all too brief *Gormont et Isembart* fragment.

	Al rei Gormont n'i mis espie,
144	joster i vait sun cors meïsme;
	pleine sa lance le sovine
	ceo dit la geste a Saint Denise.
	Ne fust la hanste qui li brise,
148	icil l'oüst geté de vie.
	Gormonz li lancet une guivre;
	parmi le cors li est saillie,
	de l'altre part s'en est eissie;
152	fiert un danzel de Lumbardie,
	qu'andous les at getés de vie.

Now if the Count had really knocked him supine, Gormont would scarcely have been able to leap to his feet and throw a spear hard enough for it to go completely through the Count and then kill a young man from Lombardy who was standing nearby. But the unique manuscript of the *Gormont* fragment dates from the thirteenth century—a good hundred years after the poem was written, and we cannot be sure what the poet actually wrote. Bayot [11] declared that the manuscript "présente, contre le sens, la mesure et l'assonance, des fautes nombreuses." It is clear, nevertheless, that in describing the twelve tilts of Christian knights against Gormont, the poet builds up interest by allowing the Christian knights an increasing degree of success: The first two are promptly killed, the third shatters Gormont's shield but breaks his own spear shaft (line 52), the fourth, fifth, and sixth break through his shield but do not wound him. (The reader will recall that Gormont is handed a new shield whenever he needs one.) The seventh one is described in the passage quoted. We shall return to it in a moment. The eighth, ninth, tenth, and eleventh all wound him in one way or another, but none of the Frankish knights succeeds in killing him. But finally Loowis, having called upon God, St. Denis, and St. Richier, does actually kill him. As for the seventh tilt against Gormont, the poet may have originally written that the Saint Denis chronicle says that he struck him a great blow breaking his spear shaft but that if he hadn't broken it, he would have surely killed him. Like other poets, he referred repeatedly to chronicles to give his story an air of authenticity. He referred to the one at St. Denis (line 146), that at St. Richier (line 330), and, once, simply to "la geste" (line 418). The fact that he declared, in line 418, that the chronicle's statement is correct suggests that at other times he might have questioned it; and he may have intended to cite the chronicle here only to contradict it. But whatever the poet wrote in the first place, the thirteenth-century scribe merely wrote: "He knocks him to the ground flat, the length of his spear [or with a great blow of his spear] and he would have killed him if his spear shaft had not broken." The scribe, like his contemporaries, was probably unaware of the original meaning of the expression *pleine sa hanste*. It is striking, however, that the hundreds of scribes and *remanieurs* happened, whether by chance or instinctively, to avoid saying that blows were struck with such tremendous force that the spear shaft was broken.

The reader will have no doubt noted that the eight passages in which our expression occurs in the *Chanson de Roland* are all in the battle of the rear guard. This fact does not suggest to me that the so-called Baligant episode was written by a different and later poet. On the contrary, if it had been written at about the time of the redaction of the Oxford manuscript, it is highly likely that the expression *pleine sa lance* would have been used over and over as a *vers-refrain*—as it was in other *chansons de geste* of the later period. The reason our poet used it in Roland's battle but not in Charlemagne's is, I think, that in the former he is primarily concerned with portraying supremely skilled and courageous human beings who are fighting magnificently while relying on their own strength; but in the latter, he is emphasizing not the courage of men but the power of God. Roland never prays for help. He even refuses to call for the help of Charlemagne. Even the Archbishop Turpin merely gives absolution and other comfortable words; but Charlemagne is frequently in communication with God, and the angel Gabriel speaks to him repeatedly in the poem. Indeed, at the climax of the battle, the angel Gabriel appears to Charlemagne, like the gods in Homer and Vergil, just in time to save him from certain death at the hand of Baligant.

In Roland's battle, the Christians are superior fighters. For 20,000 men to destroy 100,000 men and confront a second 100,000 without fear, they must be supermen. The poet describes very carefully and clearly the atmosphere of the two camps before both battles. Marsile's men have no worries because they have overwhelming numbers and because Ganelon has told them that if they massacre Roland and the rear guard, they will be rid of Charlemagne. They know their losses may be large (Ganelon told them so) but they are convinced that they can not lose. As for Roland, he is much too simple-minded to be worried. Olivier is "sage" and, consequently, very much worried; but Roland refuses even to listen to his wise advice to call for help.

In Charlemagne's battle, the Christians are no better fighters than the pagans. But they perform rites of the Christian religion, pray to the true God for help, and have holy relics and a holy battle cry. The pagans perform silly pagan rites, call upon idols of wood and stone, have no holy relics, and they have a battle cry that has no significance. But they are described as marvelous fighters. The poet says of Baligant: "Deus! quel baron, s'oust Chrestientet!" (line 3164). The greater the strength, courage, skill, and power of the pagan army, the greater the miracle of a Christian victory.

In describing the fight of Roland and his men, the poet must have quite intentionally set out to show the greatness (and insignificance) of man without God; therefore, he made the most of their physical vigor, skill, and courage. In the battle between Charlemagne and Baligant, he wanted to show the superiority of God and of Christian faith over the pagan gods and the Mohammedan religion. That Roland finally admitted his mistake, prayed for forgiveness, and was carried off to heaven by angels does not alter the fact that 20,000 Frankish knights had been killed because he foolishly failed to call for help.

The difference between the meaning of the word *hanste* and *lance* is, and always was, clear; but it is perfectly comprehensible that the former should be replaced by the latter in our expression without necessarily changing its meaning. But the problem becomes more complicated when we remember that *plein* (*plenus*) and *plain* (*planus*) are entirely different words which were frequently used interchangeably in manuscripts in which the spellings *-ei-* and *-ai-* were interchangeable. After all, the best manuscript of the best Old French epic (the Oxford *Roland*) writes *la pleine tere* instead of *la plaine tere* ("level ground"). Then there were a number of expressions like *plein pié, plein doit, plein pas*, and so on, that were commonly used as expressions of distance; but since they were often written *plain pié, plain pas*, and so on, they could easily be taken to mean "a plain foot," or "a mere foot," or whatever you please. The meaning of the entire complex of words was further complicated by the constant use of such expressions as *cols pleniers, lance pleniere, en plein champ, de plein, plein eslais, lonc une lance, tant con hanste li dure*—all of which soon became clichés. In the *Chanson de Willame*, the word *espee* is repeatedly used instead of *espié* (lines 1804, 1811, and 1839); it seems unthinkable that a scribe could write that the shaft of an *espee* was broken in one line and in the very next line write that the knight drew his *espee* (*Williame*, lines 1842, 1843). But that is precisely what happened.

Given such a large number of expressions whose meanings were becoming more and more academic as the Middle Ages wore on and as the manner of fighting evolved, it is not in the least surprising that scribes who were copying manuscripts in the thirteenth century did not distinguish between the expression *pleine sa hanste* and *plaine sa lance*. But it is perhaps as important for Old French specialists today to distinguish between a term of eleventh- and thirteenth-century warfare as

it is to distinguish between technical terms having to do with
architecture, law, finance, literature, philosophy, or religion.

1. References to the text of the poem are always to the edition of Joseph Bédier (Paris, 1922).

2. Frédéric Godefroy, *Dictionnaire de l'ancienne langue française et de tous ses dialectes, du IXe au XVe siècle* (10 vols.; Paris, 1881–92).

3. T. A. Jenkins (ed.), *La Chanson de Roland* (Boston, 1924). D. J. A. Ross supported this interpretation with many citations and two handsome illustrations of mounted combat from a fourteenth-century MS. Unfortunately, the illustrations do not show that the unhorsed knight was knocked from his horse the full length of a spear. Be it said, however, that in order to show the distance of a spear shaft between the knight and his horse, the illustrator would have had either to reduce the scale of his composition or to simplify it considerably (*Medium Aevum*, XX (1951), pp. 1–10). I am indebted to U. T. Holmes, Jr., for this reference and the one to the articles of W. D. Elcock which is mentioned in footnote 8 *infra*.

4. Lucien Foulet, "Glossaire," in *La Chanson de Roland*, commentée par Joseph Bédier (Paris, 1927).

5. Bédier's translation of the poem is included with the edition of the text.

6. *La Chanson de Roland*, commentée par Joseph Bédier, p. 160.

7. For the customary nomenclature used here, see Bédier, *La Chanson de Roland*, pp. 65–73.

8. Emile Littré, *Dictionnaire de la langue française* (4 vols.; Paris, 1863–83). W. D. Elcock expressed the opinion that of the various interpretations that had been suggested, Littré's was the one "most strongly supported by medieval evidence"; but instead of accepting Littré's explanation, he argued that our expression had survived from an earlier exercise in which knights practiced maneuvering a spear and that it had the same meaning as *lance baissiée* (*French Studies*, VII [1953], 35–47).

9. Jean Rychner, *La Chanson de geste, essai sur l'art épique des jongleurs* (Geneva, 1955).

10. Readings cited here are taken from the variants listed in E. Stengel, *Das Altfranzösische Rolandslied* (Leipzig, 1900).

11. Alphonse Bayot (ed.), *Gormont et Isembart* ("Classiques Français du Moyen Age" [Paris, 1914]), p. xiii.

―――― *Henry and Renée Kahane* ――――

Carestia

THE AREA of *carestia* ("scarcity of food," "want," "high cost of living") and its variants in form and meaning extends from Italy to Portugal.[1] The origin of the term is still unknown, in spite of the various attempts listed by Corominas (*s.v.*, *carestía*) and Wartburg (*FEW*, II, 373). We think that it reflects a typically Byzantine institution.

In an essay, "On the Question of Byzantine Feudalism" (*Byzantion*, VIII [1933], 587), A. A. Vasiliev states:

> In the East the Greek word *kharistikion* corresponded in meaning to the Latin word *beneficium*, and the Greek word *kharistikarios* corresponded to *beneficiarius*, i.e. a man granted land on condition of paying military service. But in Byzantium, especially beginning with the tenth century, the system of distribution of land as *kharistikia* was usually applied to monasteries, which were granted both to laymen and to clergy. Possibly this peculiarity of Byzantine *beneficium* (*kharistikion*) should be connected with the iconoclastic epoch, when the government in its struggle against the monks resorted to the secularization of monastery lands, which gave the emperor a rich source for land grants. This circumstance in all probability is the reason why the original meaning of *kharistikion*,

a grant of land in general not specifically monasterial, was lost and the term *kharistikion* was used specifically as a monastery grant.

The result to which the charisticary system led is briefly described by H.-G. Beck, *Kirche und theologische Literatur im byzantinischen Reich* (München, 1959), p. 136:

> The charisticary received the monastery as a kind of fief; with this, he was curator (ἔφορος) of the monastery. . . . If in its beginnings the institution seems to have been in the interest of weak monasteries, soon misuse occurred: the charisticaries saw in their monasteries prebends which they were able to exploit at will for their own purposes.

In short, in the phrasing of F. Dölger (*Byzantinische Zeitschrift*, XL [1940], 559), "the charisticariate is the invasion of the laic aristocracy into the sphere of monastic possessions." [2]

A treatise by the eleventh-century patriarch John of Antioch, which is directed against the transfer of monasteries to the charisticaries (Krumbacher, *Geschichte der byzantinischen Literatur*, p. 156), presents a good description of the havoc that it brought about. The treatise is found in Migne, *Patrologia Graeca*, CXXXII, 1115–50; we quote two passages:

> Τέως σήμερον, τὰ ἐλεύθερα θάλλουσι καὶ ἐπιδιδόασι· τὰ δὲ δοῦλα καταλύονται . . . Οὐ γὰρ τὰ καταλελυμένα δωροῦνται· ἀλλὰ μᾶλλον τὰ συνιστάμενα καὶ εὐθαλῆ τὴν πρόσοδον ἔχοντα.

("At this very day, the free monasteries flourish and grow but the ones enslaved [under the charisticary system] break up. For not the ones in decline are given as benefits but rather those in good status with thriving income." page 1137)

The charisticary sequestered everything that belonged to the monastery:

οὐ μόνον οἰκήματα, προάστειά τε καὶ ζῶα καὶ παντοίας προσόδους, ἀλλὰ καὶ ναοὺς αὐτούς· καὶ καθηγούμενον καί μονάζοντας δούλους ἡγεῖται, καὶ πάντας καὶ πάντα, ὡς ἰδιόκτητα πράγματα ἔχει . . . Τοῖς δὲ θείοις ναοῖς τε καὶ μοναχοῖς, ἀπόμοιράν τινα σμικροτάτην, ἐκ πάσης τῆς προσόδου ἀπένειμε· κ'ἀκείνην ὡς ἴδιον ψυχικόν, μετὰ πολλῶν αἰτήσεων αὐτοῖς παρεχόμενος · · · αὐτίκα γοῦν πέπαυται καὶ ἀπέσβη · · · καὶ αὐτὰ τὰ τῶν μοναχῶν σιτηρέσια καὶ ἀναγκαιότατα.

(". . . not only the buildings, the suburban estates, the animals, and the revenues of every sort, but also the churches themselves. He considers the abbot and the monks as his serfs, and holds everybody and everything as his private property. He allots to the churches of the Lord and to the monks a mimimal portion of the whole revenue, and this he gives them just like alms, after much begging. Immediately even the most urgent food supply of the monks ceases and vanishes." [1140])

This particular context of the exploited and impoverished Byzantine monasteries explains easily the use of the term *carestia* as it is preserved in the West. Although some of the semantic shades, such as the "want" or the "high cost of living" may be due to the secondary influence of *carere* ("to be without") and *carus* ("costly"), as suggested by Corominas, the common use of them still reflects the effect of the charisticary system on the life of the monks.

The variant of the term, which was borrowed by the West, is (as far as we see) not recorded in the ecclesiastical literature. It is, however, listed, in Latin transliteration, in the ninth-century *Glossarium amplonianum secundum* explicitly as a Graecism: "*caristia* graece quasi gratia" (*Corpus Glossariorum Latinorum*, ed. G. Götz, Leipzig, [1881–91], V, 274, 50). This corresponds to the Greek *χαριστεία or *χαριστία ("benefice," "grant") based on χαρίζω as, say, καρπιστεία and καρπιστία are based on καρπίζω. The suffixes -εία and -ία, to be sure, overlap a good deal in Hellenistic Greek (Mayser, *Grammatik der griechischen Papyri*, I:3, 9). Documented derivatives in medieval Greek: χαριστική ("donative," "prebend"), (Sophocles, s.v.) and χαριστικάριος ("he who receives the χαριστική ['prebendary']"), (Du Cange, s.v.).

A variant of *χαριστεία had already been borrowed by the West once before. Latin *caristia* (neuter plural) is the designation of a popular Roman feast, during which families gathered on picnics and presents were given (Pauly-Wissowa, *Real-Encyclopaedie der Classischen Altertumswissenschaft* ([Stuttgart, 1894–1961], s.v., *caristia*). M. Leumann (*Die Sprache*, I [1949], 208) suggests that the Latin term was based on the Greek χαριστεῖον ("thank-offering"), (Liddell-Scott, s.v.); Ernout-Meillet (*s.v. caristia*) posit the variant *χαριστία. It does not seem that the word continued in Romance.[3] In the East, however, the ancient term survived in the Byzantine ecclesiastical and feudal terminology as the designation of grants and benefices. How the Byzantine word was transferred to the West is not clear. It may have spread from Byzantine southern Italy, or, since it was still in use in the twelfth century (Laurent, *Revue des études byzantines*, XII [1954], 106–7), it may have been heard by the crusaders.

The derogatory shade of meaning apparently did not develop in Byzantium. What, to the Greek speaker, was just a technical term of administration (unpleasant though it may have been) became to the foreigner who heard it in a certain context and saw it in a certain setting a word that expressed want, hardship, and starvation.

1. Including Rhaeto-Romance *chalastria*, etc. (Schorta in his *Dicziunari Rumantsch Grischun*, III, 174).

2. Bibliography on the charisticary system is given by Ostrogorskij, *Byzantion*, XXII (1952), 452, no. 1; and H.-G. Beck, *Kirche und theologische Literatur im byzantinischen Reich* (München, 1959), p. 136.

3. An immediate connection between this Graeco-Latin *caristia* and our Romance *carestia*, hesitatingly posited by Corominas, is improbable for semantic reasons, as already pointed out by Yakov Malkiel, "Linguistic Problems in a New Hispanic Etymological Dictionary," *Word*, XII (1956), 47.

―――――――――――――――*Part II*―――――――――――――――

Old Provençal

―――――Jean Boutière―――――

Quelques Observations sur le Texte des *Vidas* et des *Razos* dans les Chansonniers Provençaux AB et IK

PARMI les quelque vingt chansonniers qui nous ont transmis, en plus ou moins grand nombre (on sait qu'aucun d'entre eux ne contient la collection complète), les *vidas* et les *razos* des troubadours, ceux que l'on désigne sous les sigles A, B, I, et K,[1] datant tous quatre du XIIIe siècle, offrent, à des titres divers, un intérêt particulier.

I et K, les plus prestigieux, présentent, avec leurs textes, généralement satisfaisants, relatifs à 85 troubadours,[2] et se suivant rigoureusement dans le même ordre, la collection de *vidas* la plus abondante, à laquelle s'ajoute l'importante série des *razos* de Bertran de Born, que l'on ne retrouve que dans F;[3] l'écriture, de main italienne, est soignée; ils sont, au surplus, ornés de vignettes, dues à plusieurs miniaturistes et de qualité fort inégale, mais dont un certain nombre sont de véritables oeuvres d'art.[4]

A et B, également copiés avec soin, se recommandent par la qualité de leur graphie et leur correction générale; mais A n'a que 52 textes, dont 50 sont parallèles à ceux de IK; la collection de B, qui paraît un extrait de celle de A, n'en compte que 37.[5] A est orné de vignettes, d'une même main, semble-t-il, mais assez ternes en général et, dans l'ensemble, bien inférieures à celles de IK.

En somme, A et B, d'une part, et d'autre part, I et K, remontent à un même archétype. Sur la base de ces évidentes parentés, les provençalistes, supprimant la conjonction entre les deux sigles, parlent couramment des chansonniers AB et IK, formules acceptables, si l'on précise tout de suite que les deux couples ne sauraient être placés sur le même plan. Une image empruntée à la physiologie rend assez exactement compte de la réalité: IK sont de "vrais jumeaux," dont les ressemblances confinent souvent à l'identité; AB, de "faux jumeaux," où l'on relève assez souvent, à côté de multiples correspondances, des différences profondes.

Les "Vidas" et "Razos" de IK

Un examen attentif de IK montre que, dans ces manuscrits, l'étude des *razos* de B. de Born—dont le total est égal à près de la moitié de l'étendue des 85 *vidas*—doit être séparée de celle de ces dernières.

Alors que les *razos* ne diffèrent guère, d'un chansonnier à l'autre, que par des variantes graphiques,[6] souvent négligeables, et par un nombre restreint de menues fautes de copie, les vraies leçons divergentes étant rares, les *vidas* ont une graphie moins constante, les erreurs des copistes y sont plus fréquentes et les deux manuscrits se séparent nettement dans un certain nombre de passages. De plus, autre caractéristique décisive, alors que l'italianisme *cum* (pour *ab* 'avec') est fréquent[7] dans les *vidas*—y compris celle de B. de Born, où l'on n'en relève pas moins de sept—il n'y en a pas un seul exemple dans les longues *razos* de ce poète. L'étendue de tous ces textes est trop considérable, les exemples de *ab* (ou de *cum*) sont trop nombreux pour qu'il puisse s'agir d'un simple hasard. Visiblement les copistes de IK [8] ont pris les *vidas* dans un manuscrit qui présentait l'italianisme *cum*; et les *razos*, dans un manuscrit qui en était exempt.

A. Les "Razos" de B. de Born

Même quand on a une longue pratique de ces textes, on est surpris de la quasi insignifiance des résultats donnés par une collation rigoureuse de I et de K.

Sans faire un inutile relevé exhaustif et en négligeant les menues lacunes—d'ailleurs assez rares—on note des divergences essentiellement sur les points suivants:

1) *Des fautes matérielles de copiste* comme: [9]

orgoillasa (=orgoillosa K) I (38, 19); on el el (*avec redoublement fautif de* el) I (73, 54); anet que (=queren K) a totas I (39, 17); etc.

2) *Des incorrections grammaticales*,[10] telles que:

sos mal (mals I) talanz K (57, 40); d'aquest (aquestz K) dos I (39, 18); tortz (tort K) ni dreg I (66, 30); etc.

3) *Des altérations comme:*

penrai I (penra K) (43, 29); servirai I (servira K) (43, 33); menassa I (menassava K) (69, 19); etc.

ou encore:

no·us cal I (non cal K) (40, 25); si·l parti (si parti I) de si K (41, 30), etc.

4) De rares cas où les deux manuscrits présentent, chacun de son côté, une mauvaise leçon:

anet que (=queren K) a totas I; anet queren que a totas K (39, 17); ni de poinz I, ni del poings K (=dels) (56, 25).

5) *Des variantes "indifférentes,"* par exemple:

aquesta domna I, aquella d. K (42, 8); quant el vit I, quant vit K (67, 5); un chantar I, c'un chantar K (68, 15); etc.

On conviendra que c'est là un bilan bien mince pour des textes occupant une trentaine de pages.

B. Les "Vidas"

Même en laissant de côté, outre les lacunes, les fautes matérielles des copistes [11] et les incorrections grammaticales, nous aurons une moisson plus riche. On relèvera ici:

1) *Pour les noms propres*, d'assez nombreuses formes, plus ou moins divergentes, dont il n'est pas toujours facile de dire s'il s'agit de simples variantes ou d'altérations. Telles sont:

Noms de villes

I	K	I	K
Folcaqier	Folcalquier (77, 3, cf. 176, 2)	Ribaurac	Ribairac (14, 3)

Maurona	Mairona (79, 2)	Rocamaior	Rocamador (331, 5)
Nerbona	Narbona (316, 4)	Tripoli	Tripol (202, 3)
Pomias	Pamias (230, 8)	Userta	Userca (109, 2)
Porcarages	Porcairagues (21, 1)		etc.

Noms de personnes

Ainermada	Aimermada (316, 3) (=Aimengarda?)	Brunecs	Brunes (327, 1)
Berguedan	Breguedan (4, 11)	Icellis	Iceillins (321, 10)
		Perols	Peiols (92, 2)
			etc.

2) *Des formes verbales à des temps différents*, dont l'une est généralement imposée par le contexte:

       entendon K (entendion I) (191, 7)
       se penava I (se penet K) (173, 9–10)
       apellava K (apella I) (267, 15)
       blasmava K (blasma I) (140, 3)
       si vanava K (se vana I) (153, 17)
       trobava I (troba K) (205, 5)

3) *Des divergences portant sur un seul mot*, comme:

I	K	I	K
dompnejar [12]	domnar (81, 3)	mesuratz	amesuratz (127, 4)
mercadier	mercadan (316, 2 92, 2; 330, 2)	Albertetz	Albertz (8, 1)
furar	envolar (228, 9)	Tollosa	Tolosan (189, 1)
servir	serven (189, 3)		

4) *Des leçons divergentes, mais "indifférentes,"* du type:

.... que (qu'el K) las agues faitas (18, 13)
.... mostren que (qu'el K) n'ac (19, 24)
.... so qu'el (que K) gazaingnava (191, 16)

ou encore, avec un ordre des mots différent:

.... de las soas cansos I, de las cansos dellei K (79, 5)
.... il n'era tristz e dolenz I, tristz e dolenz en fo K (173, 9)
.... e s'en parti d'ella I, e d'ela s'en parti K (222, 17)

5) Enfin, dans un très petit nombre de passages, *des différences plus importantes*, comme:

.... de la terra d'Alverne [13] I, de la terra del Dalfi K (228, 1-2)
.... e de cans e de ausels I, e de cans d'ausels K (234, 5)
.... fo de Sirier [14] de Mantoana I, fo de Mantoana, de Sirier K (321, 1)

Tous les faits qui précèdent, pour notables qu'ils soient, n'altèrent pas sensiblement la physionomie respective de I et de K, qui restent de "vrais jumeaux." Egalement bien connus de A et de B, ils ne sont que vétilles à côté des divergences que nous allons trouver, souvent, entre ces derniers manuscrits.

Les Manuscrits "A" et "B"

L'étroite parenté de ces chansonniers éclate dans une multitude de variantes qui leur sont communes et manquent aux autres manuscrits. Mais rares sont les *vidas*—telle celle d'A. Daniel [15]—où A et B offrent, comme IK la plupart du temps, un texte identique de bout en bout. Leur version respective de la *vida* de R. de Berbezill, par exemple, toute pareille dans la plus grande partie de son développement, présente quelques menues discordances; et, dans l'ensemble, les textes de A et de B se séparent toujours sur quelques points, l'un d'eux restant, dans ce cas, souvent isolé, tandis que l'autre se rattache à un ou plusieurs manuscrits d'une autre famille.

A défaut d'une étude exhaustive, qui ne saurait trouver place dans cet article, voici quelques exemples propres à montrer jusqu'où peut aller la scission.

Il n'y a pas à s'arrêter longtemps aux différences ne portant que sur quelques mots, comme:

> longa sazon A (EIK), lonc temps B (R) (109, 7-8)
> mout l'amet e la lauzet A, mout l'amava e [la] lauzava B (IKPR) (258, 11)
> fills d'un paubre homen que era pescaire A (EIK), fills d'un paubre pescador B (R) (252, 3-4)

Voici déjà, dans la *vida* du même Perdigon (253, 2-3), des divergences plus importantes:

.... Vengron li las malas [aventuras],

  A (IK)   B

qez el perdet los amics e las car el perdet l'onor e·ls
amigas, e·l pretz e l'onor e amics.
l'aver.

Le développement de A prend encore plus d'ampleur dans ce passage relatif à Peire Vidal (237, 19-21) :

  A (EIKN²)   B

.... e si entendia   .... e pregava

 en (manque B) totas las bonas dompnas q'el vezia,

e totas las pregava d'amor e e totas l'enganavan.
totas li dizion de far e de
dir tot so q'el volgues.

Dans les derniers passages précités, A, plus développé que B, s'accordait avec plusieurs autres manuscrits, notamment IK. Il n'en est pas toujours ainsi.

Dans la *vida* de P. de Capdoill (258, 5-7), par exemple, c'est le texte, plus court, de B qui se rattache à celui des autres chansonniers :

 Pons de Capduoill .... fo fort escars d'aver (avers A);

  A   B (EIKP)

mas mout s'en sabia gen mas si s'en cobria ab gen
cobrir ab son bel acuilli- acoillir et ab honar de sa
men et ab far honor de sa persona.
persona.

Il en va de même pour la *vida* de B. de Ventadour (25, 23-31), particulièrement caractéristique à cet égard:

.... Don (Et B) ella lo receup

A	B
e l'onret e l'acuillic e·l fetz mout grans plazers.	e l'acuillic molt fort.

Lonc temps estet

en la cort de la duquessa et enamoret se d'ella e la dompna s'enamoret de lui; don En Bernartz en fetz maintas bonas chansos.	en sa cort et enamoret d'ella e ella de lui; e·n fetz maintas bonas chanssons d'ella.

... Qan lo coms fo mortz, En Bernartz

abandonet lo mon e·l trobar e·l chantar e·l solatz del segle; e pois se rendet a l'orden de Dalon	si re rendet a l'orden de Dalon ....

Mais A n'a pas le privilège de présenter les versions les plus longues; les exemples inverses ne sont pas rares.

Voici un passage de la *vida* de P. Rogier (233, 32-35):[16]

A (E)	B
Lonc temps estet ab En Raembaut;	El estet lonc temps ab En Raembaut d'Aurenga; e puois s'en parti de lui; et
et estet en Espaigna	anet s'en en Espaigna estar

ab lo bon rei Amfos d'Aragon; et ab lo bon comte Raimon de Tolosa.	ab lo bon rei Amfos d'Aragon; e pois estet ab lo bon comte Raimon de Tolosa, tant quant li plac et el volc.
Gran honor al mon ac	Mout ac gran honor el mon ....

On lit vers la fin de la *vida* d'Uc de Saint Circ (332, 23-34) :

.... Uc .... estet en Espaingna .... ;

A(IKN²P)	B
e pois en Proenssa ab totz los baros. ... Chanssons fetz fort bonas e bons sons e bonas coblas ... E mout saup ben alevar las soas dompnas e ben decazer.	e pois s'en venc en Proenssa et estet ab los barons .... Assatz fetz de bonas chanssons e de bons vers e de bonas coblas e bons sons .... E ben saup alevar las soas dompnas e ben decazer, qand el lo volia far, ab los sieus vers et ab los sieus digz.

Par ces quelques exemples, qu'il serait fort aisé de multiplier, on voit bien qu'en cas de scission entre A et B, c'est tantôt l'un de ces manuscrits, tantôt l'autre, qui se rattache à des familles différentes et c'est le texte le plus long—sans doute amplification de la version originale—qui reste, en général, isolé.

Le cas le plus typique est, sans doute, celui de la *vidarazo* de Raimon Jordan, où l'on voit B, d'abord sensiblement plus étendu qu A, présenter, vers la fin, un texte beaucoup plus bref.

Voici les principaux passages (281, 9 *et sq.*):

L'amor d'amdos (d'els dos B) fo ses tota mesura

A	B
tant amet l'uns l'autre. E·l vescoms s'en anet una vetz en garnimen on	tant se volgron de ben l'us a l'autre. Et avenc si qe·il vescoms si anet una vetz en garnimen et si
	fo una grans batailla.
Don el i fo nafratz a mort. E fon dich pelz sieus enemics q'el era mortz; e la novella venc a la dompna; et ella, de la gran dolor qe n'ac, si se rendet a l'orden dels eretges. E, si cum Dieus volc, lo vescoms gari ...,	E·l vescoms si fo nafratz a mort. E fo dich per sos enemics q'el era mortz; e venc a [la] dompna la novella q'el era mortz; et ela, de gran dolor qe n'ac, si s'en anet ades, e si·s rendet en l'orden dels eretges. E, si cum Dieus volc, lo vescoms garic de la nafra e meilloret ...
... Fon li dich cum la dompna s'era renduda	
per tristessa de lui;	per la tristessa qu'il ac de lui, quand ill auzi q'el era mortz;
don (dond B) el perdet solatz e ris et alegressa, e cobret	
plains e plors	plains e plors et esmais, ni

et non anet ni venc dentre la bona gen	non cavalguet ni anet dentre la bona gen.

... Et ella lo receup

alegramen	ab gran plazer et ab gran honor q'el (sic) li fetz. Et el fon gais et alegres de l'onor e dels plazers q'ela·ill fetz;
Don el fon gais et alegres dels plazers e de l'onor qe·il fetz e·ill dis;	

et ella mout alegra de la bontat e de la valor q'el (q'ill B) trobet en lui;

	ni non fo pas enpentida dels plazers ni de las amors qu'ill l'avia mandadas, e la saup ben grazir.

... Et anaissi

lo vescoms se parti de lieis, gais e joios et alegres,	se parti lo vescoms de la dompna, gais e joios,

et tornet

en trobar et en chantar et en alegressa; e tenc cortz e cavalget e trepet e venc et anet e briget ab los valens homes et ab las bonas gens; e retornet en trobar et en chantar et en far bons vers e bonas chanssons, atressi ben cum el solia denan.	en chantar et en alegressa;

Et adoncs el comensset far per ma dompna Elis una cansson qe ditz:	e fetz adoncs la chanson que dis:

    Vas vos soplei, en cui ai mes m'entenssa.

Cette *vida* de R. Jordan présente l'écart extrême pouvant séparer A et B. Il n'y en a guère que deux autres qui nous aient été transmises sous des formes aussi divergentes et qu'il a fallu, puisqu'elles étaient inconciliables, publier, comme ici, en deux colonnes: celle de Guillem de Balaun (n° XLVI) et celle de Guillem de Cabestaing (n° XLIX, C), l'une et l'autre d'après les manuscrits H et R.[17]

Comme, en ce qui concerne R. Jordan, IK ont un texte à peu près rigoureusement identique,[18] qui s'apparente le plus souvent à B, mais parfois aussi à A, tout en présentant par endroits des leçons propres, le dernier éditeur des *Vidas*[19]—prenant acte de la faillite, ici complète, du couple AB—s'est résigné à publier, avec éclectisme, un texte composite emprunté, suivant le paragraphe, à A, à B ou même à IK.

De tout ce qui précède, il paraît ressortir que les "jumeaux" IK (qu'il s'agisse des *razos* de B. de Born ou des *vidas*, en dépit des quelques différences relevées dans ces dernières) sont trop semblables pour être séparés de leur archétype par de nombreuses copies. Entre l'archétype et la forme actuelle respective de A et de B, ont dû exister de multiples copies intermédiaires, expliquant les divergences profondes que l'on constate, si fréquemment, entre les deux manuscrits et dont la *vida* de Raimon Jordan est une très frappante illustration.

Pour l'édition d'une *vida* donnée, on peut presque toujours envisager une base IK. Le plus souvent, on ne saurait parler d'une base AB: entre les deux manuscrits s'impose un choix, dont les critères sont loin d'apparaître toujours clairement.

    1. I (Fr. 854) et K (Fr. 12473), ainsi que B (Fr. 1592), appartiennent à la Bibliothèque Nationale de Paris; A est à Rome (Vatican, Lat. 5232). Sur ces manuscrits, voir G. Groeber, "Die Liedersammlungen der Troubadours," *Romanische Studien*, II (1897), 337-668 (étude encore precieuse pour les anthologies, mais beaucoup moins importante pour les *vidas* et les *razos*; il en est à peu près de même pour l'excellent travail de S. Santangelo, *Dante e i Trovatori provenzali* (Catania, 1921); A. Jeanroy, *Bibliographie sommaire des Chansonniers provençaux* (Paris, 1933); Pillet-Carstens, *Bibliographie de Troubadours* (Halle, 1933); C. Brunel, *Bibliographie des manuscrits littéraires en ancien provençal* (Paris, 1935).

    2. La collection de IK compte, en réalité, 86 *vidas*; mais le copiste de I a omis celle de Marcabru; et celui de K, celle de Blacasset.

    3. Rome, *Biblioteca Chigi*, L, IV, 106; in-4° parchemin du XIVe siècle.

    4. Après un commerce de plus de 30 ans, je n'en ai vu toute la beauté qu'en projetant les diapositives en couleurs spécialement exécutées pour les besoins de mon enseignement à la Sorbonne.

    5. Des 52 *vidas* de A, seules celles de B. d'Alamanon et de P. de la Mula manquent à IK; B n'a en propre que la *vida* de G. Figueira.

    6. Les deux manuscrits s'accordent souvent pour des graphies bizarres et inattendues; sauf exceptions rares, ils reproduisent fidèlement les mauvaises lectures de leur modèle, les fautes de langue, les altérations, plus ou moins profondes, qui rendent certains passages incompréhensibles.

    7. Je publierai ailleurs les résultats d'une étude sur cet italianisme caractéristique.

    8. Il est important de se rappeler que IK sont de "main italienne."

    9. Les citations son faites d'après Jean Boutière et A. H. Schutz, *Biographies des Troubadours* ... (Toulouse et Paris, 1950). Le premier chiffre des références désigne la page; le second, la ligne.

    10. Je ne relève pas les menues fautes de déclinaison, non plus que les formes du type: *recep, receup; vol, volc;* etc.

    11. Par exemple: fez direre K (80, 3), ber bertran K (178, 11), aisia faisia K (188, 26), voluntat du un I (310, 18), sauzautet I (225, 7), Salart (= Sarlat) K (93, 7), gentils bras (=bars I) K (76, 1); etc.

    12. G. Favati (éd.), p. 369, trouve les deux leçons inacceptables, alors que la première a été généralement accueillie par les précédents éditeurs.

    13. Il s'agit, à vrai dire, d'une faute matérielle du copiste de I, qui a répété *Alverne* du membre de phrase précédente: .... *si fo d'Alverne, de la terra* ....

14. Le manuscrit donne, en réalité, *de desirier de Mantoana*, qu'il est facile de corriger.

15. Et encore A contient-il, avant la citation de Daniel, un membre de phrase (*en una canson*) qui manque à B, comme d'ailleurs à tous les autres manuscrits.

16. Ce passage manque à IKN², dont le texte s'achève par la citation des vers du poète.

17. La *vida* de Balaun n'a été conservée que par ces deux manuscrits, celle de G. de Cabestaing est dans plusieurs autres, notamment dans AB, qui présentent entre eux peu de divergences, sont—dans leur première partie—étroitement liés à IK, mais, sur toute leur étendue, très différents de H et R.

18. Pourtant, dans un passage du début, K fait groupe avec B (*seigner de Saint Antoni(n) e vescoms*), alors que I se rapproche de A, dont le texte est cependant plus étendu: *seigner e vescoms de Saint Antoni I, s. e v. d'un ric borc de Rozerge que a nom S. A. A.* S'ajoutant au fait qu'il y a, dans IK, un *com* ("avec") à côté de trois *ab*, les variantes ci-dessus paraissent montrer que la *vida-razo* de R. Jordan se rattache à l'archétype des *vidas*, et non à celui des *razos* de B. de Born.

19. G. Favati, *Le Biografie trovadoriche* (Bologna, 1961), p. 284 *et sq.*

———Stanley C. Aston———

The Name of the Troubadour Dalfin d'Alvernhe

THE CURIOUS NAME of Dalfin d'Alvernhe has given rise over the years to considerable discussion.[1] Three questions involved may be summarized thus: Whence did the name Dalfin derive?[2] Was Dalfin the only name borne by the troubadour, or was he also called Robert?[3] When and how did the change from Dalfin, used as a personal name, to Dalfin, used as a title, take place? M. Fournier has devoted much of his article "Le Nom du troubadour Dauphin d'Auvergne" to this third problem and has shown convincingly, as Prudhomme had earlier suggested less thoroughly, that there was a progression from the personal name of the troubadour-baron to the use of the name as a patronymic by his son Guillaume (1235–*ca.* 1240) and grandson Robert I (1240–62) and thence to its use as a title.[4] M. Fournier has primarily followed the sure evidence of Latin *acta*, while discussing in general terms the apparently conflicting evidence of numerous vernacular troubadour texts in which the name Dalfin is usually preceded by the definite article. These texts were adduced by Stronski to support his conclusion that Dalfin was a surname and already had, in twelfth-century troubadour texts, the value of a title; and, although his general conclusion has been countered effectively by M. Fournier, some element of doubt still remains, in as much as the latter did not submit the vernacular texts to detailed examination.

For convenience the vernacular texts are discussed below under three headings: (I) the *vidas*, (II) vernacular documents, and (III) vernacular texts. It is obvious that the extant manuscripts are generally of a much later date than the texts themselves, and some of their statements, for example, the gratuitous attributions inserted by some scribes at the head of their texts (e.g., "lo dalfins e en Peirol," etc.), can be disregarded as evidence. Our aim here has therefore been, first, to examine the manuscript tradition in order to see how far the readings may represent different lines of evidence; secondly, to deduce, when possible, the earliest probable date of the material of the texts in question; and, thirdly, to compare the resulting evidence with the conclusions of M. Fournier in order to evaluate the importance to be attached to the vernacular texts in a consideration of the third problem indicated above.

The "Vidas" [5]

The *vidas* and the *razos* pay eloquent tribute to the esteem in which Dalfin was held, both as poet and patron, by contemporary troubadours, and the references to him are relatively numerous. The actual date of composition of the extant *vidas* and *razos* is not of prime importance here; the versions which have come down to us could conceivably have been derived from material copied from earlier sources; and the important thing, therefore, is, first, to deduce from the information contained in the extant text the earliest dates at which the material transmitted in the manuscripts could have been composed and, secondly, to examine the interrelationship of the manuscripts themselves.

1. Dalfin d'Alvernhe

>   (A) *Vida* (MSS: ABIK [Boutière and Schutz, p. 84]).
>
>   "Lo Dalfins d'Alverne si fo coms d'Alverne. . . ."

Dalfin died in 1235. The *vida* itself makes no mention of his death and is probably subsequent to this date. The only possible indication of a date is contained in the passage, "E per la larguesa soa perdet la meitat e plus de tot lo sieu comtat; e par avareza e per sen o saup tot recobrar, e gazaignar plus que non perdut." In my forthcoming edition of Dalfin, I have accepted the possibility [6] that this may be an oblique reference to the assumption of the title of count of Clermont by his cousin Guy II of Auvergne (various acts, *ca.* 1202) and to the resumption of the title by Dalfin (documents 1223 A.D., *et seq.*). If this assumption is correct, the material of the *vida* would be subsequent to 1223.

>   (B) *Razo* of 95.3 and 119.4 (MS: H [Boutière and Schutz, p. 85]).
>
>   "Lo Dalfins d'Alverne si era drutz. . . . Et un dia ella mandet al baile del Dalfin. . . . E·l Dalfins si·l respondent a la cobla. . . ."

The date of the poems in question is *ca.* 1213, and the *razo* must obviously be later than the poem.

(C) *Razo* of 92.1 and 119.5 (MS: H [Boutière and Schutz, p. 86]).

"Lo Dalfins fetz aquesta cobla d'En Bertram de la Tor. . . . "

A number of objections can be raised to Stronski's identification[7] of this Bertran with Bertran I de la Tour d'Auvergne (1110–ca. 1191), and the reference is more probably to Bertran II, who had succeeded to the title by 1206[8] and who probably died in 1222.[9] The exchange of *coblas* should probably be placed between these dates.

(D) *Razo* of 119.1a and 353.1 (MS: H [Boutière and Schutz, p. 87]).

" . . . E·l Dalfins d'Alverne . . . si era drutz de Na Contor. . . . "

And the text of the first line of Peire Pelissier's *cobla*.

"Al Dalfin man q'estei dins son hostel. . . . "

To which, according to the *razo*, "Lo Dalfins respondet a Peire Pelissier."

Nothing is known of Peire Pelissier beyond the details given by the *razo* (Boutière and Schutz, p. 370), but he may have exchanged *coblas* with Blacatz (97.3), whose compositions date from 1200 to 1227.[10] The Lady Contor was one of the three daughters of Raimon II of Turenne (1143–91); she married the Viscount Elias de Camborn, who died young between 1184 and 1187. There is no reason to suppose that Dalfin's "affair" with the lady, if it ever took place, is necessarily to be set near these dates. Taking into account the possible dates of Peire Pelissier, the *coblas* may well not be earlier than 1200.

(E) *Razo* of 119.8 and 420.1 (MSS: I, K [Boutière and Schutz, pp. 88 ff.]).

" . . . Dont lo Dalfins e sos cosis lo coms Gis. . . . "

The date of the exchange of poems between Dalfin and Richard I is probably 1194–95, but the texts themselves offer no internal evidence as to the name Dalfin, since the only reference to him is the simple vocative "Dalfin" at the beginning of 420.1.

2. Guillem de Saint Leidier (MSS: ABEIKPRSga"a' [Boutière and Schutz, p. 178]).

"Et entendet se en la marqueza de Polonhac, qu'era sor del Dalfin d'Alverne e de Na Sail de Claustra, e moiller del vescomte de Polonhac. . . ."

Of the manuscripts, only P ("de dalfin delauerne") omits the definite article. Sail de Claustra, sung by Periol, may have died about 1202,[11] Heraclius III of Polignac, in 1198 or 1201. There are no references to Dalfin in the poems of Guillem de Saint Leidier, who probably died between 1195 and 1200.[12]

3. Peire d'Alvergne (MSS: ABEIKN²R [Boutière and Schutz, p. 220]).

" . . . segon qu'en dis lo Dalfins d'Alverne. . . . "

There is no mention of Dalfin in the poems of Peire d'Alvergne. The *vida* is probably the work of Uc de Saint Circ,[13] and therefore dates from the thirteenth century.

4. Peire de Maensac (MSS: IK [Boutière and Schutz, p. 228]).

"Peire de Maensac si fo d'Alverne, de la terra del Dalfin (de la terra daluerne I) . . . e mena la en un castel del Dalfin d'Alverne . . . e·l Dalfins lo mantenc. . . ."

Peire may have been the jongleur of Dalfin.[14] If Chabaneau's identification of his brother Austorc de Maensac (attested in 1238) is admissible, it would probably place the date of Peire de Maensac in the thirteenth century. The lady sung by Peire, the wife of En Bernart de Tierce, may have been the "Na Biatritz, la bella de Tierne" chosen for arbiter by Gui d'Ussel in P.C. 136.6. Peire is also addressed in the *sirventes* of Robert, bishop of Clermont, (P.C. 95.2), the date of which is probably *ca.* 1212–13.

5. Peirol (MSS: ABEIKRA[1] [Boutière and Schutz, p. 250]).

"Peirols si fo . . . d'un castel que a nom Peirols, qu'es en la contrada del Dalfin. . . . E·l Dalfins d'Alverne. . . ."

Whatever the date of the composition of the *vida*, it must be after the departure of Peirol from Clermont, which may be placed in the first decade of the thirteenth century.[15]

6. Perdigon (MSS: AEIKRA[1]a[2] [Boutière and Schutz, pp. 252–55]).

" . . . que·l Dalfins d'Alverne lo tenc per son cavallier. . . . "

and from manuscripts E and R

" . . . e·l Dalfins d'Alverne li ac touta la terra. . . . "

It is obvious from the texts that the *vida* must have been composed after the death of Perdigon, which his editor [16] puts at *ca.* 1220.

7. Uc Brunet (MSS: AEIKRa¹a² [Boutière and Schutz, p. 327]).

" . . . E briget com lo rei d'Arragon . . . e com lo Dalfin d'Alverne. . . . "

The text again indicates that the *vida* was composed after the death of Uc. This troubadour was the friend of Daude de Pradas, the first mention of whom is found in 1214.

8. Uc de Saint Circ (MSS: ABIKN²P [Boutière and Schutz, p. 332]).

" . . . com las tensos e com las coblas que feiren com lui, e·l bons dalphins d'Alverne."

The phrase "e·l bons Dalfins d'Alverne" is missing in ABP.

The text of the *vida* shows that it was composed "pois qu'el ac moiller"; his marriage may well have taken place after Uc's arrival in Italy, which his editors [17] place about 1220.

What evidence, then, do the *vidas* and *razos* offer as to the name of our troubadour? With only one exception (manuscript P in the *vida* of Guillem de Saint Leidier), they uniformly designate him as "lo Dalfins" or as "lo Dalfins d'Alverne." Two points, however, are to be noted. First, the great majority of the references are to be found in a small group of manuscripts (ABEIK) which are nearly always closely allied in troubadour texts, while the other manuscripts, with the possible exception of the individualistic R, often show affinities with this major group; one is therefore tempted to ask whether there is more than one line of tradition here. Secondly, and leaving aside the actual dates of the surviving texts, the information given in the texts indicates that, with one or two doubtful exceptions, any original material which might have formed the basis of the extant texts could not in all probability be earlier than 1200.

Vernacular Documents

Official documents such as charters or legal *acta* are generally surer evidence than troubadour texts. Two such vernacular documents, which conform to designations found in contemporary Latin *acta* (*Dalfinus comes, Delfinus comes Arvernie*), offer valuable testimony. The first, an agreement between Anselm d'Olbi and Dalfin, bears no date but is from about 1200;[18] it begins: "N'Anselmes d'Olbi avia grahusas de terras am lo comte dalfi e acorderunt s'en. . . ." Subsequent references in the text are to "el coms," "lo coms," "al comte." The second[19] is dated 1201, and refers to Dalfin first as "el Dalfis coms d'Alvergne," and later in the text as "el Dalfis," "al Dalfi," and sometimes as "el coms," "lo coms," etc. These texts would indicate that, about 1200, Dalfin was used as a personal name, but that already in vernacular *acta* the article was prefixed to the name. One may agree with M. Fournier that to attribute to the simple name accompanied by the article the value of a title, which it could not have in the complete phrase "el Dalfis coms d'Alvergne," would be arbitrary; nevertheless, the juxtaposition of article and name in vernacular *acta* is formal evidence that the practice had come into use at this period in the vernacular speech.

Vernacular Texts

References to Dalfin in troubadour texts are numerous; the list given below does not claim to be exhaustive, but is thought to be fairly complete.[20]

1. Dalfin d'Alvernhe

> (A) *Coblas* exchanged with Peire Pelissier (P.C. 119.1a and 353.1), MS: H.

"Al Dalfin man qu'estei dinz son hostel." (P.C. 353.1, line 1)

For observations on the date of the coblas, see *supra*.

> (B) *Tenso* with Uc (Bausan) (P.C. 119.1 and 448.1), MSS: DGMNQRa¹.

Here the name Dalfin occurs only in the vocative at the beginning of the two poems of Uc.

> (C) *Tenso* with Peirol (P.C. 366.10), MSS: EGIKNQa¹d.

Again the name Dalfin occurs only in a vocative at the beginning of alternate stanzas.

> (D) *Coblas* exchanged with the bishop of Clermont (P.C. 95.3 and 119.4), MS: H.

"Ben saup del Dalfin lo talan." (P.C. 95.3, line 5)

The date of this exchange is *ca.* 1213 (see *supra*). In the *sirventes* of the bishop addressed to Peire de Maensac (95.2), the bishop does not address Dalfin by name but calls him "el coms."

(E) *Coblas* exchanged with Bertran de la Tor (P.C. 92.1 and 119.5), MS: H.

"Mauret, al Dalfin agrada." (P.C. 92.1, line1)

This Bertran is probably Bertran II de la Tour (see *supra*).

(F) *Sirventes* exchanged with Richard Coeur-de-Lion (P.C. 119.8 and 420.1), MSS: ABDIKR.

The name of Dalfin again occurs only as a vocative, except in the *razo* (see *supra*).

2. Elias de Barjols [21] (P.C. 132.5 [Stronski (ed.), p. 2]), MSS: CE.

>   N'Aymars me don sa coindia
>   En Trencaleos
>   sa gensoze', En Randos
>   donar, qu'es la senhoria
>   e·l Dalfis sos belhs respos.

(Stanza III, lines 17–21)

Stronski, relying on his identification of Bertran de la Tor "qui ne vivait plus en 1191," places this poem before 1191. If, as is more probable, the reference is to Bertran (see *supra*), the date is more likely to be after 1200. All the other poems of Elias are later than 1191, and the references to other persons in the poem do not preclude this date.

3. Gaucelm Faidit

(A) P.C. 167.61 (A. Kolsen [ed.], *Trobadorgedichte*, p. 34), MSS: AVa.

> Tant m'es al cor s'amors que a presenssa
> Dopte disses son bel nom en dormen,
> Que de mi·m gart e de tot'autra gen,
> Seign'en Dalfin, e s'agues entendenssa
> Que ja nuill temps li plagues m'amistatz,
> Tot lo maltraich volgra sofrir en patz.
>
> (Stanza VI, lines 49–54)

Variants: "seigner dalfin," A; "senjen dalfin," V; "segnier dalfin," a. The variants show that A and a often stand together against V.

(B) *Tenso* with Uc de la Bacalaria (P.C. 167.44 [Mahn (ed.), *Werke*, pp. 2, 99]), MSS: ADIKMORTa^{1}d.

> Gaucelm, lieis tenc per valen,
> E vuelh que·l fassa, ab que·il sia,
> E que·i apel eyssamen
> Lo Dalfin que sap la via
> E l'obra de drudaria.
>
> (Stanza VIII, lines 72–76, second *tornada*)

Line 75 is found in ADIKOTa^1. It is missing in M; R has "lo merga"; T confuses the two *tornadas*. The reference to Maria de Ventadour (died 1221) and the dates of Uc de la Bacalaria suggest that the poem dates from the first or second decade of the thirteenth century.

4. Guiraudo lo Ros

(A) *Tenso* with a count (P.C. 240.6a [Suchier (ed.), *Denkmäler*, I. 333]), MS: N 287–461 (290b).

> Seingner, en lei son trastut bon usatge,
> e sai de ver, ses nuilla falizo,
> qu'il e·l dalfis mantenran ma razo;
> que chascus sap d'amor lo dretz viatge.
>
> (Stanza VIII, lines 55–56, *tornada*)

Guiraudo lo Ros is mentioned in the celebrated *sirventes* of the Monk of Montaudon (*ca.* 1194), and the date of his poetic activity probably centers around the last decade of the twelfth century.[22]

(B) P.C. 240.5 (Mahn [ed.], *Werke*, p. 174), MSS: CDᵉERa¹e.

> Senher Dalfi, tant sai vostres fags bos
> Que tot quan faitz platz et agrad'als pros.
>
> (Stanza VII, lines 43–44, *tornada*)

The *tornada* occurs only in CERe. The text offers no indication of the date of composition.

5. Guiraut de Borneill [23]

(A) *Sirventes* (P.C. 242.27 [Kolsen (ed.), I, 474]), MSS: ACDHIK.

> E si anatz lai vas Rodes
> Ni passatz entre·ls montanhers,

> Lachs frechs no·us tenha ni tempers
> Quez al Dalfi no siatz la kalenda
> E no·us chalra preiar, qu'el vos entenda.
>
> (Stanza VIII, lines 68–72)

This poem, addressed to the *jongleur* Cardalhac, is followed up in Dalfin's *sirventes* (119.7) addressed to the same person. The text of Guiraut offers no indications of the date of composition, but the reference to Elias Rudel (II) de Bergarac (whose existence has been attested to have been between 1201 and 1251) [24] in Dalfin's poem indicates that the latter should probably be dated after 1200.

(B) *Sirventes* (P.C. 242.45 [Kolsen (ed.), I, 300]), MSS: ABCDHIKMNQRSgTUVa.

> Leu chansonet'e vil
> M'auri'a obs a far
> Que pogues enviar
> En Alvernh' al Dalfi.
>
> (Stanza I, lines 1–4)

Although the manuscripts fall into fairly well defined groups, they are all more or less uniform in their versions of these four lines.

It is difficult to see any good reason for identifying the Eblon named in line 6 of the poem with Eble de Saignas (P.C. 128) and hence for following Stronski in his assertion [25] that the poem "paraît remonter assez loin dans la deuxième moitié du XII· siècle." If the Sobre-Totz of the *tornada* is to be identified with Raimon Bernart de Rouvenac [26] who is probably attested in a charter of 1197, the date of the poem may well be nearer to the end of the century.

(C) *Sirventes* (P.C. 242.55 [Kolsen (ed.), I, 412]), MSS: ABCDIKNPQRSgUVCe.

> So di·l Dalfis que conois los bos chans.
>
> (Stanza X, *tornada*)

This tornada of one line is found only in ABDIKNPSge. There is no internal evidence in the poem to indicate its date of composition.[27]

6. Peirol

(A) *Canso* (P.C. 366.1 [Aston (ed.), XIII]), MSS: ACD'D'IKNRTa.

> En Vianes anera plus soven
> mas per midonz remain sai Alvergnatz,
> prop del Dalfin, car sos afars mi platz.
>
> (Stanza VIII, *tornada*)

This *tornada* is found only in ACD'IKN, which are almost identical in their readings. The poem probably dates from the last decade of the twelfth century and the references to Vienne in the poems of Peirol [28] may be significant (see *infra*).

(B) Various *cansos* (P.C. 366.9, 12, and 27 [Aston (ed.), XXIV, XII, XI]) in which Dalfin is apostropized in a *tornada*.

> Dalfi, s'auzes mon voler
>   dir' a ren que sia,
> tant am vostra seignoria
> que vos en saubratz lo ver.
>
> (XXIV, Stanza VII, lines 53–56)

This *tornada* is found in only seven versions (ABCEMRa) of the twenty-one manuscripts.

> Dalfi, solatz et amors
> e cortes sens vos essenha
> cossi joys e pretz vos venha.
>
> (XII, Stanza VIII, lines 46–48)

The *tornada* is found in only two (Ca) of the sixteen manuscripts.

> Dalfi, ses duptansa
> joy' e pretz vos enansa
> mielhas c'amors no fai me.
>
> (XI, Stanza VII, lines 61–63)

Of the eleven manuscripts (ACD'IKLMNRSa), all except D' contain the *tornada*.

(C) *Tenso* (P.C. 366.10 [Aston (ed.), XXVIII]), MSS: EGIKNQa¹d.

See *supra*, section 1(C).

(D) *Tenso* (P.C. 366.29 [Aston (ed.), XXXI]), MSS: ACDGIKLMNORSTa.

> Amors, si li rey no·i van,
> del Dalfi vos dic aitan;
> ja per guerra ni per vos
> no remanra, tant es pros.
>
> (Stanza VI, lines 46–49, *tornada*)

The *tornada* is missing in IKR.

The *tenso* was written during the preparation for the Third Crusade, and may be dated almost certainly in 1188.[29]

This is apparently the earliest certain date at which the use of "Dalfin" with the definite article is found in troubadour poetry.

7. Perdigon (*Tenso*, P.C. 167-47 [Chaytor (ed.), p. 32]), MSS: ACDGIJKMNQSa¹.

> Totz temps duraria·l tensos,
> Perdigons, per qu'ieu vuelh e·m platz
> qu·el Dalfin sia·l plaitz pauzatz
> qu'el jutge e l'acort en patz.
> (Stanza VII, line 61-64, *tornada*)

There is almost complete unanimity in the readings of the manuscripts. The dates of Perdigon's poetic career are to be set between 1195 and 1220;[30] those of Gaucelm Faidit between 1185 and 1220.[31] It seems probable that the date of composition of the *tenso* should be placed early in the thirteenth century.

8. Raimbaut and Albertet de Sisteron[32] (*Tenso*, P.C. 16.4 and 388.1 [Boutière (ed.), p. 92]), MSS: Oa¹.

> Q'ieu vic qe·l dalfiz fon plus pros
> Entendeir', enanz qe drutz fos.
> (Stanza IV, lines 39-40)

Albertet's career and hence the date of the *tenso* is to be placed between the extremes of 1200 and *ca.* 1225. His datable poems lie between 1210 and 1221.[33]

9. Raimon Vidal

In the *Abrils issia* of Raimon Vidal (Bartsch [ed.], *Denkmäler* p. 144), probably composed *ca.* 1210, there are eight references [34] to Dalfin, seven of which use his name with the definite article. The one exception indicates, however, that the author knew another current usage:

> En Blacas noy fai a laissar
> Ni del Baus en Guillaume lo blon
> Ni d'Alvernhal senor Dunon
> Ni·l comte Dalfi [35] que tan valc.
>
> (Bartsch, *op. cit.*, p. 165, line 37, and p. 166, lines 1–3)

10. Uc de Saint Circ

(A) *Tenso* (P.C. 457.1 [A. Jeanroy and Salverda de Grave (eds.), p. 28]), MSS: ACDGIKLNN²R.

> Dalfin, de clara razo
> Ai er faicha ma chansso,
> Per so que puosca eslire
> E devire
> Cum eu ai
> Vas lieis mon fin cor verai
>
> (Stanza VI, lines 56–61, *tornada*)

The *tornada* is found only in ADIKN². The poem is ascribed by the editors to Uc's Toulouse period (1211 to 1220).[36]

(B) *Tenso* (P.C. 457.24 [A. Jeanroy and Salverda de Grave (eds.), p. 136]), MSS: ADTa¹.

> N'Ugo, eu voill que lo Dalfis
> D'Alvergne, que sap ben d'amor
> Cum ella vai e ven e cor,

> Jutge si·m veda l'entendenssa
> Per mo mal o per ben volenssa.
>
> (Stanza VII, lines 79–83, *tornada*)

The *tornada* in this form is found only in A and D. The other two manuscripts have in the first two lines: T, "N'Ugo lo rei valentc e fis / D'Aragon en cui pres saizia . . ."; and a, "N'Ugo, lo reis valenz e fiz / D'Aragon a cui es aclis. . . ." The editors assign this *tenso*, also, to Uc's Toulouse period.

The evidence offered by the vernacular texts is both more varied and more weighty than that provided by the *vidas*. In the first place, the manuscripts are far more numerous (twenty-five, or possibly twenty-six); and, although the greatest number of examples are to be found in ACDIKN, the manuscripts offer different lines of tradition and hence some degree of corroborative evidence. Secondly, although a considerable number of texts may date from after 1200, and hence be evidence of current thirteenth-century vernacular usage, there is one (the *tenso* of Peirol, P.C. 366.29) which shows the use of the article with Dalfin's name at the early and certain date of 1188, and a few (texts of Elias de Barjols, Gaucelm Faidit, Guiraudo lo Ros Guiraut de Borneill, Peirol) which may possibly date from the last decade of the twelfth century.

These texts, too, offer a variety of designations. Thus, alongside the common "lo dalfis," etc., we find: "senher dalfis," offered by manuscripts Aa(V) in Gaucelm Faidit, P.C. 161.61, and by C(E)R e in Guiraudo lo Ros, P.C. 240.5; "·l comte dalfi," along with the more common "lo dalfis," etc. (in Raimon Vidal); and "lo dalfis d'Alvergne"[37] (in Uc de Saint Circ, P.C. 185.2).

Conclusion

The evidence of the vernacular texts for the use of the definite article with the name "Dalfin" is quantitatively imposing but is subject to qualifications. Most of the texts are not earlier than the thirteenth century, by which time, as M. Fournier has shown, various forms had begun to develop in the Latin texts. Yet one may distinguish between the authoritative usage of official chancellery *acta*, on the one hand, and the freer fashions and conventions of literary usage, on the other. In the vernacular, four forms occur, two of which are rare. In "senher [en] dalfis," "dalfis" is clearly a personal name, while the isolated "·l comte dalfi" of Raimon Vidal corresponds to the "Delphinus comes" of contemporary Latin *acta*. Two usages, however, "lo Dalfins" and "lo Dalfins d'Alvernhe," are clearly evident. The former is earlier and more common and is found alike in *vidas*, vernacular documents, and literary texts. It is evident from the text of Peirol (P.C. 366.29) that the combination of article and name was definitely used as early as 1188, while a few of the other texts cited, including the vernacular document of 1201, may add some corroborative evidence for such a usage before or about 1200. Nevertheless, the use of the term "lo Dalfins" does not justify Stronski's categoric assertion that the word "Dalfin" at this time could only be a surname which had already assumed the value of a title; this question has been thoroughly examined by M. Fournier.[38] To see an analogy between usage in the Viennois, where the name "Dalfin" had been borne by the counts for more than half a century, and usage in the Auvergne, where the son of Guillaume le Jeune is the first to bear the name,[39] is not necessarily justified, even though the close family connection between the families and the close contacts of the two counts, for which some literary evidence may be found in the references to Vienne in the poems of Peirol (P.C. 366.1 and 26), may have given a natural impulse to the adoption of the terminology "lo Dalfis." M. Fournier has found, I think, the true explanation when he points out that the use of pseudonyms has always existed in the literary circles associated with a courtly society. Dalfin's unusual name offered an obvious and easy sobriquet which Dalfin himself early recognized,[40] and in recognizing it publicly in his crest, no doubt gave it wider currency. The use of the term "lo Dalfis" in troubadour texts represents, in all probability, a literary usage which, to judge by the vernacular document of 1201, may well have become more widely used by the turn of the century.

More puzzling on the surface, perhaps, is the terminology "lo Dalfins d'Alvernhe," found both in the *vidas* and *razos* and in the poem of Uc de Saint Circ (P.C. 457.24). The latter poem dates certainly from the thirteenth century and the evidence of the tornada found in A and D against the contrary "reis d'Aragon" of T and a¹ may possibly be suspect. The evidence of the *vidas* and *razos* is more extensive and seemingly more definite; yet here again it is possible to suggest a simple explanation, without maintaining, as does Stronski, that the name had already become a title.

The *vidas* and *razos*, in the forms as we have them, certainly belong to the thirteenth century; but even if one admits that the extant texts could be based on earlier material, such material, if it existed, could scarcely be earlier than 1200 and would, for the most part, belong to the first or second decades of the thirteenth century. The phrase "lo Dalfis d'Alvernhe" could well be a confusion. Latin *acta* attest the use of

"Delfinus comes Arvernie" as early as 1196, and of "Dalphinus de Arvernia" by 1225;[41] and a vernacular document, the use of "el Dalfis coms d'Alvernge" in 1201. Is it not possible that the vernacular equivalent "Dalfis [coms] d'Alvernhe" of the Latin *acta* and the current vernacular usage of "lo Dalfins" may have been combined to give rise to another usage, "lo Dalfins [coms] d'Alvernhe"? And that it is this new usage which is reflected in the *vidas* and *razos* and in the document of 1201?

M. Fournier has relied on the sure evidence of Latin *acta*, from which the gradual development of Dalfin in Auvergne from a personal name, via a patronymic, into a title is clear. One may conclude that a detailed examination of the vernacular texts is far from disproving his thesis and, indeed, does much to support it.

---

1. A convenient résumé of the problems and the principal points of view is given by P. F. Fournier in his excellent article "Le Nom du troubadour Dauphin d'Auvergne," *Bibliothèque de l'Ecole des Chartes*, XCI (1930), 66–99, to which the same scholar added a supplementary note in the *Bulletin Historique et Scientifique de l'Auvergne*, 2ᵉ série, No. 3 (1930), p. 114. The most important articles for the controversy are: A. Prudhomme, "De l'Origine et du sens des mots Dauphin et Dauphiné . . . ," *Bibliothèque de l'Ecole des Chartes*, LIV (1893), 429–56 (also see A. Thomas' review of Prudhomme in *Annales du Midi*, VI [1894], 251–52); S. Stronski, "Recherches historiques sur quelques protecteurs des troubadours," *Annales du Midi*, XVIII (1906), 473–93; S. Stronski, "Le Nom du troubadour Dalfin d'Alvernhe," *Romania*, XXXVI (1907), 610–12; A. Jeanroy, review of article by A. Thomas, *Annales du Midi*, XX (1908), 565.

2. Whether the name Dalfin borne by Dalfin d'Alvernhe's father-in-law, Guigues IV, count of Albon and Vienne (1132–42), derived from a hagiographical tradition (Prudhomme, *op. cit.*, p. 435; and G. de Monteyer, "Les Origines du Dauphiné de Viennois: D'où provient le surnom de baptême Dauphin?", *Bulletin de la Société d'Etudes des Hautes-Alpes*, 44ᵉ année, 5e série, vol. IV) or whether it derived from the Anglo-Saxon connections of the counts of Albon (De Monteyer, *op. cit.*; P. F. Fournier, "Le Nom du troubadour," p. 89,n.2; P. A. Becker, *Dalfin d'Alvernhe der Troubadour*

[Leipzig], 1941, p. 34, presumably following De Monteyer) is immaterial for our purpose here.

3. Articles by Thomas, Stronski, and M. Fournier ("Le Nom du troubadour," p. 75 ff., and his supplementary note in *Bulletin Historique et Scientifique de l'Auvergne*) have shown that the name "Robert" derives from the late and uncertain copies of an act of 1215 and is not authenticated. For an ingenious suggestion regarding a possible source of error in a faulty reading of the manuscripts, see Becker, *op. cit.*, p. 36.

4. The first documentary evidence for the title "Arvenie delphinus" is found in the will of Robert III (1262–1282), dated 1281.

5. Quotations in this section are taken from the texts contained in J. Boutière and A. H. Schutz, *Biographies des Troubadours* (Toulouse and Paris, 1950).

6. Suggested by P. A. Becker, *op. cit.*, p. 64 ff.; cf. also citations given by Fournier, *op. cit.*, p. 74.

7. *Annales du Midi*, XVIII, 477 ff.

8. Baluze, *Hist. gén. de la maison d'Auvergne*, I, 278.

9. Baluze, *op. cit.*, I, 278–79; II, 494.

10. Jeanroy, *Poésie lyrique*, I, 177.

11. See S. C. Aston, *Peirol: Troubadour of Auvergne* (Cambridge: Cambridge University Press, 1953), p. 6.

12. A. Sakari, *Poésies du troubadour G. de S. D.* (Helsinki, 1956), p. 17.

13. Jeanroy, *Poésie lyrique*, I, 105.

14. Stronski, "Recherches hist.," p. 478 n.

15. Aston, *op. cit.*, p. 12.

16. H. J. Chaytor, *Les Chansons de Perdigon* (Paris, 1926), p. vi.

17. A. Jeanroy and J. Salverda de Grave, *Poésies de Uc de Saint-Circ* (Toulouse, 1913), p. xv.

18. C. Brunel, in *Les Plus anciens chartes en langue provençale*, No. 349 (Paris, 1926), p. 344, mentioned P. F. Fournier, *op. cit.*, p. 74.

19. R. Grand, in *Les Plus anciens textes romans de la Haute-Auvergne* (Paris, 1901), p. 27, mentioned P. F. Fournier, *op. cit.*, p. 74, and, for a full discussion, see especially p. 86. The text of this document has not been immediately accessible to me; and I have, therefore, had to rely on the details supplied by M. Fournier, p. 86.

20. Examples of the use of *dalfin* which refer definitely to the counts of Vienne (for example, the *sirventes* of the Trobaire de Villa-Arnaut, Pillet-Carstens, *Bibliographie des Troubadours*, 446.2, the date of which is 1257) have not been included here.

21. S. Stronski (ed.), *Le Troubadour Elias de Barjols* (Toulouse, 1906).

22. It is not altogether certain that the poem is to be attributed to Guiraudo lo Ros (P.C. 240) as distinct from Guiraudo (P.C. 239). Jeanroy,

Poésie lyrique, I, 383, places the activity of the latter ("qui se confond probablement avec Guiraudo lo Ros") in the first third of the thirteenth century. Stronski, *Annales du Midi*, XVIII, 481, assumes Guiraudo lo Ros, whom he assigns to the twelfth century, and states that Dalfin's relations with him "sont nécessairement d'une date ancienne." It is not clear what meaning is to be attached to this statement, nor indeed what authority justifies it.

23. A. Kolsen (ed.), *Sämtliche Lieder des Trobadors Giraut de Bornelh* (2 vols.; Halle, 1910–1935).

24. Stronski, "Recherches hist.," p. 479, n. 2.

25. *Ibid.*, p. 480.

26. Kolsen, *op. cit.*, II, 275.

27. The picturesque story contained in the *razo* of the poem (Boutière and Schutz, *op. cit.*, p. 199), which is based on a faulty interpretation of St. VIII, is to be disregarded (see Boutière and Schutz, p. 394).

28. Cf. P. C. 366.26 (Aston, *op. cit.*, XVI) in addition to 366.1.

29. Aston, *op. cit.*, p. 8.

30. Chaytor, *op. cit.*, p. vi.

31. Jeanroy, *Poésie lyrique*, I, 370.

32. J. Boutière (ed.), *Studi Medievali*, X (1937), 1–129.

33. *Ibid.*, p. 12. It is possible that the *dalfiz* referred to here may be Gui-André of Vienne.

34. Pp. 148, 161, 162, 163, 165–66, 167, 168, 170.

35. Stronski, *Annales du Midi*, XVIII, 483, n. I, sees here the juxtaposition of two titles, and cites as parallels *lo rei emperador*, *·l comte dalfin Gigo* (found in the *sirventes* of 1257 of the Trobaire de Villa-Arnaut [P.C. 446.2]; the phrase there designates, however, the count of Albon and Vienne, and, as Fournier indicates [*op. cit.*, p. 84], this usage is attested in the Viennois from 1223 onward). One could adduce against Stronski numerous examples of the use of title and proper name (for example, *lo coms Gis* in the *razos* to P.C. 119.8 and 420.1; see Boutière and Schutz, p. 89).

36. *Op. cit.*, p. xii.

37. The *tornada* concerned occurs only in AD (cf. variants of Ta[1]); corresponding terminology (*Arvenie delphinus*) is not attested in a Latin text until 1281.

38. *Op. cit.*, p. 85 ff.

39. One may point out here that, although it is customary to date Dalfin's succession to the countly title as early as 1169, there is some documentary evidence (Baluze, *op. cit.*, II, 69) to indicate that his father, Guillaume le Jeune, was still alive in 1181. Dalfin can scarcely have been born before 1155–1160. The earliest extant act attributed to him dates from 1193. See also P. A. Becker, *op. cit.*, p. 30.

40. The oldest example of Dalfin's seal, which dates from 1199, shows that by this date Dalfin has replaced the old arms of the house of Auvergne with the emblem of the dolphin. See A. Prudhomme, *op. cit.*, p. 453; and P. F. Fournier, *op. cit.*, p. 87. The houses of Albon and Forez adopted the same device shortly afterwards.

41. P. F. Fournier, *op. cit.*, p. 74.

Three Little Problems of Old Provençal Syntax

Omission of a Relative Pronoun

IN HIS *Vermischte Beiträge*, second edition, pages 111–13, Tobler deals with the following Old French syntactical phenomenon. Where the first of two co-ordinate verbs is accompanied by a personal pronoun which should be repeated before the second verb, but in a different case, this second pronoun is frequently dropped, as in the following sentence: "Il lor dona armes et apareilla honorablent." Here a *les* is to be supplied before *apareilla* from the foregoing *lor*. At the end of his article, Tobler gives one example of the same phenomenon, but in connection with a relative, instead of a personal, pronoun. We want here, in a way, to complement Tobler's article by presenting some Provençal parallels to his last example, i.e., the omission of a relative pronoun.

1. Lo reis cui es Castrasoritz
e te de Toleta·l palais
lau que mostre de sos eslais . . .

(Bertran de Born, P.C. 80.32
[Appel (ed.), No. 21, IV, 2])

As *cui* (line 1) is dative, the nominative *qui* is to be supplied after *e* (line 2).

2.   Qar cel cui destreing grans dolors
     e sap qu'aver no pot secors
     mas per un metge sol, cre . . .

     (Gauc. Faidit, P.C. 167.5 [Kolsen (ed.),
     Arch. Rom., XVII, 365], IV, 8)

Here the *cui* (line 1) is an accusative, so one should expect to find the nominative *qui* before *sap* (line 2).

3.   . . . dont ad autor
     trac mon segnor
     de Peitieus, cui es honransa
     e pretz capdell' et secor.

     (*Ibid.*, P.C. 167.31 [Kolsen (ed.), *Arch. Rom.*, XVII, 1] VI, 10)

The *cui* of line 3 has the value of a dative, while another case of the relative pronoun is missing after *e* (line 4). This should be *que* (accusative), if one assumes, as does Kolsen, that the subject of *capdell' e secors* is *pretz* (line 4); it should be *qui* (nominative) if the subject is the *segnor de Peitieus*.

4.   Per que falh qui· desdui,
     pos aisi leu s'esdui
     so c'om plus vol ni·lh platz.

     (Giraut de Bornelh, P.C. 242.73
     [Kolsen (ed.) No. 73] VI, 9)

The subject of *vol* (line 3) is *om*, its object *que* (*c'*). In the second part of the line, what was nominative in the first part (*om*) becomes dative in the second: ·*lh* (=*li*). So a relative pronoun in the nominative should stand between *ni* and ·*lh*. The form of that nominative, its gender being neuter, would, it is true, have the same form as the *que* (*c'*) in the beginning of the line, but they differ from logical and grammatical standpoints.

> 5. Selh cui joys tanh ni chantar sap
>   e sos belhs ditz vol despendre
>   a tal dona·ls fass' entendre . . .
>
>   (Raim. de Miraval, P.C. 406.18 [Kolsen (ed.), *Beiträge*, 25], I, 1)

Here the nominative *qui* is to be supplied after *ni* (line 1), the *cui* of the same line having the value of a dative. This *qui* would also be the subject of *vol* (line 2).

> 6. Cel qu'eu asor   e volc esdevenir
>   per nostr' amor   fyll de Santa Maria
>   e mal sentir,   turmen, pen' e paor,
>   e mort sofrir   e ressors al terç dia,
>   prec . . .
>
>   (Cerveri, P.C. 434a.62 [Riquer (ed.), No. 40, V, 1])

In line 1 *que* is accusative, the object of *asor*, whose subject is *eu*. But the subject of the second verb (*volc*) is a missing *qui*, which should refer to *Cel*, i.e., Christ. This nonexistent *qui* is also the subject of the third finite verb of this passage, viz., *ressors* in line 4.

7. Ar a Brunesenz so que vol,
    que de so de que plus si dol
    e mais en est siegle dezira,
    de que soven plain e sospira,
    si fai mut ricamenz pregar.

("Jaufre," ed. Clovis Brunel [Paris, 1943], line 7849)

Since the *que* of line 2 depends on the preposition *de*, one should expect another *que*, direct object of *dezira* (line 3), after the *e* of the same line. This anacoluthon would have been more obvious still if the poet had used *don* instead of *de que* in line 2. It is, moreover, noteworthy that, after the anacoluthon of line 3, the poet resumes, with the *de que* in line 4, the original construction of line 2.

The above examples no doubt show a certain negligence from a strict grammatical standpoint. Could one, therefore, say that the authors of these passages did not know their language well, or would they, if somebody had called their attention to this way of speaking, have admitted that they had made mistakes? We do not think so. For such an assumption, the examples seem too great in number and the writings from which they are taken too different in character and time of composition. Such anacolutha, just as the Old French ones mentioned in the beginning of this section, where it is a personal pronoun that was omitted, sprang from common usage in medieval times, and it was—and could be—left to the reader or listener to adjust grammar and sense.

Complementary Relative Clauses

There are relative clauses that seem absolutely superfluous because the nouns to which they refer are perfectly clear in their meanings. I have found such clauses only in non-lyric writings.

> 1. En cenaire,[1] nos mantenem
>   mielz la nostra lei *que tenem*
>   que vos non faz, si nos ajut
>   le nostre dieus per sa vertut.
>
> (Jeu de Sainte Agnès, ed. Jeanroy [Paris, 1931], line 158)

The possessive pronoun preceding *lei* makes the following relative clause still more dispensable.[2]

> 2. Ben sui certa que mais non ti veirai.
>   Dona mi .I. bais al partir *qu'en farai*.
>   Que Dieu ti don s'ajuda.
>
> (*Ibid.*, line 381)

The spectators are witness of this farewell; *al partir* alone would, therefore, seem sufficiently clear.[3]

> 3. [Que] anc non vist sa par dolor
>   *qu'el fay*, e sons payres major.
>
> (Sant Honorat, ed. Ingagärd Suwe [Uppsala, 1943], line 552)

> 4. Fuion s'en de rrandon de paor *c'an aguda*.
>
> (*Ibid.*, line 4106)

> 5. . . . Per que la batet fort:
>   de gran ira *que ac* l'aduys pres de la mort.
>
> (Sant Honorat, ed. A-L. Sardou[4] [Nice, 1875], LXX, 6)

6. Atressi m'avias dat un sol fiyll *que avia;*
    Sarrasin lo mi tolgron de denfra l'abadia.

(*Ibid.,* XCIV, 67)

Is this only an awkward condensation of two different ideas: "you had given me a son" and "he was the only one I had"? In this case, the relative clause would not be unjustified.

The following examples, taken from a prose work, show that our pleonastic relative clauses are not due to prosodic reasons.

7. E, ploran de gaug *que avian,*[5] disseron a Thomas. . . .

(Philomena, ed. Schneegans in *Gesta Karoli Magni* [Halle, 1898], line 236)

8. Et Helias del dol *que ac* laissec se cazer del cavalh.

(*Ibid.,* line 1719)

9. E Matras, ples de vergonha, d'ira e de tristessa *que ac,* entret s'en en la ciutat.

(*Ibid.,* line 1868)

10. E Karles, can ausia que venian, isxic lor defora e, can los vic, de gran gaug *que n'ac* la cara li·n tornec colorada.

(*Ibid.,* line 2697)

11. . . . que, per erguelh *que an,* no volon estar am la cort.

(*Ibid.,* line 2755)

12. . . . de gran meravelha *que·s doneron* foron totz esbalausitz.

(*Ibid.,* lines 3030–31)

What may have been the origin of these pleonastic relative clauses? We venture to give an explanation. In Chapter XXXVI of Volume I of his *Vermischte Beiträge zur französischen Grammatik* (2nd ed.; Leipzig, 1906–21), Tobler deals with "Aussage bestehend aus Nomen und Relativsatz." He gives numerous Old and modern French examples; e.g., the following one in modern French: "Et le médecin qui n'arrivait pas." He also quotes two Old Provençal passages, of which we reproduce here the one from *Croisade Albigeoise* (line 8678): "Li Frances s'en partiron, mas laichero·i pens.⁶ Mans mortz e mans perdutz, e lor coms que n'es mens."

Something similar was, in our opinion, the root of our relative clauses. Tobler's French examples are characterized as statements, although some of them border on exclamations, and the nouns to which the relative clauses refer designate, almost exclusively, living beings. I could imagine that there had been, in the spoken language, similarly constructed sentences—a noun and a relative clause—whose nouns expressed an emotion in themselves and were referred to by adequate relative clauses. Such sentences, then, would have been genuine exclamations, not mere statements. I am thinking of expressions such as "*Ai, la dolors que fetz!", "*Oi, la paors que an aguda!", "*E lo gaugs qu'en senti!"⁷ Those relative clauses, originally complementing exclamations, were then, we presume, so intimately connected, in the speaker's mind, with nouns expressing an emotion that they were also kept where those nouns appeared in statements, thus penetrating into the written language, especially into works of a less sophisticated kind than troubadour lyrics. Our theory would seem to be corroborated by the fact that all our examples with the exception of three (1, 2, and 6), which are dubious anyhow, have an emotive noun as the antecedent of those pleonastic relative clauses.

Senseless as those clauses may appear to us today, they may have had a certain stylistic value at their time. They separate the emotive noun, which represents an essential element of the sentence, from what follows. This procedure forces the reader or listener to dwell on that noun and its emotional value, thus bringing the latter out in full relief.

A Special Use of the Preposition "A"

The oldest example known to me, a deed of 1103,[8] may illustrate this special use of the preposition *a:* "Ab aquels fin[9] ni societad non auria, fors pels[10] castels a recobrar." We find here two prepositions, *per* and *a*, the former indicating the purpose of the action expressed by the infinitive *recobrar*, the latter seemingly quite superfluous. This *a* appears only if the infinitive is preceded by what seems to be its object (here, *los castels*).

Tobler and Lommatzsch (I, 22–24) offer a great many examples of the Old French parallel of our *a*. For Provençal, such a statement has not yet been made, though some editors of Provençal texts have pointed to the special nature of this *a*, while others failed to recognize it and prefixed it to the following infinitives, thus forming compound verbs beginning with *a*.[11] The following quotations will show that our *a* was no less frequent than in Old French.

A. *The governing preposition is "per":*

1. Quecx, *per* enugz *a* dir fos natz
 e per parlar vilanamentz.
 ("Jaufre," ed. Breuer [Göttingen, 1925],[12] line 144)

2.   Malvas rei, *per* te *az* aunir
     o ai fait. . . .

                    (*Ibid.*, ed. Brunel, line 585)

3.   Q'escut ni espasa ni lansa
     non penrai *per* vos *a* contendre
     ni per vostre plaser defendre.[13]

                    (*Ibid.*, line 3639)

4.   Seiner, *per* nos *a* salvar
     muris e·us laises clavelar.

                    (*Ibid.*, line 5747)

5.   E tuit escoutavan goglars [14]
     per la sala, si que·ls manjars
     n'an laissat *per* els *a* ausir.

                    (*Ibid.*, line 9817)

6.   Qe cel que venc a naissement
     per totz nos autres *a* salvar. . . .

                    (*Ibid.*, line 10947)

7.   Be·m miravill qu'usquecs no·s pena
     de far be e de viure gen
     per gaug *ad* aver solamen.

                    (Sordel, Docum. hon., ed. De Lollis,
                    p. 219, line 454)

8.   . . . feyron venir
     rics metges *per* lyes *a* guerir.

     (Ste Enimie, ed. Clovis Brunel [Paris, 1916], line 230)

9. Car ins en Tarn, de bruncs en broncs,
   cazon belencs, rocas e rancs . . .
   pel fer drago *a* sebelhir.[15]

   (*Ibid.*, line 1233)

10. Ab aquels fin ni societad non auria, fors quant *per* lo castel *a recobrar*.

    (Brunel, *Chartes*, I, No. 10 [A.D. 1103]) [16]

11. Finem ne societatem cum illo vel cum illis non auria, fors quant *per* lo castel *a* recobrar.

    (*Ibid.*, No. 18 [A.D. 1130])

12. Ab aquel ne ab aquella ne ab aquels ne ab aquellas fin ne societad non auria, for *per* lo castel *a* recobrar.

    (*Ibid.*, No. 25 [around 1138])

13. Aquest do faim e guirpem . . . , eu Beatritz e mei effaint, a jassen, per totz terminis, *per* tota lor voluntat *a* ffar.[17]

    (*Ibid.*, No. 108 [A.D.] 1166])

14. Aquel glorios Dieus que son cors det a venda *per* totz nos *a* salvar. . . .

    (Folquet de Mars, P.C. 155, 26, ed. Stronski, No. 28, V, 2)

15. Si capellan per trop beure anoal [?]
    ni legistas *per* tort *a* mantenir. . . . [18]

    (Peire Card[?], P.C. 335, 37, ed. Lavaud, V, 12)

16. Avans de jorn deu hom levar
per son auzel *a* regardar.

(Daude de Pradas, *Dels Auzels Cassadors*, ed. Schutz, line 702)

17. Restrenha e se e sa maynada de beure e de manjar *per* lo sieu *ad* estalbiar.

(V. et Vert.,[19] fol. 18 [Sternbeck])

18. Per qu'er escur so qu'ar es clar
lai on Dieus mostra·l martir
qu'elh sostenc *per* nos *a* garir.

(Peire d'Alvernhe [20] [Sternbeck])

19. ... m'es bon e belh hueymais que m'entremeta d'un sirventes *per* els *a* conortar.[21]

(Bertran de Born [Sternbeck])

20. ... *per* nos *ad* essenhar a fugir la lauzor e la favor del pobol et tot movement de vana gloria.

(V. et Vert., fol. 55 [Sternbeck])

21. Quan venc en terra *per* lo mon *a* salvar. ...

(Declaramens de motas demandas [Sternbeck])

22. ... per mort e passio *per* nos autres peccadors *a* salvar.

(*Ibid.*)

23. ... *per* nos, mals sers desconoissens, *a* restaurar de mort.

(V. et Vert., fol 36[Sternbeck])

24.   *Per* los murs *a* fendre
    fan engenhs e castels.[22]

     (Raimb. de Vaqueiras [Sternbeck])

In the following two passages, the governing preposition (*per*) is followed by an adverb, not a noun. They show that our construction has lost any meaning.

25. En motas de manieras si prohet li certez del[s] sieus vers raubamens; car alcunas personas *per* plus fort *a* prohar li plantavan alenas e la poinhian amb agulhas.[23]

     (Appel, *Chrest.*, No. 119, 118 [Santa Doucelina])

26. Tota nostra compaynha es lassa, e mays val que sian pausatz *per* mielhs *a* batalhar.

     (Philomena [Sternbeck])

B. *The governing preposition is "de"*:

27.   Qecs, ja no estaretz en pas
    ni·us laisares *de* mal *a* dir.

     ("Jaufre," ed. Brunel, line 619)

28.   Per que fa ades bon servir
    a om estrain, qui·l ve venir
    o d'aculir, o de parlar
    o *de* sun aver *a* donar.

     (*Ibid.*, line 5820)

29.   De favas *a* desgranar
       de notz *a* scofellar,
       lamcant hom las escofena,[24]
       e *de* gran ga [25] *a* nadar,
       e *de* figas *a* pellar
       lo vencerai ses contena.

              (Marcoat, P.C. 294.1 [Jeanroy (ed.),
              Jongleurs, p. 12, lines 13–18)

30. En entencio *de* lui *a* diffamar. . . .

              (V. et Vert., fol. 3 [Sternbeck])

31. Aquo fon tot son mestier *de* sas fedas *a* pastorgar.

              (Trad. d'un évangile aprov. [Sternbeck])

32.   Es tengutz . . . *de* tot *a* restaurar.

              (Statuts de Montpellier, de 1204 [Sternbeck])

33.   Enquer no·us passa,
              fi·m ieu, la maniera
              de mi *a* chuflar.

              (Guir. Riquier, P.C. 248.22 [Mahn (ed.), IV,
              190], III, 3 [Sternbeck])

34.   Verges, en vos ai mes auzar
              *d'*aquest escrig *a* romansar.

              (Passio de Maria [26] [Sternbeck])

C. *The governing preposition is "en"*:

35.   Qe non pot aver alegrier,
                 ans l'ave lo jorn a lassar
                 catre ves e [=en] gran dol *a* far.

              ("Jaufre," ed. Brunel, line 3156)

36.   Que·s lassavon.III. ves lo dia
      e la nueg *en* gran dol *a* ffar.[27]

                                    (*Ibid.*, line 6459)

37.   E que vos en par
        de ric home quan pesa
           en grant tort *a* far? [28]

                      (Peire Cardenal, P.C. 335.38
                      [Lavaud (ed.), No. 61], V, 3)

D. *The governing preposition is "a"*:

38.   E Brunissens ab sas donselas
      sun si *al* dol *a* far enpresas.

                            ("Jaufre," ed. Brunel, line 3928)

39.   E l'enfan sun d'aisi mogut,
      e sun gran e fort e cregut,
      e sun si pres *al* mal *a* faire.

                                    (*Ibid.*, line 3541)

40. Enaissi apren hom a mal a fugir et a conoysser . . .
    tot pecat.

                            (V. et Vert., fol. 28 [Sternbeck])

A great number of the above quotations are taken from the romance of "Jaufre." Indeed, Breuer says in his edition (page 371 n): "In 'Jaufre,' the infinitive, where it follows its object, is always accompanied by *a*." [29] Such consistency in the use of *a* has not always been observed by other writers. We have already pointed out two such cases (see footnotes 13 and 18). Here are some additional examples:

41. A mos ops la vuelh retenir
per lo cor dedins refrescar
e *per* la carn renovellar.

(Guillem, IX, P.C. 183.8 [Jeanroy (ed.), No. 6], VI, 4 and 5)

42. Et om no deu temer
mal *per* Deu gazanhar.

(Guir. de Born., P.C. 242.74 [Kolsen (ed.), No. 51], VI, 8)

43. Selui qu'el mon volc venir
per nostres peccatz delir. . . .

(Peire d'Alv., P.C. 323.21 [Zenker or Del Monte (ed.), No. 19], III, 2)

44. Guiraut, ieu chant *per* mon cor alegrar.

(Guir. Riquier-Bonfils, P.C. 248.16 [quoted after Raynouard, *Lex. Rom.*, IV, 508])

Among the governing prepositions, *per* is the one used in the majority of examples quoted above, whereas in Old French, according to Tobler-Lommatzsch, *de* prevails in this function. For *ses*, *sobre*, and *sus*, we cannot provide examples, as Tobler and Lommatzsch do for Old French *sans*, *sor*, and *sus*. These prepositions seem to have been rare anyhow, in view of the few examples provided by Tobler and Lommatzsch. For *sus*, for instance, they have only one: "Sus a perdre leur terre." But does this example really belong here? The object (*leur terre*) does not precede but rather follows the infinitive, and *a* stands immediately after the governing preposition.[30]

We do not remember having ever met with this *a* in Provençal *cansos*, and the situation seems to be similar in Old French since Tobler and Lommatzsch quote only one example, the first one, taken from the song manuscript of Bern. The reason for this phenomenon may be that the construction *a* with infinitive belonged to a more popular way of speaking— as in epic poetry, for example, *sirventes* and so forth; it was spurned in the more sophisticated style of courtly love poetry.

There is no commonly accepted explanation of the origin of this seemingly superfluous *a*.[31] The latest theory, so far as I know, is that of Ernst Gamillscheg.[32] He speaks of this *a* as an "a-prefix isolating the content of the infinitive." I prefer to go back to an incidental remark of Tobler's [33] and to see in the infinitive with *a* a qualifier of what could logically be regarded as the object of the infinitive.[34]

Let us take example 37: "E que vos en par De ric home quan pessa En gran tort a far?" Here the original meaning of the infinitive with *a* seems to be recognizable: the rich man meditates on great harm (that is) to be done (by him). Lavaud's translation seems to reflect the same interpretation of this passage.[35] In example 29, "E de gran ga a nadar E de figas a pellar Lo vencerai ses contena," the poet is sure that he will surpass his adversary with regard to a great ford (which is) to be swum through or with regard to figs (which are) to be husked. And in a last example (16), "Avans de jorn deu hom levar Per son auzel a regardar," the owner of a bird has to get up before dawn because of his bird (which is) to be looked after.

We do not know whether the Provençal (or Old French) writers really conceived of such an *a* with infinitive as a qualifier, a kind of attribute, to the preceding noun, if, indeed, they gave any thought at all to the nature of the construction. It may have been a stereotyped, fossilized way of speaking at the time that the first examples appeared in writing, which was misused in later times, as in examples 25 and 26.

Our *a* with infinitive cannot be traced back to classical Latin because this language did not know the infinitive preceded by a preposition, for Latin used the gerundive to express the same idea.[36] One may compare the following Latin examples: [37]

1. " . . . paratiores ad omnia pericula subeunda," which the authors render as "readier to undergo all dangers." More literally it would be, however, "readier for all dangers (that are) to be undergone." Translated into Provençal, the sentence could have run thus: "*plus volontos a totz perilhs a sotzportar." But with this difference only: in Latin the qualifier of the noun (*pericula*) is the adjectival gerundive (*subeunda*); in Provençal, it is the infinitive with *a*.

2. "Veniunt ad pacem petendam." The authors' translation is, "They come for peace (which is) to be sought," or in Provençal, "*Venon per patz a demandar." Here again the Latin gerundive (*petendam*) corresponds to the Provençal infinitive with *a* (*a demandar*).

Do not the above comparisons between Latin and Provençal sentences corroborate the theory that our infinitive with *a* is—or originally was—like the Latin gerundive, a qualifier of the preceding noun?

Three Little Problems of Old Provençal Syntax 181

1. *Cenaire* ("senator").

2. It is, however, possible that the poet added the relative clause only to have a word rhyming with *mantenem*. If so, this example would not belong to the stereotyped kind of clauses we are dealing with here.

3. The pronominal adverb *en* may refer to a person one is speaking to. Cf., "Pueys fus joglars de dir vers e chansos; Ar iest poiatz a major onramen, Que·l conzs n'a fag ['the count has made of you'] cavaier salvatge"—Bertr. d'Alam., P. C. 76, 1 (ed. Salv. de Grave, p. 76) I, 8. So the *en* of our second example probably means "of you" (sc., leave-taking) with which the saint is addressed by her sister. This *en* needed a verb, because it could not join the substantivized infinitive *al partir*, to which it logically belongs. Therefore, I assume, the author formed the relative clause *qu'en farai*, which then is less senseless than it would seem at first sight.

4. Of Miss Suwe's edition only the first volume was published, her text ending with line 4127.

5. Latin translation of the *Philomena* significantly does not take care of the relative clause: *gaudio flentes dixerunt ei*.

6. *Pens* ("as pawns").

7. Similar exclamations might well be uttered in modern English: "Oh, the ordeal [that] he had to go through!" or, "And the fun [that] we had!"

8. Clovis Brunel, *Les plus anciennes chartes en langue provençale* (Paris 1926), Vol. I, no. 10.

9. *fin* ("accord"), (Brunel).

10. *pels* (*per los*).

11. So did Raynouard, at whose time this kind of *a* was still unknown to scholars. H. Sternbeck (*Unrichtige Wortaufstellungen und Wortdeutungen in Raynouard's Lexique Roman* [Berlin, 1887], p. 36), in correcting Raynouard's *a*-prefixed verbs, brought to light a larger number of examples. We have incorporated his findings in our list, marking them with the name of their discoverer.
Sternbeck's book was not available to me when I was writing this paper. My thanks go to Mr. Frederick Goldin of Rutgers University, who had an opportunity to look it up and who has provided me with a report on what Sternbeck had to say on page 36 of his dissertation.

12. Brunel, following another manuscript, has a different text.

13. It is worth mentioning that, in the third line, the poet fails to use this *a* (before *defendre*).

14. *goglars* (*joglars*).

15. Brunel's text shows *asebelhir*.

16. See footnote 8, *supra*.

17. Brunel reads *affar*.

18. Lavaud translates line 2 thus: ". . . les légistes pour injustice à sou-

tenir." It is noteworthy that, in the following line, "ni albergier per lor oste trair," the poet does not make use of the *a* dealt with here.

19. Raynouard's abbreviation for "Vices et Vertus," a moral treatise (fourteenth century) translated from the Old French "Somme le Roi" (1279).

20. Quoted after Zenker's edition, No. 17, line 59.

21. All editions have *per lor assegurar* (Appel [ed.], No. 11, line 6).

22. Erhard Lommatzsch, *Leben und Lieder der Provenzalischen Troubadours* (Berlin, 1959), II, No. 22, line 106 (P.C. 392, 32).

23. Prohet, Prohar (*proet*), *proar* (Latin *probare*) ("to examine); *alena* ("awe").

24. The verbs *desgranar, escofelar,* and *escofenar* are synonyms meaning "to husk."

25. Dejeanne, in his edition (*Ann. Midi*, XV, 362), translates *ga* by "rivière," but the word means "ford."

26. Later on published by Mushacke in his *Altprovenzalische Marienklage des XIII. Jahrhunderts* (Halle, 1890).

27. Brunel reads *affar*.

28. Lavaud translates: ". . . Il songe a de grandes injustices a commettre."

29. There is, however, one exception at least; see footnote 13.

30. Similar cases are also listed under *por* and *sans* (Tobler-Lommatzsch, I, p. 24, lines 3, 4, 9, 13, 15).

31. See the literature in Tobler-Lommatzsch, I, p. 22, 45–23, 3.

32. *Historische Französische Syntax* (Tübingen, [1957]), pp. 468–69.

33. "Göttinger Gelehrte Anzeigen" 1875, Stück 34, reprinted in *Vermischte Beiträge*, V (1912), 404.

34. Sternbeck (see footnote 11), starting from the same remark of Tobler's, came to a similar result.

35. See footnote 28. The same is true of his translation of example 15 in footnote 18.

36. See also Gamillscheg, *op. cit.*, p. 463.

37. These are taken from Allen and Greenough, *New Latin Grammar* (Boston, 1931), § 503.

———————Edward B. Ham———————

Flamenca Gleanings

SINCE the notes suggested here are limited to the *Roman de Flamenca*, only one example is singled out from Professor Schutz's many solutions to problems in Provençal lexicography and its *courtois* terminology: his conclusive explanation [1] of *nozol* ("night owl") as a "derivative of *nocte* (*noctula >*noctiola, etc.," in line 2114 of *Flamenca*. This gives firm support to his treatment of the same word in line 771 of the *Auzels Cassadors* by an author whom Professor Schutz has so ably rehabilitated, Daude de Pradas.

During the past hundred years, there have been, from time to time, inklings that medieval French texts can guide more than one latter-day hopeful down the garden path of enchanted—and enchanting—conjecture. Notably, when a poem has been saved only by a single and defective manuscript, its wording even now is usually still teeming with unresolved puzzles: puzzles which, moreover, have not only baffled leading scholars, but which have also inspired some among them to rewardingly resonant blunder. My attempt here is no more than a tentative commentary on five samples of such stab and stumble as encountered in *Flamenca*. Not merely in passing, it will be remembered that, like *Aucassin et Nicolette* and Beroul's *Tristan, Flamenca* is yet another jewel with the misfortune of having been preserved in only one manuscript and having been sorely mistreated by a copyist still known favorably only for his penmanship.

In line 1540 of *Flamenca*, Oskar Schultz-Gora found Archimbaut, the jealous husband, cursing Flamenca's handmaidens with a two-fold blight of "asthma and death."[2] In line 1638, Adolf Tobler saw Guillem, flawless hero in the poem, kicking up to nine feet, only to reach and sample some nasal mucus.[3] While a straightforward proverb (line 2191) says simply that recital of one's troubles brings only yawns to listeners, the yawns have been interpreted all the way from "dawn song" to "real pleasure": the latter suggestion coming from Adolf Mussafia.[4] The poet's intentionally preposterous *digastendonz* in lines 1557 and 2441 has been manhandled by so many experts that some further manhandling on my part may not be amiss. As is also the case with the verb *pas(s)ar* in lines 1540 and 5058–59.

Inasmuch as philologists of the special stature of Tobler, Mussafia, Schultz-Gora, Paul Meyer, and René Lavaud[5] have faltered absurdly over only an occasional word in *Flamenca*, their speculations will always require the most serious attention. It is precisely thanks to their pioneering that anyone today can venture a few inches further into *Flamenca* mysteries. Thus speculation at this time is limited to the five lexicographical problems just listed. My choices have been determined both by the past mistakes of others and by the relative absence of philological grimness required for their rectification.

1. For some five hundred lines prior to line 1540, Archimbaut has been suffering from baseless jealousy of his bride

"Flamenca" Gleanings

Flamenca, whom he has confined to a tower, together with her chirrupy maids-in-waiting, Alis and Margarida. Customarily, when he shepherds the three of them, cautiously and suspiciously, to the thermal baths, he keeps glowering watch at the entrance.

On one occasion he reproaches Flamenca for staying too long, but Margarida tries to assure him that his wife was merely waiting for her and Alis to finish their own ablutions. Archimbaut's response (according to the reading recommended here, cf. *infra*):

1540	"Pasa!" fai s'el, — las mas emort, —
	"Mais volés bain que non fan aucas,
	Aitan ben sas grans com sas pauchas;
1543	Mais de vos non es meravilla."

While the manuscript has *emort* as a single word, the *e* has ever since been treated and edited as a conjunction. But the presence and location of such a conjunction has never yet been satisfactorily explained: a scribal blunder perhaps? In 1926, Lewent proposed a regrouping of the letters (plus alteration of two of them) to make the poet say that Archimbaut was biting his lips: sensible, but somewhat arbitrary. Meyer, Mussafia, Chabaneau, and Hubert agree that the jealous groom is biting or gnawing his hands: the interpretation for which I hope to add new support. The more so, since Archimbaut has some five thousand verses to go before once again recovering normal composure. The Lavaud-Nelli translation ignores the supposed conjunction and has Archimbaut biting his thumbs. The prize suggestion of all, however, dates from 1903 when Schultz-Gora suggested deleting two letters, reading *asma e mort*, and thence crediting Archimbaut with devising the malediction of asthma and death. Solemnly, Schultz-Gora added that "it is not surprising that the *Flamenca* author knew the word [asthma] or that the copyist knew it not at all." Up to now, no one has exclaimed at this interpretation, except for Lewent's charitable notation that it is "brilliant but much too bold." Now that the experts have been taken to task, what does the present paper have to offer? Two possibilities only: (1) without changing any of the letters as they are given in the manuscript, keep *las mas emort*; or (2) move the alleged conjunction and read *e las mas mort*. The first suggestion, which I prefer, calls for an easily and entirely possible *emordre* (< *ex* + *mordere*), while the second requires needless editorial tampering.

2. *Pas(s)ar* in lines 1540 and 5058–59. The second part of line 1540 creates only one of the difficulties of interpreting this line, the first two syllables of which are spaced in the manuscript as *pas ai*. Meyer keeps this reading, but suggests in his variants that it might be emended to a *passatz*, which Lewent subsequently accepted as an imperative in the sense of *vorbeigehen, weitergehen*.[6] Hubert-Porter and Lavaud-Nelli also read *pas ai*, which the latter translate "c'est bon," and explain literally as "j'ai paix = je ne dis plus rien." The view that this interpretation seems farfetched will be developed presently.

If the poet intended a form of *pasar*, should the reading be *pasa* or *pasatz*? *Flamenca* has but few indications of Archimbaut's manner of addressing Alis or Margarida: he uses *tu* when speaking to Alis in line 6158, but not in lines 6151 and lines 7065–74. Elsewhere, except in line 1540 where he is answering Margarida, Archimbaut never addresses either girl singly. Consequently, and the more so as emendation of *pasai* to *pasa* is less drastic than to *pasatz*, it is the former which is recommended here.

In support of the verb *pasar* in line 1540, it is essential to examine a certain remark by Guillem, later on in the poem:

5056   Dirai vos o, bel sener Dieus:
          Del paradis quem devés dar
          Pogras ab mi fort ben passar.
5059   Passar? Ans i faria gietas!

Influenced by *passar* and *gietas* taken together, various scholars have interpreted the passage as involving a suggestion of compromise. However, what seems unquestionably the correct translation has been recently supplied by Guido Favati: "Il paradiso che mi dovete dare potreste anche fare a meno di darmelo. Farne a meno? Lo getterei anzi via!" [7] *Gieta* plainly denotes something to be rejected and thrown away.

In no case is Archimbaut (in line 1540) advising Margarida that he "has peace" or that he "is saying nothing more" (he goes on talking, for three more lines): would he be "having peace" and gnawing his hands, simultaneously? Just as *passar* in lines 5058-59 indicates that Guillem is asking to be spared any gift of Paradise, so also, in line 1540, Archimbaut is brusquely telling Margarida to spare him her excuses (cf. modern French *passons!*).

3. Guillem is represented as being seven feet tall and, with either foot, readily capable of reaching *una candela o un muquet* (line 1638), "nine feet above floor level." Mistral's Provençal dictionary explains *mouquet* as a small candle stub

or candle end (cf. *supra*, note 3). Meyer cites a further Mistral entry, in which *mou* (variants: *mouc, mouch, mousc*) has two meanings: "candle stub," and "nasal mucus." While Meyer, in 1901, had no difficulty in making the sensible choice, he seems not to have noticed Mistral's *mouquet*. However, in 1866, albeit only thirty-one-years old, Tobler stated categorically that in *Flamenca* "*muquet* is undoubtedly identical with modern Provençal *mouquet*, a word derived from *muccus*, equivalent to Old Provençal *moc* 'sanies naris.'" Less ridiculous, but manifestly still incorrect, and perhaps anachronistic as well, is the meaning "lighted wick," which turns up in the Lavaud-Nelli translation. By all odds, "candle stub" or "candle end" is the most likely rendering (as if the *Flamenca* poet particularly cared), but the vague possibility that "candle snuffer" may have been intended should not be overlooked, given etymological connection with the scissor-like instrument known in French today as *mouchettes* (cf. Godefroy, by the way, for an example as early as the fourteenth century).

4. The proverb in line 2191 specifies, as mentioned *supra*, that talk about one's troubles brings only yawns to any listener. While this verse lacks the exegetical glow of asthma or mucus, it does underscore a zest for emendation which all too frequently beguiles editors and critics. The *Flamenca* manuscript reads "Autrui dol albadallas son," but in 1901, influenced by Mussafia from decades before,[8] Meyer abandoned his sound 1865 sense and changed the line to "Que l'autrui dol badallas son," with his new-found *badallas* rendered as "plaisanteries [cf. Miss Prescott, p. 43], bagatelles, choses dénuées d'importance." Even the Lavaud-Nelli transla-

tion supports this needless liberty by fastening upon *badallas* the unlikely meaning "vaines criailleries."

The frequency, as attested for instance in Mistral, of words beginning with *aba-* or *ba-* interchangeably (cf. also *FEW*, I, 282: *bataculare*) should have maintained respect for the manuscript. Probably, however, the first *l* in *albadallas* should be dropped: it seems to reflect a misplaced anticipation of *al* in the third syllable.

The meaning of *abadalla* is suggested by the verb *badalhar* ("yawn"), which, for modern Provençal, Mistral and von Wartburg enter as *abadalha*. The odd translation "aubade" goes back to Leroux de Lincy in 1842, who recorded a saying which now appears as No. 214 in Morawski's *Proverbes français:* "Autruy deul querelle semble." Conceivably, this could suggest support for *abadalla* ("bataille"), except that the double *t* in the etymon *battualia* did not change to *d* in either southern or northern France.

5. *Digastendonz,* the final problem in this paper, appears in two *Flamenca* passages:

1557	E tot o fes digastendons
2440	Adoncs venc le fers aversiers
2441	Per digastendonz totz derriers

It will be recalled that, early in the poem, the queen of France fanned to flame Archimbaut's incipient jealousy regarding his still innocent bride. His psychopathic self-torture was needless, as Flamenca had given him no cause. Since soon after his marriage, says the poet (lines 1550–60), Archimbaut "never bathed, nor did the idea of bathing even cross his mind; he never pared his fingernails nor cut his hair. This way he thought he had done enough to spy upon his wife successfully. No one could have persuaded him to shave: he looked like a Greek or a Slavic prisoner. All this he did *digastendons*." And immediately and decisively at this point, Archimbaut added: "My lady will have greater terror of me if she sees me with beard and moustache, and she will think twice before welcoming a lover."

Except for dourly supervised attendance at Mass and visits to the thermal baths, Flamenca is constantly confined, as noted *supra*, to the tower chamber, with Alis and Margarida. When Guillem for the first time sees Archimbaut bringing Flamenca to the church, the husband comes in as a monstrous ferocity who lacks only a hunting spear to make him look like a scarecrow fit to frighten off wild boars: in the poet's words, Archimbaut's entry is staged *per digastendonz*. It should be added, in passing, that literal translation of *aversiers*, line 2440, is more accurately "devil" than "monstrous ferocity," a point which is developed explicitly in lines 3894–99, but which need not be elaborated here.

Without comment, Meyer, in 1865, gave up entirely on *digastendonz*, and his reviewers followed suit unanimously, with equally resourceful silence. In 1901, the *Flamenca* editor was more venturesome, but only three contemporaries took comparable risks. Meyer came forward with what, still today, may be the tempting suggestion that *digastendonz* might be a popular expression, *digas t'en donz*, on the order, for instance, of current *qu'en-dira-t-on* or *m'as-tu-vu*. Meyer added that this might indicate a state of mind. Years ago, Chabaneau asked if *digastendonz* could not equally well represent some sort of physical attitude, and then wondered if the reading could be *gigas t'en donz* ("donne-t'en des jambes"), from which he proceeded by way of "à la course, à la hâte," to conclude that *digastendonz* meant "brusquement"—in his view a reasonably natural extension. More important, however, is Chabaneau's excellent suspicion that the word could have been something created by the poet himself. In an early incarnation of his Provençal chrestomathy, Carl Appel proposed tentatively that *per digastendonz* means "in order to cause vexation," a rendering retained in all subsequent editions. Following on, soon after Meyer's *Flamenca* in 1901, Mussafia dismissed (*loc. cit.*, p. 10; cf. note 4, *supra*) these several hypotheses as "forced and unconvincing." He insisted that "the situation in v. 2441 requires 'intentionally' for *per digastendonz*, perhaps with a pejorative connotation, maybe something like 'maliciously, with secret and evil intention.' This is especially evident in v. 1557 and tolerably clear in v. 2441." In the *Supplement-Wörterbuch*, Levy supported this opinion, which, actually, is not very different from Appel's.[9]

In subsequent years, so far as I know, no critic coped with *digastendonz* until the Lavaud-Nelli translation. As far as it goes, their rather free interpretation is more or less acceptable, but their explanatory note is discouraging. They render the two verses as follows: (line 1557) "Et tout cela il le faisait pour intimider"; (line 2441)" [Arriva] après tout le monde, avec son air provocant." Their note, however, treats *digastendonz* as a "familiar" [*sic*] adverbial locution, to be broken down, as Meyer proposed sixty years ago, into *digas t'en, donz*. However, they translate this latter (literally, as they would have it, and with the intrusive comma after *t'en*) as "dis là-dessus, seigneur," meaning nothing more impressive than their explanatory "qu'as-tu à en dire?" As a possible alternative to the "seigneur," they do grant that the final syllable could have represented "donc." But, "seigneur"!

From line 2441, it is clear that *digastendonz* is meant as a noun, so that, however reasonably adverbial it may appear in line 1557, the chances are that also in this earlier verse it is already a noun, merely in apposition either with the pronoun o ("cela") or with Archimbaut as subject.

It is not unknown that the *Flamenca* poet had a gift for vivid meridional vehemence, and that he was a firm enough Latinist to give himself additionally handsome dividends, wherever available. But what is vivid or vehement about juxtaposition of colorless *digas* and zestless *t'en* with an adverb as anodine as *donc*? If, as Chabaneau momentarily—and so well—suspected, the poet was fabricating something,[10] even if only along *dis-t'en donc* lines, surely he would have sought something at least as energetic as, for example, the initial word in Raymond Queneau's *Zazie dans le Métro* (Paris, 1959), a novel which begins with the portentous point which follows: "Doukipudonktan, se demanda Gabriel excédé. Pas possible, ils se nettoient jamais." Although outright proof is lacking either way, it seems difficult not to expect something more energetic than mere *dire* or *donc* within a word as strenuous as *digastendonz*.

Nonce-words have been a prerogative of countless authors over the centuries, and well before Rabelais. In his *Persa*, Plautus perpetrated *numquampostreddonides* "one who never will return anything"; in the final moments for Troilus before his first operative meeting with Criseyde, Chaucer has him in a *kankerdort*, a word of baffling origin, but of unmistakable meaning; T. H. White refines American *hooey* into *hoolarium*;[11] the American language has taken to itself innumerable items such as *discombobulate* (and its offshoot *discombooberate*), *boondoggle*, *gobbledygook*, *foofaraw*, *hornswoggle*, *disirregardless*, H. Caen's *beatnik*, and so on indefinitely. Is the creation of *digastendonz* anything more than a matter of thirteenth-century fancy?

Just as many nonce-words are readily explained in terms of etymological contrivings or in terms of contemporaneous distortions involving only the language in which such nonce-words arise, *digastendonz* lends itself to similarly ready explanation. It is inconceivable that the *Flamenca* poet was unaware of his own Provençal g(u)*astar*, of Latin (*de*)*vastare*, of pejorative implication in suffix *-on(s)*, of Provençal *dons* ("lady"). Did he, then, take pedestrian pause and consciously assemble these ingredients in order to contrive a new word tailored, the while, to the firmest traditions of a Meyer-Lübke or a von Wartburg? It may be suspected that he subjected himself to no such rule-bound philological process.

Even for anyone non-Provençal, the sound-effects of *digastendonz* harmonize excellently with the style "stiff and strong" which infects the description of Archimbaut's jealous vagaries in both of the passages where the word occurs. Surely, the poet hit upon *digastendonz* by way of the kind of casual flash which brings on the creation of any new and successful syllabic concatenation. In any case, however consciously or otherwise, he arrived at this particular devising, it is interwoven with elements which pinpoint a literal meaning more specifically than anything suggested hitherto. Therefore, why not, to etymological windward of *digastendonz*, something on the order of *devastante* plus *dominas* which, in both passages, can yield the meaning "terrifyer of ladies"? As already mentioned, in line 1558 immediately following *digastendons*, Archimbaut says that his grisly appearance will make Flamenca cringe only the more. The incidental factor that *dominas* and *donz* do not match inflectionally is of no concern in a fanciful nonce-word: after all, note the commonplace *mi donz* ("my lady") in line 1558, just as anywhere else in medieval Provençal. Incidentally, Professor H. E. Keller has reminded me that *digastendonz* is not listed in FEW, XIV, 202–7 (*s. v. vastare*).

A final word about *digas t'en donz* as the earlier, and still possible, explanation. While this fits perfectly in terms of letter-by-letter derivation, it is not only colorless in the context, but also *s'en dire* merits little if any acceptance or support per se: so far as I know, medieval examples are lacking, either in southern or northern France. Furthermore, the question always remains: what, in lines 1557 and 2441, would be the point of a *digas t'en donc* ("say to yourself in the matter")? Racked with jealousy, would not a hirsute Archimbaut, unwashed, unbarbered, and unshaven, deserve better from the pen of his author-creator? With *digastendonz* in the sense of "terror to women," the *Flamenca* poet discharges a literary debt to his Archimbaut, resoundingly.

1. *Modern Language Notes*, LXIV (1949), 468–70.

2. *Zeitschrift für Romanische Philologie*, XXVII (1903), 496. Cf. also Kurt Lewent, *ibid.*, XLV (1926), 599; H. F. M. Prescott (trans.), *Flamenca* (London, 1930), p. 30; *The Romance of Flamenca*, English verse translation by Merton Jerome Hubert, and revised Provençal text by Marion E. Porter (Princeton, N. J., 1962), p. 105.

3. Cf. his 1866 critique, reprinted in *Vermischte Beiträge*, V, 280; Miss Prescott (*op. cit.*, p. 32) renders *muquet* by "candle end."

4. For this and other mentions in this paper, cf. Mussafia's elaborate notes in the *Sitzungsberichte der Wiener Akademie*, CXLV, No. 10 (1902). Cf. also Camille Chabaneau, *Revue des Langues Romanes*, XLV (1902), 5–43.

5. Cf. Meyer's second edition of *Flamenca* (Paris, 1901), and the translation by Lavaud and René Nelli in *Les Troubadours* (Paris, 1960).

6. *Zeitschrift für Romanische Philologie,* XLV (1926), 598; and *Bruchstücke des provenzalischen Versromans Flamenca* (Halle, 1926), p. 72.

7. *Studi Mediolatini e Volgari,* VIII (1960), 117, n. 87. Cf. also Antoine Thomas, *Journal des Savants* (1901), p. 374; and Tobler-Lommatzsch, IV, 1639.

8. *Jahrbuch für Romanische und Englische Literatur,* VIII (1867), 116.

9. Lewent (*Bruchstücke,* p. 62) suggested that *digastendons* (line 1557) may be an adverb meaning "deliberately." Miss Prescott (p. 31) rendered line 1557: "and all this for pride and spite"; and lines 2440–2441 (p. 48): "last of all, in came the Adversary—a perfect scarecrow."

10. Cf. also Hubert and Porter, p. 436.

11. *Making of the President* (New York, 1961), p. 354.

The Lady from Plazensa

> Una domna leyal
> Sai ieu qu'es de Plazensa
> Mas estai en Valensa
>   Per mielhs gardar Sanhflor
>   E Mirabel que te,
>   E Cortezo, per que
>   Gazanha Benaven
>   E Belhjoc franchamen,
> E ten Guarda e Verona mandan,
> E·s bateget lo jorn de sant Johan.[1]

IN THIS STANZA, Aimeric de Peguilhan (10, 40: *Per razo natural*) describes and praises a lady, otherwise unidentified, but in all likelihood a patroness: "I know a loyal lady who is from Piacenza, but she lives in Valensa, in order better to guard San Flor and Mirabel, which she holds, and Cortezo; therefore she wins for herself Benaven and Belhjoc freely, and she holds in fee Garda and Verona. She was baptized on Saint John's Day."

Since proper names often serve to localize and identify the innumerable vague "ladies" that people the Provençal lyrics, it might seem that we could hardly fail to discover what lady it was that Aimeric had in mind here. We know where she is from, when she was baptized, where she lives, and the names of seven other towns or castles that belong to her. Unfortunately, even a superficial probing among these names reveals that they are less informative in a literal sense than one might expect. This is no new discovery of mine, but a conclusion reached by various scholars long ago. The place names are genuine, and every one can be pinned down to a specific city or town, though sometimes it would be hard to say which of several similarly named localities is meant; but no matter which choices we make, we find that it is impossible to relate them all to any historical person or family. No real lady could conceivably have been connected with all these places. Why, then, did the poet name them as belonging to her?

Writing in 1899, Nicolà Zingarelli answered this question. First he went through the list of names, localizing each in the most likely fashion; then he added:

> . . . senza che alcuno di questi sia allusivo a rapporti reali con la dama. Quando il poeta dice che guadagna Benevento, e tiene Garda, e comanda in Verona, non bisogna credere che ella possedesse queste città: come quando il buon predicatore rimproverava ai suoi uditori perché andavano tutti a *Piacenza* e nessuno a *Verona*, non voleva dire che vi andassero davvero! E così dove il poeta dice che la sua dama si battezzò il dí di san Giovanni bisognerà intendere un'allusione a *joja*, gioia, se non a quello speciale significato di "grazioso" che annettevano gli ecclesiastici e teologi, e Dante stesso, al nome di Giovanni.[2]

The cities, therefore, are set down in these verses, not for themselves, but only for the sake of their names. If the lady is said to be from Plazensa, it is because she is pleasing (*plazen*).

She lives in Valensa only in the sense that she is worthy (*valen*). The other names suggest other attributes of the lady: San Flor ("holy flower"); Mirabel ("fair glance"); Cortezo ("courtesy"); Benaven (perhaps "benevolence"); Belhjoc ("good manners"); Garda ("prudence"); Verona ("sincerity"). In short, this list of place names is nothing but a series of puns, whose purpose is to suggest various good qualities of the lady in question.

Aimeric de Peguilhan was not the first to employ this device, nor is he the best known practitioner of it. Peire Vidal, in the poem *Tant an ben dig del Marques* (364, 47), says this about another lady (probably Azalaïs of Montferrat, married to Manfred of Saluzzo):

> Que fag e dig e parvensa
> A de Monbel e d'Argensa
> E de Monrozier color
> E sa cambr' es de Vallflor.[3]

In his edition of Peire, Anglade renders this: "dans ses actes, dans ses paroles et dans son maintien, elle ressemble [aux dames de] Montbel e d'Argence, elle a la couleur de celle de Montrosier et sa maison est de Valfleur."[4] De Bartholomzeis rejects this interpretation:

> I due editori stampano bensì i nomi di luogo con la maiuscola, ma si direbbe non abbiano afferata la ragione della menzione di essi. . . . In realtà si tratta anche qui di giuochi di parole: "Monbel" (Mombello del Monferrato) e "bello"; "Argenza" (Argence, sul Rodano . . . o Argenta nell' Emilia) e "gent" gentile; "Monrosier" (il Monterosa: "rosa" la pianta) e "color roseo"; "Valflor" . . . e "fiore."[5]

The reason why De Bartholomaeis uses the expression "si tratta *anche qui* di giuochi di parole" is that he takes an earlier passage (lines 1–8) of this poem in the same way:

> Tant an ben dig del marques
> Joglar truant e garbier,
> Que tuit en son vertadier,
> Qu'ieu no sai que m'en disses;
> Pero sua es valensa,
> On bons pretz nais e comensa,
> E·i renovela valor
> E·n fai dir vera lauzor.[6]

Speaking of line 5, De Bartholomaeis says:

> Tanto il Bartsch quanto l'Anglade stampano "valensa" col *v* minuscolo. Non già che qui si tratta della Valenza del Monferrato, e tanto meno di qualcuna delle altre Valenze d'Italia e degli altri paesi. Il nome della cittadina che rientrava ne' domini del Marchese, serve al trovatore per un gioco di parole ("valen"): uno di que' bisticci di cui, in questo e in altre poesie, P. V. fa addirittura un abuso.

Likewise, De Bartholomaeis sees a punning allusion to a city in these lines (21–24) of the same poem:

> E·m fier al cor ses falhensa
> Ab un cairel de plazensa
> Fabregat el fuec d'amor,
> Temprat de dousa sabor.

"She strikes me in the heart with a dart from Piacenza (*or* a dart of pleasure)."

Torraca, writing in 1901, anticipates De Bartholomaeis in taking *Valensa* (line 5 of this poem) as a place name:

. . . Era costume di questo trovatore far giochi di parole con nomi di luoghi; qui gioca sul nome della città di Valenza, tra Casal Monferrato e Alessandria, e sul nome astratto *valenza*, che in provenzale significa *valentia*, e piú sotto giocherà in simil modo.[7]

"Piú sotto" refers to lines 37–40 (Monbel, Argensa, Monrozier, Vallflor), which we discussed above. Torraca does not see a pun in line 22, "Ab un cairel de plazensa," which he translates simply "con un dardo di piacere."

Avalle, the most recent editor of Peire Vidal's poems, agrees with Torraca and De Bartholomaeis about the punning allusions in lines 37–40, but he specifically rejects De Bartholomaeis's use of capital letters in lines 5 and 22, and takes both *valensa* and *plazensa* as abstract nouns.[8] I think he is wrong on these two points, but these are hardly matters that one can prove or disprove.

In another poem, *Pus ai ubert mon ric thesaur* (364, 38), Peire Vidal offers a whole catalogue of place names which both De Bartholomaeis and Avalle interpret as puns, though they disagree with each other and with earlier editors (Bartsch, Anglade, Torraca) as to whether certain specific expressions are place names or not.[9] Also, De Bartholomaeis believes that all the places named (even the most unlikely-sounding ones, like *Esquiva-mendics* and *Melhs-m'en-venha*) really did exist, while Avalle feels that Peire invented some of the names to make his point; he adds, however, "ma la questione è oziosa." Anglade does not comment on the names except insofar as he tries to identify them one by one; the presumption is that he took them quite literally as places owned by or connected with the persons mentioned in the poem.[10]

In three stanzas, Peire piles up place names in praise of a lady, in whom Avalle sees once more Azalaïs of Saluzzo. Here are some of the pertinent verses:

25 Per sieu tenh Vertfuelh e Monlaur
    E servo·l plus de cent castell
    E tres ciutatz ses tot revell;
    . . . .
37 Color fresc'a ab cabelh saur
    Et anc non obret de pinzell,
    Mas Mongalhart e Daurabell
    Li platz qu'a sos ops retenha.
    Beljoc no vent ni empenha,
    E mi fai Montamat tener
    E Bon-repaus per miels jazer;
    E per m'amor platz l'Ostals-rics
    Et es sieus Esquiva-mendics;
    Et al marques non es destrics,
    Si·m dona Segur e Clavai
    E a liei Cardon' e Monjai.

By themselves, Vertfuelh and Monlaur might not appear unusual; but in context with all the names that follow in the next stanza, it seems likely that they are intended to give the idea of a triumphal wreath ("green leaf") and *laur* ("laurel"). Here is Anglade's translation of lines 37–48:

Elle a une couleur fraîche avec une chevelure blonde sans s'être jamais servie du pinceau; mais il lui plaît de garder pour elle Montgaillard et Daurabell. Elle ne vend ni ne met en gage Beaujeu, elle me fait tenir Montamat et Bon Repos pour mieux coucher. Pour mon amour lui plaît la Riche Maison (ou Hostalrichs), et Esquive-Mendiants lui appartient; et ce n'est pas un embarras pour le marquis [de Montferrat] s'il me donne Ségur et Clavai et à elle Cardona et Monjai (Monjoie?).[11]

There is no special comment on any of this, though in the glossary, *Esquiva-mendics* is explained "nom d'une localité imaginaire." It seems perfectly clear, however, that all these places, whether real or not, are mentioned for the sake of their names alone. The lady does not use a brush (for makeup); she keeps Montgalhart and Daurabell for her use—*galhart* ("gay," "merry"); *daurar* ("to gild"); *bell* ("beautiful")—and evidently needs no other cosmetics. She does not sell or mortgage Beljoc (probably "good manners," as I suggested for Aimeric de Peguilhan, though, of course, *joc* can mean many things). She lets me hold Montamat and Bon-repaus—*amat* ("beloved"); *bon-repaus* ("good rest"), with the added clarification *per miels jazer*. For my sake she likes Ostal-ric ("rich dwelling"), and Esquiva-mendics is hers—*esquivar* ("to avoid, refuse"); *mendic* ("poor," "miserly," "perfidious"). Segur is "sure," "safe," and *Clavai* perhaps connected with *clavar* ("to lock"). Cardona suggests *car* ("dear") and *don* or *dona* ("gift"), while Monjai is "Mount Joy."

The rest of this poem, particularly stanza VI (lines 61–72) is so obscure and has been interpreted in so many ways that it does not make a very convincing instance of the punning use of place names, although that is how Avalle and De Bartholomaeis take it.[12] Apparently Peire Vidal has turned from praising his lady to attacking Marquis Manfred Lancia (*Lanz'aguda*):

> E Lanz'aguda tegna·l Maur,
> Ab Dur-os et ab Negra-pell,
> E Trencan-nut e Mal-coutell
> E Crebacor e Compenha
> E Roignas ab que s'estrenha.
> Mal-matin conques e Mal-ser,
> Quan det trega per pauc d'aver.
> Sieus es Villans e Montantics,
> Malas-meissos e Viels-espics,
> E Cava-dens e pueis Lombrics,
> E Cordolors e Fastic-fai
> E Malamortz e Vida·l-trai,

Anglade prints many of these expressions with small letters and takes them for common nouns, which he translates as best he can. Places are known with names like some of these, and Avalle lists them. Others may have been fanciful inventions of the poet. The sense of several of the names is obvious: *crebacor* ("heartbreak"); *Compenha* ("mud") (cf. *compenh*) and, of course, Compiègne; *Roignas* suggests *ronha* ("itch," "filth"); *Mal-matin* and *Mal-ser* ("bad morning" and "bad evening"); *Villans* ("rustic," "boor"); *Montantics* ("old") (*antic*); *Malas-meissos* ("bad harvests"); *Viels-espics* ("old ears of grain"); *Cava-dens* ("tooth-hollower"); *Lombrics* ("worms"); *Cordolors*, *cor* ("heart") and *dolor* ("pain"), the compound usually taken in the sense of "compassion"; *Fastic-fai* ("make-disgust"); *Malamortz* ("bad death"); *Vida·l-trai* ("take his life").

These are the two poems in which Peire Vidal makes the most obvious use of place names for the purposes we are discussing. In fact, these are the only two I can find that contain clear instances of such puns.

Among the other troubadours, similar usages are less common than I had at first supposed. I have come across only three or four other cases, and not all of those are beyond contradiction. Here, for example, is a stanza (lines 13–24) from Peire Guilhem de Luserna's poem *Qi Na Cuniça guerreja* (344, 5):

> E qill mou guerra ni tenza
> Non cosel c'an en Proenza
>   Dompnejar,
> Qe ben poira semblar
> Folz, e portar penedenza
> Per la soa malvolenza,
>   Don m'anpar;
> Pero de Luzernas gar,
> C'orgoill ni desconoissenza
> No i troban luec ni guirenza,
>   Quil affar
> De lai son tuit de Plasenza! [13]

De Bartholomaeis has this comment: "I nomi di 'Proenza,' 'Luzerna' e 'Plasenza' non contengono, come alcuni critici hanno creduto, allusioni geografiche, ma sono addotti puramente per giuochi di parole." *Proenza*, of course, suggests *pro* ("good," "excellent," "meritorious"); the common noun *luzerna* means "lamp"; and *Plasenza* suggests "pleasure." The editor of Peire Guilhem, Guarnerio, prints *plasenza* with a small letter and does not comment on the puns implicit in *Proenza* and *Luzerna*. In another poem (344, 3), the same poet says:

> per q'eu me voill ab ioi tenir
> et ab los pros de Proenza.[14]

Here, the pun is made quite explicit, but the editor does not call attention to it.

In one of the poems of Peire Bremon Ricas Novas, there are these lines (he is speaking of *joglars*):

> C'un sai de part Plazenssa
> que, si·m conseguia,
> per aitan cum val Argenssa
> viu no·m laissaria.[15]

Plazenssa is not especially convincing as a pun, but *Argenssa* is surely to be connected with *argen* ("silver," "money"): "he would not leave me alive for all the money in Silverland."

The same word, *argen*, was probably in the mind of Torcafol when he wrote:

> Qui·us tolia Vivares,
> l'Argentieira e·l Solas,
> on lor comtatz mainz orbes,
> mesures vos hom lo vas;
> que quant Pons-tortz vos passia
> e Sainz-Laurens vos vestia,
> siatz totz paubres e ras,
> que sieus es anquer, si·os plas.

After trying to identify the first three names, the editor (Appel) adds: "Mais est-ce bien de noms de lieux réels qu'il s'agit ici, ou n'est-ce plutôt un exemple de cette sorte de jeu de mots dont parle Tobler dans 'Verblümter Ausdruck und Wortspiel in altfranzösischer Rede,' p. 2?" [16] In addition to the *argen* in *Argentieira*, the poet is in all likelihood thinking of *viure* ("to live") or *viu* ("alive") in connection with V*ivares*, and *solatz* ("joy," "companionship") with *Solas*: "If one took away from you life, money, and companionship. . . ."

And now, finally, two poems by Peire Cardenal. The first is a *cobla*, or poem of one stanza (461, 96), which appears in the manuscript without any indication of authorship, but among the authentic poems of Peire:

> Domna que va ves Valensa
> Deu enan passar Gardon;
> E deu tener per Verdon
> Si vol entrar en Proensa.
> E si vol passar la mar
> Pren un tal governador
> Que sapcha la Mar major,
> Que la guarde de varar
> Si vol tener vas lo Far.[17]

The editor, René Lavaud, translates thus:

> Une dame qui va vers Valence (vers la valeur) doit auparavant passer le Gardon (doit dépasser "je garde don," ne pas être avare); et elle doit se diriger le long du Verdon (suivre le "vrai don," être généreuse) si elle veut entrer en Provence ("prouesse," excellence). Et si elle veut traverser la Mer

("l'Aimer," l'Amour), elle prend le pilote tel qu'il connaisse la Mer Majeure ("l'Amour Majeure," le grand Amour) et qu'il la garde d'échouer si elle veut aller vers le Phare (le Phare est le port de Messine; au fig., le Phare lumineux, le Port du bonheur. Le pilote sûr sera l'amant sincère, le troubadour initié).

In a longer poem, the sirventes *Qui·s vol tal fais cargar* (335, 44, lines 33–35), Peire Cardenal has this to say about certain men of rank:

> Aquist ric home non son ges de Valensa
> Ans son de Gap e d'Albrac, deforas Fransa;
> De Bauzac e de Cruas es lur semensa.

Ces puissants hommes-là ne sont pas de "Valence" (valeur) mais plutôt de "Gap" (jactance) ou d'"Albrac" (boue), hors de la "France" (franchise); de "Beauzac" (tromperie) et de "Cruas" (cruauté) est leur race.[18]

In both of these poems, the wordplay on place names is fairly obvious, but Peire Cardenal does not seem to have used this device anywhere else. Furthermore, as far as I can discover after some searching, this closes the list of Provençal poems containing such puns.

Only six poets, then, indulged in this verbal play to a degree that would make a modern reader aware of what they were doing. The six are: Peire Vidal, Aimeric de Peguilhan, Torcafol, Peire Bremon Ricas Novas, Peire Guilhem de Luserna, and Peire Cardenal. It would seem that Peire Vidal invented this little word game; for his poem seems to be the first in point of time. Perhaps "popularized" would be a better word since this sort of play on place names, like puns in general, can hardly be said to have been invented. Such things go beyond literature, even beyond writing. But Peire Vidal probably did give this particular kind of pun a certain vogue among his fellow poets; and the ones who followed his lead were also quite close to him in time. All, in fact, were his contemporaries or only slightly his juniors. It seems that all the poems we have quoted here were written between approximately 1195 and 1240. Peire Vidal was a popular poet. His poems were well known and his metrical forms widely imitated.[19] It is not surprising that a mannerism like this one, appearing in the songs of so influential a poet, was also the subject of a certain amount of imitation.

The actual place names used for this purpose reveal some imagination now and then, but *Valensa* and *Plazensa* keep cropping up again and again, not to mention *Beljoc* and the towns based on the word *argen*. Perhaps it was the limited number of real localities available for punning references that kept other poets from indulging in Peire Vidal's game. Rather than declare that their ladies too were from Valensa or Plazensa, they decided to praise them in other ways. All in all, the decision, conscious or unconscious, was a wise one, because the joke was beginning to wear a little thin.

1. *The Poems of Aimeric de Peguilhan*, ed. W. P. Shepard and F. M. Chambers (Evanston, Ill.: Northwestern University Press, 1950), p. 194.

2. Zingarelli, *Intorno a due trovatori in Italia* (Firenze: Sansoni, 1899), pp. 36–37.

3. *Peire Vidal, Poesie*, a cura di D'Arco Silvio Avalle (Milano-Napoli: Ricciardi, 1960), poem xj, p. 107.

4. *Les Poésies de Peire Vidal*, éditées par Joseph Anglade (Paris: Champion [Classiques Français du Moyen Age], 1923), poem xxxv, p. 110.

5. Vincenzo De Bartholomaeis, *Poesie provenzali storiche* (Roma, 1931), I, 46.

6. Quoted from Avalle's text, p. 107. All the poems of Peire Vidal will be quoted in the reading of Avalle.

7. Francesco Torraca, *Le donne italiane nella poesia provenzale* (Firenze: Sansoni, 1901), p. 5.

8. Avalle, pp. 107, 108.

9. Avalle, Number xxxv, p. 288; De Bartholomaeis, I, 161.

10. Anglade, Number xlv, p. 143. Ernest Hoepffner, in his posthumous *Le Troubadour Peire Vidal* (Paris, 1961), pp. 140–41 and 171 ff., agrees fundamentally with Avalle and De Bartholomaeis that Peire is punning on place names both here and in the poem *Tant an ben dig del Marques*; as one might expect, there is some disagreement on details.

11. Anglade, p. 145.

12. Avalle, pp. 294 ff.; De Bartholomaeis, *loc. cit.*; Hoepffner (pp. 172 ff.) takes a number of the "place names" as common nouns.

13. De Bartholomaeis, II, 60; Pier Enea Guarnerio, *Pietro Guglielmo di Luserna* (Geneva, 1896), p. 34.

14. Guarnerio, p. 31.

15. *Les Poésies du Troubadour Peire Bremon Ricas Novas* . . . par Jean Boutière (Paris and Toulouse, 1930); *Lo bels terminis* (330, 9), lines 29–32, page 60.

16. *Revue des langues romanes*, XXXIV, 20. The article by Adolf Tobler to which Appel refers here was reprinted in an expanded version as an "Anhang" to Tobler's *Vermischte Beiträge* (Leipzig, 1906), II, 211–63. In this article, Tobler brings together a large number of puns and other bits of wordplay from Old French, including some like the ones we have been considering in Old Provençal. By way of preface, p. 214, he mentions in passing a few of the Provençal examples that we have cited, as well as some from other languages. There is, I think, little likelihood that there was any influence from our Provençal poets on these other writers; and most if not all of those named by Tobler are somewhat later in time than our poets. The place names cited by Tobler from Old French are: Blangy, Monpancier, Bauliant, Bordelois, Chanteleu, Clugny, Ronchieres, Roncheroles, Cornouaille, Empire, Femenie, Gales, Matefelon, Mentenai, Niceroles, Niort, Noyon, Tremblay, and Vaucelles. In general, these seem to me less convincing as puns than our Provençal examples.

17. *Poésies complètes du Troubadour Peire Cardenal*, publiées par René Lavaud (Toulouse, 1957), p. 28.

18. *Ibid.*, p. 113.

19. See, for example, in I. Frank's *Répertoire métrique*, I, 111 ff., the number of poems that have the same metrical form and rimes (*al, ir, ieu, en*) as Peire Vidal's poem *Anc no mori per amor ni per al* (364, 4).

———————Robert White Linker———————

The Vocabulary of the New Testament in Provençal

IN 1887, Clédat published a facsimile of the manuscript of the New Testament in Provençal.[1] This adaptation was supposedly made for the use of Albigensians, according to the ritual that ends the manuscript—or it could have been for Waldensians.[2] Foerster identifies dialectal traits contained in it as "du pur provençal parlé sur la rive droite du Rhône, probablement dans le département de l'Aude ou du Tarn," an opinion to which Chabaneau suscribed.[3] Very little work has been done on this manuscript, and an examination of its vocabulary should be of interest in determining the basic meaning of some Provençal words which, in the translation of a sacred text, would have been used quite literally. It will be obvious that many of the Provençal forms correspond closely to the Latin etyma from which they were originally derived; others display a change of prefix or an added suffix. More interesting are those cases in which a word entirely unrelated translates the Latin expression.

In the Gospel according to St. Matthew, the first word that attracted my attention was *encantadors* used to render *magi* (Matt. 2:1). This leads one to all kinds of speculation. *Escarnitz* is the frequent translation of *illusus*, and this applies to *escarniro* for *illudebant* (Matt. 9:29), and *illuserunt* (Matt. 27:31). But *escarnis* is used also for *hic blasphemat* (Matt. 9:3) and *escarniro* for *deridebant* (Matt. 9:24). There is the *blasma* which translates *blasphemat* (Jas 2:5). *Gaug* is the common equivalent of *gaudium*. Verbs of rejoicing are in *alegratz vos e esgauzetz* for *gaudete et exultate* (Matt. 5:12), while these are reversed and *s'esgauziran* represents *gaudebunt* in Luke 1:14. *Congaudent* is expressed by Provençal *essems s'engauzisso* (I Cor. 12:26).

Human attitudes toward others are represented by such translations as *enganador* for *hypocritae* (Matt. 6:2, 5, 16), *engan* for *dolum* (I Pet. 2:1). Seduction falls together with hypocrisy in *enganantz* for *seducens* (Jas. 1:26). Persecutors are *encauzador* (for *persequentibus*) (Matt. 5:44); persecution is *encausz* (for *persecutionem*), (Matt. 5:10); the verb *encauzaran* translates *persecuti vos fuerunt* (Matt. 10:11), and *persequentur* (Matt. 10:23). Contrasting with these more unpleasant terms are *amantz* for *diligentibus* (Jas. 1:1 and 2:5), *amadi* for *dilectissimi* (Jas. 1:16), *mout amadi* for *dilectissimi* and *amatz* for *dilectus* (Matt. 12:18).

Before proceeding to compare other words, it might be proper first to comment on the general treatment of prefixes. The Latin negative *in-* is replaced either by *no-*, or by a complete change of word. Other Latin prefixes are similarly altered, as the following will indicate. *Injustitiam* is *no dreitura*; but *impietatem* is *felonia* (Rom. 1:18). *Praedestinatus* is translated by *davant azordenatz* (Rom. 1:1), *circumfertur* by *enaviro portada* (Jas. 1:6), *accipiat* by *recipia* (Jas. 1:7). *Inconstans est* becomes *no es ferms* (Jas. 1:8); *indiget, besonha*, and *consummatum, acabatz* (Jas. 1:15); *immaculata, no solhada* (Jas. 1:27); *immundorum, nonedes* (Matt. 10:1);

while *lagesa* translates *immunditia* (Jas. 1:21). *Invisibilia* is rendered by *noveziblas cosas* (Rom. 1:20). *Trans-* remains in *trasmudamentz* from *transmutatio* (Jas. 1:17); with a change of the verb, as in *traspassare* from *transibit* (Jas. 1:10). *Com-* is replaced by *essems* in *essems sofro* from *compatiuntur* (I Cor. 12:26).

In the field of domestic relations, *puer* and *puella* give way to *macips* (Matt. 8:6) and *macipa* (Matt. 9:24). *Patrem familias* becomes *paire de las mainadas* (Matt. 10:25), and *domesticos* becomes *privat*.

Other translations, too varied to be grouped but whose comparisons are of some interest, follow in alphabetical order:

> *adesmari: aestimabo* (Matt. 11:16)
> *afillament: adoptionem* (Eph. 1:5)
> *amonestansa: exhortationem* (II Cor. 1:4)
> *amonestatz: adominitus* (Matt. 2:22)
> *aparelara: praeparabit* (Matt. 11:10)
> *aparelatz: parate* (Matt. 3:3)
> *apremement: pressura* (II Cor. 1:4)
> *aridam: secam* (Matt. 12:10)
> *assaiatz: tentaretur* (Matt. 4:1)
> *atrobara: inveniet* (Matt. 10:39)
> *azesmatz: existimate* (Jas. 1:1)
> *aziraras: odio habebis* (Matt. 5:43)
> *azombramentz devegada: vicissitudinis obumbratio* (Jas. 1:17)
> *baletz: saltabis* (Matt. 11:17)
> *canavera: arundinem* (Matt. 11:7)
> *cobezeza: concupiscentia* (Jas. 1:14)
> *cofort: consolationis* (II Cor. 1:3)

coforta: consolatur (II Cor. 1:4)
companha: societas (Phil. 2:1)
conortz: consolation (Phil. 2:1)
cosollada esser: consolari (Matt. 2:18)
cossiratz: cogitans (Matt. 6:27)
cossiratz: cogitatis (Matt. 9:4)
cossirers: cogitationibus (Rom. 1:21)
cossirosi: soliciti (Matt. 6:28)
davant: ante (Rom. 1:2)
degiradas: varias (Jas. 1:14)
delivrec: eripuit (II Cor. 1:10)
departitz: segregatus (Rom. 1:1)
derazenintz: detractiones (I Pet. 2:1)
derescaps: iterum (II Cor. 1:16)
detiratz: abstractus (Jas. 1:14)
devedatz: prohibitus (Rom. 1:13)
doncas: numquid (I Cor. 12:30)
efeubetatz: simulationes (II Pet. 2:1)
enapres: mox (Phil. 2:23)
enlazatz: illectus (Jas. 1:14)
enoges: taederet (II Cor. 1:8)
enpeutada: insitum (Jas. 1:21)
entro: usque (Rom. 1:13)
escaunels: scabellum (Matt. 5:35)
esgardament: conspectu (Eph. 1:4)
esmanza: opinio (Matt. 4:24)
essausament: exaltatione (Jas. 1:9)
establisment: constitutionem (Eph. 1:4)
eveia: invidias (II Pet. 2:1)
eveiatz: aemulamini (I Cor. 12:31)
evanezira: evanuerit (Matt. 5:13)

for: autem (Matt. 5:37,39)
forzadament: violenti (Matt. 11:12)
franqueza: libertatem (Jas. 1:25)
fretanssas: tolerantiam (II Cor. 1:6)
garda vos: attendite (Matt. 7)
gazanh: redemptionem (Eph. 1:14)
haesitans, haesitat: dopte, dopta (Jas. 1:6)
intrallias: viscera (Phil. 2:1)
laizat, no: immaculati (Eph. 1:4)
lebra: vir (Jas. 1:12)
leudaria: telonio (Matt. 9:9)
linhages: genera (I Cor. 12:28)
linhages: tribubus (Jas. 1:1)
lobra: vir (Jas. 1:8)
loquer: bravium (I Cor. 9:24)
malaveigz: infirmitatem (Matt. 10:1)
malaventz: male habentes (Matt. 4:24)
malevara: volenti mutuari (Matt. 5:42)
maleza: malitia (Matt. 6:34)
malvestat: ignominiae (Rom. 1:21)
manentz: dives (Jas. 1:10)
mercia ac: misertus (Mark 1:41)
mesconoisser: ignorare (Rom. 1:13)
mesprezara: contemnet (Matt. 6:24)
mesura: modum (II Cor. 1:8)
mezala: asse (Matt. 10:29)
nomenativara: exiit fama (Matt. 9:26)
nominativero: diffamaverunt (Matt. 9:31)
para: praebe (Matt. 5:39)
plaissetz: planxistes (Matt. 11:17)
prezara: sustinebit (Matt. 6:24)

primeirament: primum (I Cor. 12:28)
recobrament: aquisitionis (Eph. 1:14)
requeira: postulet (Jas. 1:5)
ric: divites (Jas. 2:6)
restaurar: instaurare (Eph. 1:10)
sadolat seran: satiorabuntur (Matt. 5:6)
sanamentz: curationes (I Cor. 12:28)
secon, el secon loc: secondo (I Cor. 12:28)
sofre, suffert (Jas. 1:12)
sofrere: patitur (I Cor. 12:26)
sofro essems: compatiuntur (I Cor. 12:26)
solatz: solatium (Phil. 2:1)
soprericat: evangelizantur (Matt. 11:5)
suau: mites (Matt. 5:4)
sufrenza: patientiam (Jas. 1:4)
tenzo: contentionem (Phil. 2:3)
temptacio: tentationem (Jas. 1:12)
tormentar: afficient (Matt. 10:21)
trebalat: vexati (Matt. 9:36)
trebalatz: torquetur (Matt. 8:6)
trebalhadas siem: tribulamur (II Cor. 1:6)
unial: unanimes (Phil. 2:2)
vas: apud (Jas. 1:27)
vergonhi: erubesco (Rom. 1:16)
viacers: velox (Jas. 1:19)
viassament: cito (Phil. 2:19)
viasz: cito (Phil. 2:24)
viazament: continuo (Matt. 4:20)

Last but not least, I should like to point out *atrobador* for *inventor* (Rom. 1:30). This and other parallels in the foregoing do not add a great amount to our knowledge of Provençal vocabulary. They do, however, indicate a fairly positive means of checking dictionary definitions now available against a Latin word whose meaning is scarcely to be doubted. Further study of material of this type could give better results than shown here, for the examples above were selected at random with no idea of making an exhaustive study in a short space. Rather interesting are some of the variations in translation of essentially the same idea, such as *no solhada* and *no laizat* for *immaculatus*, the appearance of *lebra* and *lobra* for *vir*, and the treatment, as indicated, of suffixes and prefixes. Surely, this approach in the comparison of Latin and Provençal rests on surer ground than inference from context in the writing of the troubadour.

1. *Le Nouveau Testament traduit au XIIIe siècle en langue provençale suivi d'un rituel cathare. Reproduction photolithographique du manuscrit de Lyons* . . . par L. Clédat (Paris, 1887).
2. *Ibid.*, p. iv.
3. *Ibid.*

———————————Part III———————————

Renaissance French

Raymond Lebègue

Flux et Reflux du Vocabulaire Français au XVIᵉ Siècle

MÊME APRÈS *l'Histoire de la langue française* de Ferdinand Brunot, on peut étudier à nouveau l'évolution du vocabulaire français depuis les Rhétoriqueurs jusqu'à l'arrivée de Malherbe à Paris (1605). Les mouvements de ce vocabulaire ont été d'une telle ampleur qu'il serait instructif de le comparer à celui des pays voisins à la même époque. Je ne saurais traiter ce problème de linguistique comparée. Je voudrais seulement tracer à grands traits la courbe du vocabulaire français pendant cette période.

Le Flux

L'enrichissement du vocabulaire français est essentiellement constitué dès le Moyen-Age d'emprunts faits au latin par les savants.[1] Puis, à partir du XIVᵉ siècle, les souverains et les grands féodaux commandent des traductions françaises d'œuvres latines. C'est le début d'un afflux de mots empruntés par les traducteurs aux langues étrangères et pourvus d'une terminaison française, afflux qui grossira au XVᵉ et surtout au XVIᵉ siècle.

Un courant parallèle est dû aux poètes: les Grands Rhétoriqueurs cultivent une poésie de Cour, farcie de mots savants, qui, en outre, ont l'avantage de leur fournir des rimes riches. C'est surtout chez eux que le latinisme devient un ornement littéraire.[2] Brunot cite des exemples empruntés à Eustache Deschamps et Chastellain; Molinet met à la rime *altitude, sainctitude, similitude, plénitude, impérative, opinative. Le Temple de Vénus* de Lemaire de Belges s'orne de rimes telles que *monocordes, décacordes, pedissèque, extrinsèque, resecque, concupiscible, signacles, substantacles, génitive, imaginative*. Dans les Mystères, qui tiennent une si grande place dans la littérature et la vie sociale du XVe et de la première moitié du XVIe siècle, les personnages divins, diaboliques, ou impériaux emploient souvent un style emphatique et des mots rares et savants: le premier interpolateur du mystère des *Actes des Apôtres* fait rimer *tartarines* avec *sulphurines* et *soubzterrines, plutoniques* avec *draconicques, traditeurs* avec *progeniteurs, propugnacle* avec *retinacle*, etc.

Les emprunts au latin seront si nombreux, soit dans la poésie, soit dans la prose cicéronienne des Rhétoriqueurs,[3] qu'on accusera maint auteur d'*écorcher, excorier, écumer*, ou *despumer* le latin.[4]

Au XVIe siècle, on traduit quantité d'œuvres latines, grecques, italiennes, etc. Les *Arts poétiques* de Sebillet, de Peletier et de Laudun d'Aigaliers contiennent un chapitre consacré à la traduction, et Dolet publie en 1540 *La Manière de bien traduire d'une langue en autre*. Pour les termes techniques, les traducteurs ont le choix entre un équivalent français (par exemple, *capitaine général de la gendarmerie*) ou le mot étranger francisé. En optant pour la seconde solution, ils ont fait entrer dans notre langue un nombre considérable de mots étrangers. Huguet n'ayant dépouillé qu'une soixantaine de traductions, son dictionnaire est loin de contenir la totalité de ces emprunts. La philosophie, la rhétorique, les sciences, la médecine, les arts, la musique s'enrichirent de mots tirés du latin, du grec, de l'italien.[5]

Les traducteurs d'ouvrages techniques n'ont pas seulement francisé des mots étrangers; ils ont fait appel au langage de nos corps de métiers et l'ont promu à la dignité littéraire. En traduisant Vitruve, J. Martin consulte les ouvriers; Du Pinet interroge les paysans, les artisans, les chirurgiens, les peintres, etc., afin de traduire exactement Pline l'ancien. L'éditeur de la traduction de L. B. Alberti écrit avec orgueil au roi Henri II: "Vous y trouverez votre langue enrichie de mille mots paravant cachés dedans les boutiques des seuls ouvriers."

Passons aux poètes. Elève des Grands Rhétoriqueurs, mais ayant choisi la cour de François I pour maîtresse d'école, Marot ne cultive pas le latinisme, et ses néologismes, loin d'être pédants, visent à l'amusement du lecteur: emprisonnerie, rimaille, rimoyer, rimonner, etc. Mais Maurice Scève, dans *Délie* et surtout dans le *Microcosme*, se permet quantité de latinismes, d'hellénismes, d'italianismes et de néologismes.[6]

On sait depuis longtemps que, dans son dessein d'enrichir la langue française, Du Bellay avait eu des précurseurs. Il est inutile, après F. Brunot, de revenir sur eux. Citons seulement ce conseil de Peletier à un poète:

>S'il y a de la pauvreté,
>Qui garde que tu ne composes
>Nouveaux motz aux nouvelles choses?

Comme tant de ses contemporains, Peletier reprend à son compte le conseil que, dans l'épître aux Pisons, Horace formulait: pour des choses nouvelles créer avec mesure des mots nouveaux.

Le Pléiade s'est donné licence de ressusciter des archaïsmes, d'introduire dans la langue poétique des mots dialectaux, de franciser des mots latins, grecs, italiens, de créer—souvent à l'imitation des poètes latins et grecs—des mots nouveaux. Pour leur classement, je renvoie à Brunot. Mais il faut noter ceci: nous connaissons très insuffisamment les innovations (et les repentirs) de Ronsard; car Marty-Laveaux, auteur de la *Langue de la Pléiade*, opérait sur l'édition de 1584: seule, l'édition Laumonier des *Textes Français Modernes* permet d'embrasser la totalité du vocabulaire de Ronsard et d'en suivre l'évolution.

En outre, Du Bellay et Ronsard ont recommandé aux poètes d'orner leurs oeuvres de comparaisons tirées des métiers; aussi les invitent-ils à fréquenter les peintres, graveurs, orfèvres, fondeurs, marins, etc., afin de connaître et d'employer "les noms propres des outils." Avec raison, Marty-Laveaux a consacré une section de son ouvrage aux mots techniques.

Nombreux furent les poètes qui, à l'exemple de la Pléiade, prétendirent enrichir la langue de mots nouveaux; Du Bartas ne fut pas seul à oublier le prudent avertissement d'Horace: *pudenter*, avec réserve![7] De tout nom propre antique on pouvait dériver, à volonté deux, trois, quatre adjectifs: Robert Garnier emploie concurremment *pelean, pelian, pelide, pharsalien, pharsalique, romulien, romulide, acheronté, acherontide*, etc.

Le Reflux

Si nous sommes bien instruits de l'accroissement du vocabulaire pendant le XVIe siècle, aucun progrès n'a été réalisé, pour le reflux, depuis la publication du tome III de *l'Histoire de la langue française* de F. Brunot. Conservant la division par siècles, Brunot faisait commencer l'épuration du vocabulaire à Malherbe. Malgré des opposants sur lesquels la *Doctrine de Malherbe* avait déjà apporté la lumière, le poète-grammairien avait impitoyablement sacrifié les mots dialectaux, les archaïsmes, les néologismes, les termes techniques, etc. C'est exact, et le vocabulaire de Malherbe est beaucoup plus restreint que celui de Robert Garnier, qui avait seulement onze ans de plus que lui.

Mais Brunot lui-même avait deviné que "les maîtres lassés battirent en retraite, alors que la foule des disciples se ruaient encore à l'assaut," et qu'ils ont capitulé devant "l'opposition sourde d'un public anonyme."[8]

Aujourd'hui que les éditions critiques et les études savantes se sont multipliées, on peut voir plus clairement les reculades des poètes et le reflux du vocabulaire.[9] *Ab Jove principium* : on connaît les innovations de Ronsard, mais on ne parle guère des désaveux qu'il s'inflige à lui-même. Il me fait penser à cette procession de S. Roch qu'il a célébrée dans un de ses derniers poèmes et où, après avoir avancé de trois pas, on recule de deux. Il francise des mots étrangers, il forge des néologismes; puis, en révisant son oeuvre, plus attentif au jugement du grand public qu'il ne l'affirme, il remplace le mot par un terme plus usuel. En attendant l'achèvement de thèses sur ses corrections, citons quelques exemples. Les superlatifs en *ime* : *folatrime, reverendime, cruelime, grandime, bonime, excellentime*, et le verbe *lunapreslautrer* (*Voyage d'Arcueil*, v. 48), ces innovations de 1553 ne se retrouvent pas dans l'édition collective de 1560. La réédition des Odes en 1555 supprime des néologismes et des archaïsmes.

Comme l'a constaté G. Raibaud,[10] Ronsard enlève des *Amours à Cassandre*, à des dates variables, *frigoreux, volter, contumax, bastant, arpin* (Cicéron). En 1578, il remplace par *haleter* le verbe à redoublement *babattre* (1552). Dans le même recueil, H. Weber note la disparition de *dessoiffer, sorceler* et *pantoyment* (adverbe) en 1567, d'*avantpenser* et *fourchument* en 1578, de *pandorin* en 1584.[11]

Mais à l'époque où il travaille à son grand poème homérique, il emploie *sacerdote, phtinopore, phocense, vates* (qui, dans *Hylas* remplace *chantres*). Les différents états de la *Franciade* témoignent de ses hésitations et de ses repentirs;[12] il biffe *thérébin* (d'après *térébinthe*), *mange-vivre, crus-vieillards* (traduit de l'*Iliade*), *cueur-masle, enmitré, acazaner, isnel, escoteux*, etc.

En 1573, J. A. de Baïf renonce à deux adjectifs composés qu'il avait employés en 1552: *douxamer, dousucré*.[13]

En 1584, dix ans après la publication de sa traduction partielle de l'*Iliade*, Amadis Jamyn remplace *pleiger, braguard, Jupin, corne-pieds, porte-trident, large-cours, crochu-bec, courbe-serre*.[14]

Robert Garnier remplace en 1574 *desammurer* et l'adjectif *orbe*, en 1580 l'archaïsme *isnel* que Du Bellay avait recommandé, en 1585 *massacrouere, insupérable, ensépulchrable*. Il y a moins de néologismes dans *Bradamante* et dans *Les Juives* que dans ses tragédies antérieures.[15]

Nous ne ferons pas mention des très nombreuses corrections de la *Sophonisbe* de Montchrestien; car nous pensons, ainsi que M. Fromilhague, qu'elles ont été inspirées à ce jeune dramaturge par son compatriote Malherbe. Mais, avant même que l'influence de Malherbe ne s'exerce, un Desportes, un Bertaut, un Du Perron évitent la plupart des néologismes de la

Pléiade, ils dédaignent les termes techniques, leur vocabulaire poétique se rétrécit. Dans les œuvres des poètes de la Cour, le reflux a commencé dès le dernier tiers du XVI° siècle.

Certes il est regrettable que la langue poétique se soit appauvrie et décolorée, et se soit dépouillée de ses caractères concrets.[16] Mais la plupart des mots que nos poètes empruntaient au latin, et ceux qu'ils créaient par dérivation ou composition, ne pouvaient entrer dans l'usage public. Qu'Horace eût employé *Pimplaea*,[17] cela ne donnait pas à pimpléan, en France, le droit de cité.

Il serait intéressant de dénombrer, par discipline, les mots que les traductions ont définitivement introduits dans la langue française. Certains traducteurs eurent la main lourde; les Français n'ont pas naturalisé *conceptacle*, *pédotribique*, *ochlocratie*, que Le Roy a employés, et qui sonnaient mal à leurs oreilles. L'apothicaire Dusseau donne à sa traduction ce titre qui n'a rien de français: *Enchirid ou manipul des miropoles*; aucun de ces trois substantifs n'a survécu. Mais un grand nombre de leurs néologismes sont restés, parce qu'ils étaient indispensables.

Sans doute, l'enrichissement de la langue française au XVI° siècle n'est pas dû uniquement aux poètes et aux traducteurs : les ouvrages scientifiques modernes, les récits de voyage, etc., y ont aussi contribué. Mais ce sont là deux courants très abondants, que les historiens du vocabulaire n'ont pas suffisamment sondés. Leur destin a été différent; aussi bien les traducteurs avaient-ils été poussés par la nécessité, tandis que les poètes cherchaient plutôt des ornements. Le grand public a été peu sensible à des ornements qui étaient appropriés aux Grecs ou aux Latins, mais non aux Français.

1. Cf. Brunot, *op. cit.*, I, 292–95.
2. *Ibid.*, I, 525.
3. Voir, par exemple, le prologue des *Chroniques* de Molinet.
4. Cf. Brunot, *op. cit.*, II, 223–27; Lebègue, "L'Ecolier limousin," *Revue des Cours et Conférences*, XL, 2ème série; le dictionnaire Huguet. Un certain nombre des mots latins qui ont été francisés, étaient d'origine grecque ou même hébraïque.
5. Cf. Lebègue, *Les Traductions en France pendant la Renaissance* (Association Budé, Congrès de Strasbourg, 1938), pp. 362–77, et *La Langue des traducteurs français au XVIe siècle* (Festgabe Gamillscheg, 1952), pp. 24–34.
6. Cf. V. L. Saulnier, *Maurice Scève*, 1948, I, 295–96, 303, 502–7.
7. Dans une tragédie du magister Pierre Mathieu, on trouve des vers tels que: Au scope de leur jour apostater leur gloire.
8. *Op. cit.*, III, 1.
9. Sur l'ampleur de ce reflux, cf. Huguet, *Mots disparus ou vieillis depuis le XVIe siècle* (1935).
10. "Sur quelques variantes des Amours de Cassandre," *Revue Universitaire*, XLVIII, I (1939).
11. *Les Corrections de Ronsard dans les Amours de 1552* (Studi . . . Lugli-Valeri, 1961), pp. 989–1015. Voir aussi Chamard, *Histoire de la Pleiade*, IV, 58, 61–63.
12. Cf. Lebègue, "Ronsard au travail," *Lettres d'Humanité*, XI (1952), 72–92.
13. Cf. Chamard, *Histoire de la Pléiade*, IV, 73.
14. Cf. Th. Graur, *Amadis Jamyn* (1929), pp. 324–25.
15. Cf. Lebègue, "Le Vocabulaire de R. Garnier," *Le Français Moderne* (1949), pp. 165–81.
16. Bien entendu, ceci ne s'applique pas aux poètes bernesques, satyriques, baroques, ou burlesques.
17. D'ailleurs ce mot devait être inintelligible à un Romain moyen.

———————*Isidore Silver*———————

Archaism in Ronsard's Theory of a Poetic Vocabulary

Je fis des mots nouveaux, je restauray les vieux. . . .

Nos Peres Peu Curieus

WHEN one considers Ronsard's theory of a poetic vocabulary in relation to the general theory of poetry that guided him and his colleagues, one is impressed by the high degree of consistency that unites the part to the whole, even though this consistency was not always realized in practice. The immense regeneration of French letters to which these poets dedicated their labors and which Ronsard, in so far as his own work was concerned, described as requiring a "stile apart, sens apart, euvre apart" (I, 45)[1] inexorably involved as well a renewal of the vocabulary of poetry. A significant renovation both of style and sense would have been impossible on the basis of the aesthetic and intellectual orientation of the Rhétoriqueurs, of Jean Lemaire de Belges, Maurice Scève, Clément Marot, or Mellin de Saint-Gelais. Some of these writers no doubt took the initial forward steps, but the common ideal shared by the members of the Pléiade, of opening definitively the highroad of European tradition that originates in the literatures of classical antiquity and especially in that of Greece, could be made a living reality, they felt, only when their theoretical postulates took form in a new poetry distinguished from the old in every important respect, including the lexical. This accounts for the great concern with the problem of language which emerges in the title of their manifesto, Joachim du Bellay's *Deffence et Illustration de la Langue Francoyse*.

Like most manifestos, the *Deffence* did not limit itself to a discussion and evocation of the positive values that it sought to bring into being. Parallel with this discussion, and in a sense justifying and motivating it, was the reiterated expression of dissatisfaction with the work of preceding generations of French writers :

> Et si nostre langue n'est si copieuse et riche que la greque ou latine, cela ne doit estre imputé au default d'icelle, comme si d'elle mesme elle ne pouvoit jamais estre si non pauvre et sterile: mais bien on le doit attribuer à l'ignorance de notz majeurs, qui ayans . . . en plus grande recommendation le bien faire que le bien dire . . . nous ont laissé nostre langue si pauvre et nue, qu'elle a besoing des ornements et . . . des plumes d'autruy.[2]

This thought was, of course, not original with Du Bellay. Long before he could have had the intention of writing the *Deffence* the idea that the poverty of the French language resulted from the neglect and disdain with which it was treated by men of education in France had already been clearly expressed by Jacques Peletier. In 1541, far in advance of his meetings with either Du Bellay or Ronsard, Peletier had stated what was to be one of the cardinal positions of the Pleiade:

> Si de bien pres on veult considerer le stile des escrivains du temps present . . . on voira clairement qu'ilz n'approchent pas de celle copieuse vehemence, & gracieuse proprieté qu'on voit luire es autheurs anciens. Et toutesfoix on ne scauroit raisonnablement dire que ce fust faulte de grant esprit. . . .

> Mais la principale raison, & plus apparente . . . qui nous oste le merite de vray honneur, est le mesprix & contennement de nostre langue native. . . .[3]

It is scarcely open to doubt that in the literary discussions that must have taken place between Peletier and Ronsard on March 6, 1543, and between Peletier and Du Bellay some time in 1546,[4] the question of the defense of the French language was either explicitly mentioned or constituted one of the implied premises fundamental to their exchange of views.

If we have mentioned Peletier it is because he was perhaps in the fullest sense the precursor of the Pléiade. He propagated the impulse toward the enrichment of the French language not only in his theoretical writings and conversations with fellow-poets but also in his poetry:

> Or pource qu'ez Latins et Grecz
> Les ars sont reduiz et compris,
> Avec les Naturelz segretz,
> C'est bien raison qu'ilz soient appris:
> Mais comme d'un riche pourpris,
> Tout le meilleur il en faut prendre,
> Pour en nostre langue le rendre:
> La ou tout peut estre traitté,
> Pourveu que bien tu te disposes:
> S'il y a de la pauvreté,
> Qui garde que tu ne composes
> Nouveaux motz aux nouvelles choses? [5]
> Si mesme a l'exemple te mires
> De ceulx la que tant tu admires? [6]

Peletier, however, was not the father of this current of thought any more than the two young men who were destined to contribute more than he to its establishment in France. A discussion of its origins and evolution in that country would be superfluous since it has been treated in masterly fashion by Ferdinand Brunot.[7] Pierre Villey[8] has shown, however, that Du Bellay's *Deffence* was very heavily indebted to Sperone Speroni's *Dialogo delle lingue*,[9] first published in 1542. The ideas that Peletier had advanced in 1541, and that later were so ardently defended by Du Bellay from 1549 onward, were thus part of the intellectual baggage of every progressive mind as the sixteenth century approached its midpoint.

Ronsard's defense of these ideas had begun some years earlier, and we may presume that even if the writings in which they appeared were not published until 1550, they were known in the poet's immediate circle soon after their composition. The ode *A sa Muse*, probably written in 1545,[10] clearly foreshadows the language and the thought of both Du Bellay's *Deffence* and of his own preface to the *Odes* of 1550. He calls upon his Muse to abandon the sense, the rhyme, and the technique of the ignorant moderns, evidently identified with those who still clung to the traditions of an earlier generation. He summons the divinity to reveal a new and brilliant poetic form, having its substantive sources in humanistic learning, whose luminous flashes of lightning would annihilate the "old ignorance of our incurious ancestors."[11] It is in the same spirit and at approximately the same time that he wrote *La Victoire de François de Bourbon*, in which he grudgingly concedes that the hymn composed by Clément Marot[12] to celebrate this victory at the battle of Cérisoles (1544) was an acceptable effort as a preliminary sketch awaiting the perfect hand of an ingenious craftsman to carry the theme to its highest possible expression (I, 83). The variants of this passage continue to the

end of the poet's life to spin the double thread of pride in the
innovation of a fresh and vigorous poetry and a sense of the
great improvement wrought by the enlightened marriage of
verse with humanist studies. In a final variant that appeared in
the first posthumous edition, Ronsard refers to himself as

> ... nay d'un meilleur âge,
> Aux lettres industrieux. . . .
>
> (1587, t. II, 33)

Between the earliest and latest assertions of these ideas, the
poet was not entirely silent. At a moment when he thought he
had received definite encouragement from Henri II to under-
take the long-delayed *Franciade*, he feigned a certain regret in
the *Elegie à Cassandre* (1554) at temporarily abandoning the
lesser forms, such as the ode and the pastoral,

> Car, à vrai dire, encore mon esprit
> N'est satisfait de ceus qui ont ecrit
> En nôtre langue, & leur amour merite
> Ou du tout rien, ou faveur bien petite.
>
> (VI, 58)

In the preface to the *Franciade*, probably composed in 1585,
and in the verses that form a sort of epilogue to this last work
in prose, the essentials of Ronsard's position regarding the
poverty of the language that he and his fellow-poets had
inherited are intact. The four decades of poetic activity on his
part and that of his immediate and more distant colleagues
have not sufficiently remedied the situation that obtained at

their first entry upon the literary scene. Ronsard tells us that it is (and presumably will remain) exceedingly difficult to write in French if the language is not greatly enriched over its present condition by the addition of new words and forms of expression. In support of this point of view, he appeals to the experience of those who have daily occasion to write French and who, therefore, have intimate knowledge of the "extreme geine de se servir tousjours d'un mot" (XVI, 348). The Muses had granted to the foremost poets of Greece and Rome the use of linguistic instruments capable of perfect utterance; but, says Ronsard, in exculpation of the shortcomings of his own epic, the daughters of Mnemosyne had been less generous with him.

> . . . dont la langue peu riche,
> Couverte de halliers tous les jours se desfriche,
> Sans mots, sans ornemens, sans honneur & sans pris,
> Comme un champ qui fait peur aux plus gentils esprits
> Des laboureurs, actifs à nourrir leurs mesnages,
> Qui tournent les guerets pleins de ronces sauvages
> Et d'herbes aux longs pieds, retardement des boeufs,
> A faute d'artisans qui n'ont point davant eux
> Defriché ny viré la campaigne feruë,
> Qui maintenant revesche arreste leur charruë,
> Luttant contre le soc d'herbes environné.
>
> (XVI, 354)

The plough, however, was never long arrested. The period that began with the publication of the *Deffence* and Ronsard's *Odes* witnessed a most intensive cultivation of the limitless potentialities of the French language, in which lexical enrichment was the inevitable accompaniment of a profound aesthetic and intellectual exploitation. Du Bellay faces the future with the utmost confidence. The language of his day, he finds, is but a slender stem that has hardly begun to put forth blossoms. How then shall it give proof of its power to produce fruit? Surely the day will come, he believes, when its roots will have plunged deeply into the nourishing soil, and the French language will attain a strength and loftiness equal to Greek and Latin.[13] The fourth chapter of Book I of the *Deffence*, entitled "Que la langue francoyse n'est si pauvre que beaucoup l'estiment," opens with an energetic statement of this theme:

> Je n'estime pourtant nostre vulgaire, tel qu'il est maintenant, estre si vil et abject. . . . Et qui voudra de bien pres y regarder, trouvera que nostre langue francoyse n'est si pauvre, qu'elle ne puysse rendre fidelement ce qu'elle emprunte des autres, si infertile, qu'elle ne puysse produyre de soy quelque fruict de bonne invention, au moyen de l'industrie et diligence des cultiveurs d'icelle, si quelques uns se treuvent tant amys de leur païz et d'eux mesmes, qu'ilz s'y veillent employer. (*Def.*, pp. 75 f.; cf. p. 81)

No doubt Ronsard's confidence in the early days of the literary movement of which he was the leader was at least as great as that of Du Bellay; but in some respects, both in theory and in practice,[14] some abatement of his enthusiasm seems to have occurred with the passage of time. Discussing the creation of compound words (e.g. *enreter, douxamer, tireloin*) in imitation of Greek and Latin procedures, Ronsard informs us in his *Abbregé de l'Art poëtique françois* (1565) that the lexical evolution of the language had suffered somewhat during the reigns of François I and Henri II through the unwillingness of the older poets to grant "aux nouveaux une telle liberté" (XIV, 32). In a note that Remy Belleau, the commentator of the *Second livre des Amours*, wrote in 1560 to explain the newly coined verbs *en-rocher, en-glacer, en-eauër, en-feuër*, we learn that Ronsard's freedom in this respect had been affected in the same manner as that of his contemporaries: "Tourner en roche, en eau, en glace, en feu," says Belleau in explanation of the above neologisms, "mots nouveaus et necessaires pour enrichir la pauvreté de nostre langue, laquelle ne manqueroit aujourd'hui d'une infinité de beaus mots bien inventez & bien recherchez, si du commencement les envieus de la vertu de l'autheur ne l'eussent détourné d'une si louable entreprise." [15] One may fairly assume that Belleau here reproduces a thought that the author of the *Amours* had communicated to him, and one that was to find renewed expression in the *Caprice au Seigneur Simon Nicolas*, one of Ronsard's last affirmations (1584) on the state of poetry in France:

> . . . ce vulgaire,
> A qui jamais je n'ay peu satisfaire
> Ny n'ay voulu, me fascha tellement
> De son japper en mon advenement,
> Quand je hantay les eaux de Castalie,
> Que nostre langue en est moins embellie:
> Car elle est manque & faut de l'action
> Pour la conduire à sa perfection.[16]

Since Belleau had died in 1577, the extension of his note which is inserted under his name in the collective edition of 1584 (page 165), may be attributed with some probability to Ronsard himself:

> En-fouë, en-eauë, en-glace) Ce sont mots inventez par l'Autheur pour la richesse de nostre langue, & fort heureusement composez. Car de feu, tournant le e en o, vient fouyer, & foüace, qui est une certaine galette ou tourteau cuit au feu. Puis fouë, qui signifie une grande flame de feu, telle que nous faisons en nos villages la vigile de la S. Jean. En-eauë) Il est certain que nos peres disoyent eauë, pour eau: tesmoins en sont les vieux Romans. Or d'eauë le Poëte a faict le verbe En-eauër, comme de glace, en-glacer. Les François le devroyent suivre en telles compositions, pourveu qu'elles fussent bien reiglées, & proprement faites.

It would be vain, Ronsard says a year or two later, to regard the classical languages as still naturally capable of giving rise to such neologisms:

> Ausquelles langues mortes il n'est licite de rien innover, disgraciees du temps, sans appuy d'Empereurs, ny de Roys, de Magistrats ny de villes, comme chose morte, laquelle s'est perdue par le fil des ans, ainsi que font toutes choses humaines, qui perissent vieilles, pour faire place aux autres suivantes & nouvelles. . . .

That constitutes no reason, in Ronsard's view, for supposing that the natural forces that once made the classical tongues so responsive to the need for linguistic innovation are unable to operate with equal power in the modern languages (XVI, 349 f.). For ancient Cybele, the Great Mother, whose domination extends throughout Nature's realm, will not deny the centuries that are to be the sustenance upon which the great literary ages of the past have been nourished (*ibid.*, 355).

Multa Renascentur Quae Jam Cecidere . . . Vocabula [17]

But the power of innovation, encouraged though it be by the benevolent collusion of quickening Nature, does not exhaust the instrumentalities that she places in the hands of poets. The innovations of yesterday may, with the passage of time and the gradual deposit of ineffably subtle associations, have become the precious archaisms of today. This appears to have been Du Bellay's thought when he wrote:

> Quand au reste,[18] use de motz purement francoys, non toutesfois trop communs, non point aussi trop inusitez, si tu ne voulois quelquefois usurper,[19] et quasi comme enchasser ainsi qu'une pierre precieuse et rare, quelques motz antiques en ton poëme. . . . Pour ce faire, te faudroit voir tous ces vieux romans et poëtes françoys, ou tu trouveras un . . . *anuyter* pour *faire nuyt, assener* pour *frapper ou on visoit* . . . et mil' autres bons motz, que nous avons perduz par notre negligence. Ne doute point que le moderé usaige de telz vocables ne donne grande majesté tant au vers comme à la prose. . . .[20]

The same ideas appear with some nuances several years later in Peletier's *Art poëtique* (1555), but he must have been turning them over in his mind since 1541 at least, when he made his translation of Horace's theory of poetry. Peletier advocates moderation and aesthetic discrimination in the use of archaic words:

> Il ne sera defendu de ramener quelquefois les motz anciens. Comme aderdre, pour aderer, dont use souvent Jean de Meung: heberger, pour loger: ost, pour une armee: pourvu que nous y soyons rares. . . . Et principalement seront bien apliquez, quand nous ferons parler quelque personnage du vieus tans François. Et pensons qu'il n'est mot si rude, qui ne trouve sa place, si nous prenons l'avis de le bien coloquer.[21]

That Ronsard shared the opinions of Du Bellay and Peletier on the value of introducing old French words into poetry will be abundantly clear in the sequel from observations that he made in 1559 and in succeeding years. But as early as 1550, his first commentator, Jean Martin, author of the *Breve exposition de quelques passages du premier livre des Odes de Pierre de Ronsard*, glossing verse 107 in the ode *A Jouachim du Bellai Angevin*, wrote as follows:

> *Beante en eus s'émerveilla*) Beante signifie autant que inhians en latin . . . & bien que ce soit un vocable antique,[22] & peu familier aus oreilles Françoises . . . il n'est pas pourtant à refuser, mais à louer, d'autant que nous n'avons un seul vocable (hors lui) propre pour desseiner telle affection. Avienne, ô bons Dieus, que quelque hardi poëte remette en usage les vieus mots François, lesquels furent nostres, & que nous avons cruellement chassés, pour donner place à ne sçai quels étrangers Italiens, & Latins. (II, 208 f.)

In these words, which may have been inspired by conversation with Ronsard or by reading of the *Deffence*, Jean Martin expressed one of the constant theoretical positions of the group of poets who were to become known as the Pléiade.

This point of view was not imposed without a struggle, a struggle that was part of the general literary conflict from which French poetry emerged with a definitively classical substance and orientation. Ronsard writes in 1559 of the "grand travail" that this effort had cost him in the early days, and of the moral courage required to stand in opposition to the "tourbe ignorante" (X, 20 f.). In spite of their defamatory zeal in rending his good name,[23] he says,

> Je fis des mots nouveaux, je restauray les vieux,
> Bien peu me souciant du vulgaire envyeux,

> Medisant, ignorant, qui depuis a fait conte
> De mes vers, qu'au premier il me tournoit à honte.
>
> (X, 21 f.)

By 1563, the slanders were coming from a different direction. The opposition now was not so much literary as politico-religious. In reply to the "injures et calomnies, de je ne sçay quels Predicans, & Ministres de Geneve," Ronsard wrote a new apology of his laborious poetic life in which some of the terms remained almost identical with those of the old:

> Je vy que des François le langage trop bas
> Se trainoit sans vertu, sans ordre, ny compas:
> Adonques pour hausser ma langue maternelle,
> Indonté du labeur, je travaillé pour elle,
> Je fis des mots nouveaux, je rapellay les vieux:
> Si bien que son renon je poussay jusqu'aux cieux. . . .
>
> (XI, 167)

In his *Art poëtique* of 1565, Ronsard reduced to theory the practice which he here describes in general language. Foremost among the sources upon which the poet must draw for his archaic words are the old romances of the Middle Ages: "Tu ne rejetteras point les vieux motz de noz Romans,[24] ains les choisiras avecques meure & prudente election" (XIV, 9 f.). Twenty years later, in his last remarks "touchant le Poëme Heroïque," he gave what he believed to be very practical advice in the hope that it would augment the lexical resources of novices in epic poetry: "Encore vaudroit il mieux, comme un bon Bourgeois ou Citoyen, rechercher & faire un Lexicon des vieils mots d'Artus, Lancelot, & Gauvain, ou commenter le Romant de la Rose, que s'amuser à je ne sçay quelle Grammaire Latine qui a passé son temps" (XVI, 352).

In extolling the aesthetic advantages of the archaism, Ronsard had, of course, no exclusive preference for the vocabulary of the old romances. These are not mentioned in a number of passages in which the claims for antiquated words are advanced. Thus, in another section of the *Art poëtique*, he wrote: "Tu ne dedaigneras les vieux motz François, d'autant que je les estime tousjours en vigueur, quoy qu'on die, jusques à ce qu'ilz ayent faict renaistre en leur place, comme une vieille souche, un rejetton . . ." (XIV, 33). The *Caprice à Nicolas*, which echoes similar verses of 1559 and 1563, merely says:

> Promeine-toy dans les plaines Attiques,
> Fay nouveaux mots, r'appelle les antiques. . . .
>
> (*LL.*, VI, 64)

And in a curious note to the first posthumous edition, whose thought and phraseology leave little doubt as to its authenticity, Ronsard commented as follows upon an old French word introduced for the first time in 1587 into the third book of the *Franciade*, at v. 251: "*Mehaigne*, perclus . . . Nos critiques se moqueront de ce vieil mot françois: mais il les faut laisser caqueter. Au contraire, je suis d'opinion que nous devons retenir les vieux vocables significatifs, jusques à tant que l'usage en aura forgé d'autres nouveaux en leur place" (XVI, 184). Finally, not long before or after the composition of this note, the poet wrote to the "lecteur apprentif" of the third preface of his epic: " . . . Je t'advertis de ne faire conscience de remettre en usage les antiques vocables . . . " (XVI, 348), a passage who primary intention, as the sequel reveals, was the preservation of ancient dialectal terms in danger of extinction.

Ferdinand Brunot, reflecting on the influence of the reforms to which Ronsard had so greatly contributed, did not overstate the case when he said: "L'effet de paroles tombées de si haut fut immense." [25] To the extent that Ronsard's archaizing tendency was concerned, his voice, if not his authority, was faithfully transmitted to the following century by one of the few poets who approach him in stature. In the preface "Aux lecteurs" to *Les Tragiques*, D'Aubigné, who regarded Ronsard as "par dessus son siecle en sa profession," recalls, in 1616, the substance of a number of conversations with the great poet [26] in which he and others participated. Ronsard told his interlocutors,

> Mes enfans, deffendez vostre mere de ceux qui veulent faire servante une Damoiselle de bonne maison. Il y a des vocables qui sont françois naturels, qui sentent le vieux, mais le libre françois, comme *dougé, tenuë, empour, dorne, bauger, bouger,* et autres de telle sorte. Je vous recommande par testament que vous ne laissiez point perdre ces vieux termes, que vous les employiez et defendiez hardiment contre des maraux qui ne tiennent pas elegant ce qui n'est point escorché du latin et de l'italien, et qui aiment mieux dire *collauder, contemuer* [sic],[27] *blasonner* que *louër, mespriser, blasmer:* tout cela est pour l'escholier de Limosin.

And D'Aubigné adds, "Voila les propres termes de Ronsard." [28] Few will be inclined to doubt the word of this man of integrity, who did not allow his religious opinions to becloud his poetic judgment as so many of his Protestant and Catholic contemporaries did. But the exactness of D'Aubigné's report of the discussions at Boncourt is to some extent attested by the "propres termes" of Ronsard both in the *Art poëtique* and in the last preface to the *Franciade*. That the poet in both of these writings argued the advantage of saving from destruction some of the archaic vocabulary of France we have amply seen in the preceding pages. There are, in addition, passages in these two prose works which anticipate the terms and tonality of the language of exhortation that D'Aubigné attributes to Ronsard. In the *Art poëtique*, for example, one reads,

> Quiconques furent less premiers qui oserent abandonner la langue des anciens pour honorer celle de leur païs, ilz furent veritablement bons enfans & non ingratz citoyens, & dignes d'estre couronnez sur une statue publicque, & que d'aage en aage on face une perpetuelle memoire d'eux & de leurs vertus. (XIV, 14)

The resemblance to D'Aubigné's account is even more remarkable in the posthumous preface to the *Franciade*. The Protestant poet's observations have, as he says, a testamentary character which is in striking harmony with the following words that may well have been written in the very garden of the Collège de Boncourt where D'Aubigné heard Ronsard express identical thoughts:

> Je supplie tres-humblement ceux, ausquels les Muses ont inspiré leur faveur de n'estre plus Latineurs ny Grecaniseurs comme ils sont, plus par ostentation que par devoir: & prendre pitié, comme bons enfans de leur pauvre mere naturelle: ils en rapporteront plus d'honneur & de reputation à l'advenir. . . . (XVI, 352)

The ultimate fortune of Ronsard's archaizing effort probably did not correspond with his intentions and hopes, any more than it did in English literature with the intentions and hopes of Edmund Spenser, who in this respect, as in some others, may have been greatly in the debt of the Pléiade. The life of language being what it is, there must be a very large element of truth in the assertion of Brunot: "En fait, la tentative des archaïsants a complètement avorté. Des mots dont on a voulu prolonger la vie, presque aucun n'a vécu." [29] It could scarcely have been otherwise. The whole tendency of Ronsard's stylistic evolution, as the variants testify countless times, was towards the classicism of the following century. In affirming, from the beginning to the end of his poetic career, his constant adherence to an archaizing principle, Ronsard's theory was in direct opposition to his underlying practice. The retention of quaint and obsolescent terms, or their introduction into this or that composition quite at the end of his life, was a tribute that his sentiment paid to the language and vocabulary into which he had been born, a vocabulary that was doomed by the inexorable movement of time and social change, but whose death he could not bear to witness.[30]

1. References unaccompanied by any letters (e.g., XVI, 354) are to Pierre de Ronsard, Œuvres complètes, critical edition by Paul Laumonier (Paris: Société des Textes Français Modernes, 1914——); those preceded by LL. are to the Laumonier (Lemerre) edition (Paris, 1914-19) of the text of 1584.

2. Deffence et illustration de la Langue Francoyse, ed. Henri Chamard (Paris, 1904), pp. 66 f; cf. p. 110: "Je ne veux alleguer en cet endroict . . . la simplicité de notz majeurs, qui se sont contentez d'exprimer leurs conceptions avecques paroles nues, sans art et ornement . . ."; see also p. 191.

3. From the preface, addressed to Christofle Perot, to the first edition, dated July 27, 1541, of Peletier's translation of the Ars Poetica of Horace. See Bernard Weinberg, "La première édition de la traduction d'Horace par

Jacques Peletier," *Bibliothèque d'Humanisme et Renaissance*, XIV (1952), 297.

4. Henri Chamard, *Histoire de la Pléiade* (4 vols.; Paris, 1939-40), I, 78-79, 94.

5. See F. Letessier, "Jacques Peletier du Mans, auteur de néologismes," *Français moderne*, XII (1944), 206.

6. André Boulanger, *L'Art poëtique de Jacques Peletier du Mans* (1555), (Paris, 1930), pp. 231-32; the two strophes are quoted from Peletier's *A un poëte qui n'escrivoit qu'en Latin*, reproduced from *Les Œuvres poëtiques de Jacques Peletier du Mans* (Paris, 1547). It is significant that the first publications of both Ronsard and Du Bellay appeared in this volume: *Ode de Pierre de Ronsart à Jacques Peletier, Des beautez qu'il voudroit en s'amie*, fol. 79 verso; *J. Dubellay à la ville du Mans*, fol. 103 verso (see Laumonier, *op. cit.*, I, 3, *appar. crit.*; Chamard, *Joachim du Bellay: Œuvres poetiques* (Paris, 1923), V, 235, *appar. crit.*).

7. *Le Seizième siècle* (*Histoire de la langue française des origines à 1900*, II [3rd ed.; Paris, 1947]), 1-91; see the summary of these pages by Chamard, *Histoire de la Pléiade*, I, 172-77. There is a good general discussion in Henri Weber, *La Création poétique au XVI° siècle en France* (Paris, 1956), I, 138-42, under the subheading "Langue savante et langue populaire." As early as 1894, in the first number of the *Revue d'histoire littéraire de la France* (1904), 27-38, Brunot had published an article entitled "Un projet d' 'enrichir, magnifier et publier' la langue française en 1509," which analyzes the "Prologue de messire Claude de Seyssel . . . en la translation de Justin . . ." and describes it as a "véritable plaidoyer en faveur de la langue française" (p. 27). More recent publications that relate to this subject are those of Mme. F. Cogan-Bernstein, "La Lutte pour la langue nationale dans l'humanisme français," *Recherches soviétiques*, No. 4 (May-June, 1956); Robert E. Hallowell, "Jean Le Blond's Defense of the French Language," *Romanic Review*, LI (1960), 86-92. I have not seen Mme. Cogan-Bernstein's study.

8. *Les Sources italiennes de la "Deffense et illustration de la langue françoise" de Joachim du Bellay* (Paris, 1908).

9. Many of the parallel passages are reproduced also in Chamard's edition of the *Deffence* for the Société des Textes Français Modernes (Paris, 1948), *passim*.

10. Paul Laumonier, *Ronsard poète lyrique* (Paris, 1923^2), p. 56.

11. *Ibid.*, I, 237.

12. "Epistre envoyée par Clement Marot à Monsieur Danguyen," in Marot, *Oeuvres complètes*, ed. Pierre Jannet (Paris, 1868), I, 71-73.

13. *Deffence*, pp. 68, 73.

14. See L. Terreaux, "A propos du vocabulaire de Ronsard," *Le Français moderne*, XXIX (1961), 112-20, for many examples of the poet's abandonment of archaic and erudite expressions, as well as of certain neologisms.

15. VII, 172, n. 4.

16. *LL.*, VI, 64; and cf. p. 62, "Bien que l'envie. . . . "

17. Horace, *Ars poetica*, 70 f.

18. In the preceding passage, Du Bellay has discussed the invention and adoption of words and the creation of compound words in imitation of Greek.

19. "Faire usage de, s'approprier," *Deffence*, p. 252, n. 1.

20. *Deffence*, pp. 256 ff.; cf. Joachim du Bellay, *Oeuvres poétiques*, ed. Henri Chamard (Paris, 1931), VI, 252.

21. Peletier, *op. cit.*, pp. 121 f. Peletier's orthography has been slightly modified to make it more consistent with normal sixteenth-century practice.

22. "C.-à-d. un archaïsme français," note by Laumonier.

23. See Marty-Laveaux, *La Langue de la Pléiade* (2 vols.; Paris, 1896–98), Introduction, I, 9 ff.; Chamard, *Histoire de la Pléiade*, I, 362 f.

24. In 1579, Henri Estienne will adopt a position analogous to that of Ronsard, but will reveal that the resistance to the introduction of archaisms is far from dead: " . . . Je puis accomparer tant de Rommans anciens qu'ha nostre langage, à un . . . chasteau: et les beaux vocables et beaux traits que nous y trouvons, aux beaux membres qu'on trouve en cest edifice, encore qu'il soit à la façon antique. Et . . . je sçay bien que les louanges que je donneray à ce vieil langage, seront subjectes à preuve, à cause que plusieurs le mesprisent. . . . "—*La Précellence du langage François*, ed. Edmond Huguet (Paris, 1896), p. 184.

25. Brunot, *Histoire de la langue française*, II, 171.

26. Pierre de Nolhac, *Ronsard et l'humanisme* (Paris, 1921), p. 238, conjectures plausibly that these conversations with the aging Ronsard took place in the garden of the Collège de Boncourt: "Tous l'entouraient, quand il faisait sa promenade quotidienne dans le jardin du collège, devenu, dit l'un d'eux, un véritable jardin d'Académus. On a trop peu recueilli de cette parole vive et savoureuse, qui instruisait et charmait ce dernier auditoire. Le poète enseignait l'amour de la langue française, à l'aide de ces brillantes images qui ont tant frappé Agrippa d'Aubigné; il traitait volontiers de la théorie de son art et de la technique du vers. . . . "

27. Read *contemner*.

28. Agrippa d'Aubigné, *Les Tragiques*, éd. crit. avec Introduction et comm. par A. Garnier et J. Plattard (Paris, 1932), I, 7 f.

29. Brunot, *Histoire de la langue française*, II, 186.

30. In a discussion of the neologisms, compound words, and archaisms of the Berlin and Paris manuscripts of Books I and II of the *Franciade*, Raymond Lebègue has said: "Tant que nous ne posséderons pas une étude chronologique et méthodique du vocabulaire de Ronsard, la langue poétique du XVIe siècle sera pour nous un domaine clos. Cette étude, l'achèvement de la grande édition Laumonier va permettre de l'entreprendre. D'ores et déjà, la publication de la *Franciade*, avec ses innombrables corrections de forme,

fournit de précieux matériaux. En composant ce poème, Ronsard s'est efforcé d'introduire dans notre littérature le vocabulaire et le style épiques de ses modèles antiques; mais les variantes témoignent de ses hésitations et de ses repentirs."—"Ronsard au travail," *Lettres d'Humanité*, XI (1952), 85. The base for the systematic study of Ronsard's vocabulary is being created by Professor A. Emerson Creore of the University of Washington, who, in September, 1962, produced through the facilities of the Research Computer Laboratory of that institution a word index to Volumes I and II of Paul Laumonier's critical edition of Ronsard as a first step in the ultimate creation of a comprehensive lexicon of the poet.

―――――*W. L. Wiley*―――――

Montaigne's Later Latin Borrowings

ONE OF THE delights for any student of Montaigne is to observe the many paradoxes in the compositions of the *gentilhomme* from Bordeaux. He speaks constantly of his poor memory, and then proceeds to quote at length from Greek, Roman, and Continental writers. He berates the reading of books, but managed to accumulate one of the finest private libraries of his day. He minimizes in his *Essais*[1] the value of factual knowledge (the counting of the number of steps in the *Santa Rotonda* [I, xxvi], for example), but will himself give details on the life of an ancient general or recite the method by which Cicero got rid of his kidney stones (II, xxxvii).

Montaigne rather constantly opposed the program of instruction in the schools of his day, with its emphasis on Latin; yet he had gained under the system, supplemented by private tutoring, a profound knowledge of the Latin language and literature, all of which he made good use of in his writings. It is with Montaigne's later interest in Roman authors, toward the end of his career, that this paper is concerned.

Some of Montaigne's most pungent remarks were directed against the study of Latin and those who taught it. One of his most spirited attacks is found in the essay *De la Praesumption*

(II, xvii), where he says: "Je retombe volontiers sur ce discours de l'ineptie de notre institution. Elle a eu pour sa fin de nous faire non bons et sages, mais sçavans: elle y est arrivée. Elle ne nous a pas apris de suivre et embrasser la vertu et la prudence, mais elle nous en a imprimé la derivation et l'etymologie. Nous sçavons decliner Vertu, si nous ne sçavons l'aymer. . . . " In the famous essay *De l'Institution des enfans* (I, xxvi), Montaigne has no patience with these *latineurs de collège*, youngsters who have spent too much time at the age of sixteen inside a schoolroom and had too little contact with life outside. In the essay *Du Pédantisme* (I, xxv), Montaigne says that he would much rather have an *écolier* spend his time playing *à la paume* than stuffing his head with Greek and Roman authorities; and he tells Diane de Foix (I, xxvi), Comtesse de Gurson, in discussing her son not yet born: " . . . Je ne veux pas qu'on emprisonne cet enfant dans un collège," where he may learn some Greek and Latin but at a price that is *trop cher*.

One of the better known facts concerning Montaigne is his own statement that he learned Latin before he learned French, from a German tutor provided by his father, and he says (I, xxvi), "J'avois plus de six ans avant que j'entendisse plus de françois ou de perigordin que d'arabesque." This process of instruction was, in Montaigne's opinion—an opinion about which there would be little argument—a painless and solid way to learn Latin. His grounding in the language was so thorough that he later impressed with his knowledge scholars like Georges Buchanan, the transported Scotsman, and Marc-Antoine Muret. In view of such basic training in the language of Rome, and of his playing the "premiers personnages" in Latin tragedies during his sojourn at the Collège de Guyenne, it is one of Montaigne's paradoxes that he advised so strongly against Latin as a part of the education of a young gentleman in sixteenth-century France. It is also something of a paradox to note the somewhat jaundiced view that Montaigne took of many of the writers of ancient Rome.

The most casual thumbing-through of any edition of Montaigne's essays will reveal that a considerable number of pages contain quotations in Latin, although he claims that he had along the way "lost his Latin"—"mais en cecy perdois je mon latin" (I,xxv)—in order not to appear too much like a pedant. Also, it is Montaigne's contention (I, xxvi) that, if he were to fill his own writings up with material from the ancients, "j'engenderois des monstres, comme font les escrivains indiscrets de nostre siecle, qui, parmi leurs ouvrages de neant, vont semant des lieux entiers des anciens autheurs pour se faire honneur de ce larrecin. . . . " Writers in this category, as a result of their petty thievery from antiquity, end up by losing more than they gain. Their own opinions and sentiments come forth only as dull reflections of the Greek and Roman authors that are quoted. Montaigne gives sharp expression to this point of view in the essay, *Du Pédantisme* (I, xxv):

> Nous sçavons dire: "Cicero dit ainsi, voilà l'opinion de Platon, ce sont les mots mesmes d'Aristote"; mais nous, que disons nous nous mesmes? qu'opinons nous? que jugeons nous? Autant en feroit bien un perroquet.

Nevertheless, as is most obvious, Montaigne's own writings were liberally seasoned with the spices of ancient authorities, though he scarcely ended up by being a parrot of antique sources.

The last edition of Montaigne's essays brought out during his lifetime was that of 1588. He continued to make revisions in his compositions until his death in 1592, and the scribblings he made on the printed text of an example of the 1588 edition (the famous Bordeaux copy) formed the basis of changes in the posthumous 1595 edition of the *Essais*. The continued inclination on the part of Montaigne, between 1588 and 1592, to add to his essays Latin quotations and references from the ancient world show that he was not worried about any inconsistency of attitude.

Before looking at the final changes made by Montaigne in his commentaries on man and the world around him, it might be well to look at the great essayist's earlier concepts of the ancients. He was not always too greatly impressed by them, nor with those who based their own conclusions too quickly upon what some Greek or Roman writer may have said. He once knew, says Montaigne (I, xxvi), in Pisa "un honneste homme, mais si aristotelicien que le plus general de ses dogmes est: que la touche et la reigle de toutes imaginations solides et de toute vérité, c'est la conformité à la doctrine d'Aristote. . . ." This point of view is wrong, to Montaigne's way of thinking, because it substitutes the authority of Aristotle's name for the basic truth of what he might have stated. In his own case, Montaigne says, he relied chiefly (II, x), "a renger mes humeurs et mes conditions," on Plutarch and Seneca from the ancients. Since he knew no Greek—"je n'entends rien au grec," he says in the essay *A demain les affaires*—he gained his knowledge of Plutarch from the French translation of Jacques Amyot, who lifted "nous autres ignorans" out of the mud of linguistic inadequacy (II, iv). In the matter of Latin poetry, Montaigne feels that Vergil, Lucretius, Catullus, and

Horace are of the first rank, and that (II, x) "les bons et anciens poëtes ont évité l'affectation et la recherche" of more modern writers.

The *gentilhomme* from Bordeaux has a great deal to say about Cicero in the last of the editions of his essays brought out during his lifetime. His admiration for the great master of Latin prose is distinctly under control. In the essay *Des Livres* (II, x), the following rather scathing estimate is given of Cicero:

> Quant à Cicero, les ouvrages qui me peuvent servir chez luy à mon desseing, ce sont ceux qui traitent des meurs et reigles de nostre vie. Mais, à confesser hardiment la verité (car, puis qu'on a franchi les barrieres de l'impudence, il n'y a plus de bride), sa façon d'escrire me semble lasche et ennuyeuse, et toute autre pareille façon: car ses prefaces, digressions, definitions, partitions, etymologies, consument la plus part de son ouvrage; ce qu'il y a de vif et de mouelle est estouffé par la longueur de ses apprets. Si j'ay employé une heure à le lire, qui est beaucoup pour moy, et que je r'amentoive ce que j'en ay tiré de suc et de substance, la plus part du temps je n'y treuve que du vent: car il n'est pas encore venu aux argumens qui servent à son propos, et aux raisons qui touchent proprement le neud que je cherche. Pour moy, qui ne demande que à devenir plus sage, non plus sçavant, ces ordonnances logiciennes et aristoteliques ne sont pas à propos.

Montaigne comes back to Cicero in this same essay, with the conclusion that there is not "beaucoup d'excellence en luy," though much "lascheté" and "vanité." As for the poetry that Cicero wrote, he should never have had the audacity to bring it out into the light of day. After all this derogatory appraisal, however, Montaigne makes another of his surprising reverses and concedes that in the matter of "eloquence," Cicero is completely beyond comparison—and "je croy que jamais homme ne l'egalera." Nevertheless, in the judgment of Montaigne, Caesar is much superior to Cicero (II, x).

Between 1588 and 1592, Montaigne, in his last days, returned to many things Roman, despite the disparaging remarks he had made earlier in his life about the Latin language and many Latin writers. The 1595 edition reflects this belated allegiance to his first "mother tongue." One noticeable feature is that Montaigne replaced at this time a number of words in his essays with other words of a more distinctly Latin sound or origin. For example, in the essay *Par divers moyens on arrive à pareille fin* (I, i), the phrase "vers la misericorde et le pardon" became in 1595 "vers la misericorde et *mansuétude*," where *mansuétude* is a rather more formalized Latinism. In the same essay, with a slight change in the 1588 phrasing, the word *pitié* evolved into the more polysyllabic *commisération* in the 1595 edition. A similar replacement was made in 1595 when in the essay *Nos affections s'emportent au delà de nous* (I, iii), *fille* became *pucelle*. In like manner, in the 1595 edition, *allongement* became *prolongation* (I, xix), "le meilleur *tiltre*" (I, xxiii) became "le meilleur *prétexte*," and "sous quel *tiltre*" (I, xxiii) became "sous quelle *enseigne*." In *Du Pédantisme* (I, xxv), the combination "*amende* son premier estat imparfaict" was replaced in 1595 by the more Latinized "*méliore* son estat imparfaict." In the essay *Considération sur Cicéron* (I, xl)— which paradoxically, has very little to say about Cicero—the 1595 edition has *commission* substituted for *charge*, and in the long essay *Apologie de Raimond Sebond* (II, xii), "de pareille *façon*" became "de pareille *témérité*." A final citation of a shift in the 1595 edition toward words of more complicated Latin derivation comes from the essay *Defence de Seneque et de Plutarque* (II, xxxii): "de *malice* et faucété" was lengthened to "de *prevarication* et faucété." These examples are in no sense a complete list of Montaigne's substitutions of a more Latinized vocabulary in the final correction of his essays during his lifetime. However, they do show that in his last years he turned back toward the speech he learned before the age of six.

The most striking feature of Montaigne's handwritten changes in the 1588 edition of his essays is the further addition of references to Greek and Roman authors and quotations from them. Among the Latin writers quoted—there is seldom any quotation in Greek because of Montaigne's admitted deficiency in that language—are, in the order of their appearance in the 1595 edition of the essays, Seneca, Ennius, Cicero, Pacuvius, Vergil, Livy, Sallust, Tertullian, Horace, Lucan, Quintilian, Martial, Lucretius, Ovid, Tacitus, Catullus, Propertius, Terence, Lucilius, and Perseus. From the Bible or the church fathers, excerpts are given (in Latin) from Saint Augustine, Saint Peter, Saint Paul, and Saint Jerome. It is mildly surprising, in view of statements made about him in the body of the *Essais*, to note the Roman most often mentioned and used by Montaigne in his last years: that writer is Cicero.

The works of Cicero are by far the most frequently quoted of any corpus of Latin material in the 1595 additions to and modifications of the *Essais*. In the altered version, done in Montaigne's own hand after 1588, added quotations from Cicero reach the rather amazing number of 131. This is, if anything, a conservative counting because it does not include lines from Cicero quoted by some other Latin writer and then used by Montaigne. The next Latin author in favor with Montaigne toward the end of his life was the younger Seneca, who appears some fifty-five additional times in the 1595 edition. The third in order among the Latin authorities used by Montaigne in his last revisions was the historian Livy—an expected type of borrowing since Montaigne had said in his essay *Des Livres* that the chroniclers of history were really his *gibier*. Livy, in any case, is quoted in the 1595 edition some thirty-one additional times. The other writers listed above are quoted from one to, possibly, a half-dozen times.

Some examples might be noted of the type of ancient material Montaigne wanted to put into the last draft of his essays. In *Nos affections s'emportent au delà de nous* (I, iii), the point is made that funereal pomp is primarily for the living, not the deceased. Additional support for this idea was given by quotations in the 1595 edition from Cicero and Saint Augustine. From the *Tusculanae Disputationes*, I, 45, comes "Totus hic locus est contemnendus in nobis, non negligendus in nostris"; and from Saint Augustine's *De Civitate Deo*, I, 12, "curatio funeris, conditio sepulturae, pompa exequiarum, magis sunt vivorum solatia quam subsidia mortuorum," an apt phrasing of the general theme.

In the essay *L'Heure des parlemens dangeureuse* (I, vi), many Latin excerpts are added to the 1595 edition, including one from Cicero's *De Officiis*, III, 17, to show that one person should not profit from another's stupidity. Cicero is employed again in the 1595 edition in the discussion of oracles (I, ix) and of auguries (I, xi), and to show that people are willing to die for their beliefs (I, xiv). In this same essay (I, xiv) is found a good description of the brittleness of luck; in the 1595 edition a neat quotation from Sallust is added to the effect that man is the architect of his own fortune—"faber est suae quisque fortunae." Horace is brought in quite delightfully (I, xvii) in the 1595 edition to illustrate the fact that many persons like to be experts in lines other than their own: "optat ephippia bos piger, optat arare caballus"—*Epistles*, I, xiv, 43.

Some typical examples of the use of Seneca in the 1595 edition might also be indicated: in the essay *Que philosopher, c'est apprendre à mourir* (I, xx), Seneca is quoted (*Epistles*, 91) on the fragility of human life; in the essay *De la Coustume, et de changer aisément une loi receüe* (I, xxiii), Seneca is used to prove that trust in an evil man only gives him an opportunity to do wrong (*Oedipus*, III, 686); in *Du Pédantisme* (I, xxv), Seneca is employed to show that our education is aimed at success in school rather than in the world (*Epistles*, 106); and in the famous essay *De l'Institution des enfans* (I, xxvi), Seneca is brought forth in opposition to a blind following of authority—"non sumus sub rege, sibi quisque se vindicet" (*Epistles*, 33); and in the same essay Seneca is adduced to support the idea that there is a great difference between not wishing to do evil and not knowing how to do evil (*Epistles*, 90).

The most extensive additions taken from Livy for the 1595 edition are to be found in the essay *Des Destriers* (I, xlviii), where some seven excerpts are included from the Latin historian on, among other matters, the ancients' use of horses, cavalry maneuvers, and reactions to certain types of wounds. Two of these excerpts are quite long, but they describe incidents rather than give expression to philosophical opinion.

Cicero is used in the 1595 edition as a support for a great variety of subjects. To his longest essay, *Apologie de Raimond Sebond* (II, xii), Montaigne adds in the 1595 edition several lines from Cicero on the inadvisability of giving wine to sick persons because of the possibility that they may become addicted to it (*De Natura Deorum*, III, 27). Cicero is quoted further along in the same essay, 1595 edition, on the nature of life's pleasures (*Tusculanae Disputationes*, II, 14); and still further on in *Apologie de Raimond Sebond*, on the attributes of the gods (*De Natura Deorum*, II, 28) and the nature of man's soul (*Tusculanae Disputationes*, I, 28). In the good essay, *De la Gloire* (II, xvi), Montaigne regrets that Cicero's treatment of the subject of glory has been lost; and in the 1595 version of the essay, he adds five quotations from Cicero to bulwark his own concepts of personal honor and glory. In *Des Coches* (III, vi), Cicero is brought in in the last version to show the many centuries and spheres that man has yet to discover (*De Natura Deorum*, I, 20). Concluding citations from the vast number of Montaigne's later borrowings from Cicero might be taken from the essay *De la Vanité* (III, ix): "Hoc ipsum ita justum est quod recte fit, si est voluntarium" (*De Officiis*, I, 9); and "Est prudentis sustinere, ut cursum, sic impetum benevolentiae" (*De Amicitia*). Montaigne took out a French phrase in order to include in his last revision this final quotation from Cicero: "It is best to hold back, even as though you were running a race, too impetuous effusions of friendship."

Montaigne said along the way (II, xvii): "Quant au latin, qui m'a esté donné pour maternel, j'ay perdu par desaccoutumance la promptitude de m'en pouvoir servir à parler."

One is permitted to wonder whether, with his inclination toward minimizing and paradoxical shifts, Montaigne was telling the exact truth about his loss of Latin as a spoken language. There is no doubt, as his later borrowings show, that he continued to read it and remember it to the end of his life. Some authors, like Cicero, whom he maligned at an earlier moment, came back to him strongly at the end of his days. This change of attitude would not have worried him in the least, since consistency—as was the case with another great essayist—was something he did not bother about at all.

1. The edition that has been employed here is *Les Essais de Montaigne*, publiés d'après l'édition de 1588 avec les variantes de 1595 . . . , par. H. Motheau et D. Jouaust (7 vols.; Paris, s.d.). This edition has provided easy comparison of the 1588 and 1595 versions of the *Essais*. I have followed the text and spellings as they have appeared in this printing.

The Coins in Rabelais

FOR A MAN who cast a sometimes bemused, sometimes caustic, eye on literally all the activities of his fellow mortals, both living and dead, it is not surprising to discover that Rabelais interspersed his writings, from time to time, with references to mankind's most common means of conducting commerce, to wit, his coins.[1] Following the pattern of his passion for learning in general, he allowed his monetary interests to range exuberantly through many epochs and many lands. In order to examine his references chronologically, we begin with currency associated with the classical world.

The first and perhaps the most exotic of these coins is the *besant*. This gold piece, originally called a *solidus*, was first minted for Constantine the Great. It endured as an important element in the currency of the eastern Roman empire until its collapse. However, the coin persisted much longer in western Europe where, because of its association with the Byzantine civilization, it became known as the *bezant* or *byzant*.[2] Rabelais writes of it in Book I during the scene of the banquet offered by Grandgousier to the victorious Gargantuans after the Pichrocolian war. The elated host, in an excess of joy, gives his guest the very ornaments of his sideboard which weighed "dis huyt cent mille quatorze bezans d'or." [3]

An original Roman coin which is associated with a celebrated classical anecdote is the *sesterce*. During the description of the temple of the priestess Bacbuc, Rabelais has occasion to mention the famous repast given by Cleopatra for Anthony when she dissolved one of her priceless pearl earrings in vinegar and water and then swallowed the concoction. Rabelais estimated that the pair of pearls was valued at many *sesterces*.[4] This coin was first minted as a small Roman silver piece which bore on its obverse side the head of Minerva. Under the Empire, it was struck in bronze and it is no doubt this coin to which reference is made here.[5]

The *talent d'or* which is often treated as a coin was never really a minted piece at all but rather a measure of weight used in metrology. The Roman talent was a money of account. However, the name was frequently applied to coins.[6] Rabelais puts the word into the mouth of Dindenault during his hearty verbal exchange with Panurge over the suitable price for a sheep. He claims, with considerable exasperation, that the finest of these animals would have commanded a talent d'or in the old days.[7]

The final piece of currency affiliated with the ancient world that is mentioned by Rabelais is the *shekel* or *sicle*. In the prologue to Book V, as he mocks himself and his art, the author observes that "a l'edification du temple de Salomon chacun un sicle d'or offrir, a plaines poignees, ne pouvoit." [8] The *sicle* is the term utilized by the French for the *siglos*. Originally this was the name for the early Persian skekel which was of gold and was known popularly as the "archer" because of the representation of a bowman on the obverse side. The

Jewish shekel to which Rabelais makes allusion in the above passage was similar to the Persian coin in name only. Since, in Biblical times, the shekel was, in all probability, a unit of weight before it became an actual coin, the reference to it made by the author would likely mean a certain weight of precious metal rather than a minted piece.[9]

Moving from the currency of classical times to that of an epoch nearer to Rabelais' own, we discover types of coins which reflect, in part, an unhappy segment of French history: the English occupation which terminated with the appearance of Jeanne d'Arc. Very shortly after her victories and the departure of the enemy from the greater part of French soil, the money which had been issued in France under English sponsorship was *décrié*. Curiously enough, however, it gained a new lease on life for literary purposes, as can be witnessed in the poetry of Villon, where this valueless money became a kind of satirical device for the representation of useless bequests bestowed on the poet's foes.[10] It is to be suspected that Rabelais often had a similar purpose in mind when he utilized these Anglo-Gallic coins.

The first of these, the *angelot*, was a gold coin, having as ancestors the English *angel*, first struck in 1470 by Edward IV, and the *angelet*, a coin of half its value. The name was derived from the figure of the archangel St. Michael who was represented on it in the act of slaying a dragon. The first angelot was struck by Henry VI in 1427. In a decree on July 12, 1436, after Henry's departure from France, Charles VII, the new French king, withdrew these Anglo-Gallic coins from circulation.[11] Under Louis XI (1461–1485), a new series of angelots appeared, issued to commemorate the foundation of the Order of St. Michael, but the most celebrated coins of that name were those of the ousted monarch.[12] This piece is found several times in Rabelais, notably during the confrontation of Panurge and Her Trippa. Among the gifts offered by Rabelais' hero to this sage are "cinquante beaulx angelotz," no doubt a quite valueless present.[13]

The *salut*, a gold coin, was minted by Henry V of England in 1422 by virtue of his authority as Regent of France. The obverse side of the coin depicted the Annunciation and the shields of France and England. Between the shields was the word *ave*.[14] This coin was also among those withdrawn from commerce by the order of July, 12, 1436. Rabelais mentions it frequently. One amusing occasion occurs after the banquet given by Homenaz for Pantagruel and his friends. The principal guest generously offers, in response to the hospitality, "neuf cent quatorze salutz d'or" to each of the serving girls as a dowry. Quite naturally a coin bearing such a design would augur well for the maternal prospects of these maidens.[15] However, since the money was long since *décrié* the good wishes rang somewhat ironically.

The *noble à la rose*, also a gold coin, is identified by some critics as being Anglo-Gallic.[16] It first appeared in 1344 during the reign of Edward III of England. Its name was said to come from the noble quality of the metal used in its minting, possessing as it did only one-half of a grain of alloy. Henry IV in 1412 reduced the quality of the coin, but Edward IV in 1465 restored it to its former weight. He also caused a rose to be stamped on each side of the piece to distinguish it from its predecessors.[17] He himself was of the house of York; but having placed a rose on both sides of the coin, he removed any stigma of discrimination against the house of Lancaster. The *nobles* that were *décriés* in 1436 were not *noble à la rose,* which were not struck, as we have seen, until 1465. The *noble à la rose* was a much imitated coin, variations of it being found in Burgundy, Austria, and the Low Countries. Rabelais makes mention of it during the discussion of the money to be paid for the construction of the Abbaye de Thélème. He writes: " . . . Pour la fondation et entretenement d'icelle donna à perpétuité vingt troys cent soixante neuf mille cinq cens quatorze nobles à la rose. . . . "[18]

Leaving money which was partially foreign, we move to examine coins cited by Rabelais which were totally alien on French soil. The first of these is the *ducat.* Probably the most celebrated of gold coins, it is believed to have been first issued by Roger II of Sicily about 1150. Its name arose from the final word of its inscription "Sit tibi Christe datus, quem tu regis iste ducatus." Virtually every European country copied this coin.[19] One of the occasions when it is mentioned by Rabelais occurs during Panurge's attempt to seduce the noble lady of Paris. He offers her, as a supreme inducement to yield to his wishes, cloth or ornaments up to the value of "cinquante mille ducatz."[20]

Another coin from the area of Italy mentioned by Rabelais is the *florin.* The first of these gold coins were said to have been made in the Republic of Florence in 1252. They bore the figure of St. John the Baptist on the obverse side and the lily and arms of the city on the other. The coin was much imitated abroad, and the Florentine lily which gave it its name was frequently replaced by armorial shields of the foreign country or the mintmaster.[21] Panurge, in the long catalogue of his accomplishments before his meeting with Pantagruel, mentions the coin when he says that he was able to feather his nest by means of "plus de six mille fleurins" acquired during the Crusades.[22]

Another coin of Italian origin was the *teston*, the name deriving from the portrait or *testa* of the monarch represented on it. As with so many coins from affluent Italy, this one was copied by other countries, among them France. As a consequence, the version of it that was, in all probability, known to Rabelais was the silver piece called a *teston* first issued by Louis XII of France in 1514.[23] One appearance of it in Rabelais occurs in the prologue to Book IV. Here the author has Couillatris exchange his silver hatchet for "beaux testons et aultre monnoye blanche." [24]

Of oriental origin is the *seraph*, a Turkish coin. Its name derives from the Arabic word *sharif* meaning "noble and glorious" that was given to the descendants of Mohammed through his daughter Fatima, and which also became the title of certain Arabic princes. In the countries where the Muslim faith was dominant, such as Turkey, Egypt, and the Barbary States, the coin was called the *sequin*, a word related to the Arabic sikka ("a coining die").[25] Rabelais referred to the coin several times, the most delightful occasion being during Panurge's account of his escape from the Turks, during which his rescuer, in despair over the failure of his special devils to prevent the burning of the house, begs Panurge to kill him. To accomplish this task, he offers the former prisoner a purse containing "six cens seraphz." [26]

A gold coin that bore a Flemish (Dutch) name was the *ridde* or *rider*, so called because it bore the figure of a knight on the obverse side. It was first minted by Philip the Good of Burgundy in 1433,[27] and was called a *cavalier* or *philippus* in

Burgundy proper. It was still allowed in legal commerce in France following the currency reforms of Charles VII. Like the teston, the ridde is mentioned by Rabelais in connection with the activities of Couillatris, who this time sells his golden hatchet for some "belles riddes" and other coins.[28]

The *malvedi*, as Rabelais describes it, was a Spanish coin of low value, the *maravedí*. Its origins were not so humble as its worth in his day would indicate, however. Its name is derived from the Almoravidian *dinar*, which was a gold piece introduced into Spain by the Moors. Sancho I of Portugal (1151–1211) was the first non-Arabic monarch to manufacture it as his own currency, in which issue he was represented on it in an equestrian pose. Alfonso VIII of Castile also minted a gold coin bearing the same name, on which the inscription was still in Arabic, though it was adapted to the title of that particular king.[29] From the fourteenth to the sixteenth centuries, the metal used in its manufacture gradually declined in value until the time of Philip II, who had it minted in copper.[30] Rabelais mentions it, in Book III, as the fantastic price, "600,000 malvedis," that was paid for a flea contained in the earring that Panurge had made for his newly pierced right ear.[31]

This brings us to coins of purely French origin. One of the most difficult of these to identify is the *pinard*. Sainéan claimed that it was a foreign piece originating in Italy.[32] Ste.-Palaye believed it to be the same as the "denier de cuivre," which was called *pinos* by the mountain people of the Haut Dauphiné and which the Italians called *pinatella*.[33] Frey speaks of a French coin called the *pignatelle*, a piece of base silver, which was originally struck in the sixteenth century.

Nor is the origin of the coin's name clear. Ste.-Palaye spoke of a coin called a *pinatelle* that was named after a mintmaster who was later hanged for producing false currency, but it appeared too late in the sixteenth century (1572) for Rabelais to have known it. Cotgrave recorded both terms, describing the pinard as "an exceedingly small piece of money" and the pinatelle as "a copper coin having small quantities of silver in it, worth about 5 liards." [34]

Rabelais writes of the pinard in a famous scene in Book II in which he describes the unusual behavior of celebrated men of the past as they wait in Limbo. Villon, for example, is observed in testy disagreement with Xerxes concerning the price of a "denrée de moustarde," and when the latter claims that it is worth a *denier*, a basic type of currency in billon or silver which had been known in western Europe since the time of Pepin the Short (the eighth century), the furious poet cries that "La blanchee n'en vault qu'un pinart!" [35]

The mention of *blanchee*, that is, "a *blanc*'s worth," provides a convenient entry into a discussion of that form of tender. It gained its title, of course, from the color of its refined silver, for when it was first struck, as the *blanc au K* in 1365, it was of the finest quality. It was usually distinguished by a cross, the inscription "Benedictum sit nomen Domini," and such symbols as suns, stars, and lilies. These symbols were frequently used to characterize different issues, and as the number of emissions was increased, the quality of the blanc deteriorated.[36] It is probably to the coins of Charles VIII and François I that Rabelais refers when he speaks, as he so often does, of *blancs*.

Sometimes Rabelais mentions a blanc that was also known as a *douzain*. This was the *grand blanc au soleil*, first issued by Louis XI in 1475, which was stipulated precisely as equaling twelve deniers, hence its name. There is, moreover, another special blanc, the *grand blanc à la couronne*, which also received a special name, the *onzain*, because it was worth eleven deniers. It came into existence by proclamation on January 4, 1474. It is mentioned only once by Rabelais, but this single instance occurs at a very crucial stage in Book I. It is the offer of this coin to one of the cake bakers of Lerne and his vigorous refusal of it that precipitates the Picrocholian Wars.[37]

The French coin designated as an *écu* dates from a gold piece of that name that was issued by Saint Louis in 1266. The coins that Rabelais had in mind when he mentioned the écu, however, were those modeled on the Italian *scudo*. Originally, it was a piece minted from the finest gold, but a silver écu appeared later on. Under Charles VII, a gold version of the coin known as the *écu à la couronne*, bearing a crowned shield, was issued in 1436; and in 1483, the *écu au soleil*, which had a sun impressed above the crowned shield, was manufactured. Both Louis XII and François I continued to mint this second type—indeed, it was the only gold currency authorized by the second of the two monarchs.[38]

In all likelihood, it was this type of coin that Rabelais had in mind when, for example, he enumerated the generous gifts bestowed by Grandgousier on his prisoner Toucquedillon.[39] On another occasion, he mentions a specific issue of this coin, that produced in the Bordeaux mint, the *escuz bourdeloys*, when he gives details on the price of an experiment conducted on roasted eggs.[40]

The *mouton* or *mouton à la laine*, a larger version of the coin known as the *agnel*, was issued by Philip IV in 1311. It was struck in France until the time of Charles VII,[41] but was, no doubt, nonexistent by Rabelais' day. One occasion when he speaks of this coin involves the magnificent ring commissioned for the middle finger of Gargantua's right hand. This ornament is said to have the value of "soixante-neuf millions huyt cens nonante et quatre mille dix et huyt moutons à la laine." [42]

The *royal*, also a gold coin, dates from the fourteenth century. Its name was derived from the picture that it bore of the king in royal robes, ensconced under a Gothic canopy or arch—a setting that resulted in the coin's also being called a *pavillon*.[43] Philip VI of Valois (1328–1350) issued a gold coin under this name, as did the Black Prince in his Anglo-Gallic series.

A coin of this name appears in Rabelais in the scene in Book II in which Panurge is given the office of "chastellenie de Salmiguondin." Among the supposed assets of this post is an annual income of "6,789,106,789 royaulx" [44]—an absurdity that was doubtless reinforced by the unavailability of such currency.

A coin that was worth very little when Rabelais' volumes began to appear was the *carolus*. It was struck by the Emperor Charles V (1519–55) and was of base silver or billon. It will be remembered that Charles succeeded to Burgundy, and that there, at Dôle, he struck money of very low value under his name.[45] Rabelais exploits this cheap money and the unpopularity of the Emperor to ironic purpose when he donates to the Sybille de Panzoust what he calls "carolus nouvellement forgéz." [46]

A genuinely valuable coin was the *henricus* or *henri d'or*, a handsome gold piece issued by Henry II in 1549. It occupies a very distinct place in French numismatics for it is the first French coin to bear a date.[47] Rabelais, doubtless as a gesture of obeissance to his monarch, has Panurge display a purseful of the freshly minted coins when he begins his bargaining for sheep with Dindenault.[48]

The *philippus* is a coin that has caused editors and critics to go rather far afield in their attempts to identify it. Contrary to expectation, the name of the coin refers neither to money issued by Philip of Macedon,[49] nor is it a general sixteenth-century term for money minted in gold.[50] The *philippus* is actually the same as the ridde issued by the Duke of Burgundy in 1433, whose coinage, as we have seen, was accepted tender in France even after the monetary reforms of 1436. One example of its use in Rabelais is found in the chapter dealing with Grandgousier's attempt to buy peace during the Picrocholian Wars. In addition to returning many cakes to replace those taken forcibly by the enemy, he orders that Marquet is to receive "sept cens mille et troys philippus pour payer les barbiers qui l'auroient pensé."

Coins that are essentially provincial are the *pite* and the *patac*. The former is usually identified with the district of Poitiers, its designation being derived from the Latin form of that name. Ste.-Palaye describes it as "petite monnaie de la valeur de la moitié d'une maille."[51] As a consequence of its infiniteisimal value, Rabelais' use of it to indicate the price of experimenting with roast eggs becomes particularly absurd when he stipulates that the cost of this culinary adventure would be "la douzaine partie d'une pithe."[52]

The problem of identifying the *patac* has caused some disagreement among critics. Sainéan claims that it is a Gascon version of the word *pithe*,[53] but Jacques Boulenger suggests that it is the same as *patars*, "monnaie picarde valant 5 liard."[54] Ste.-Palaye calls it simply "petite monnaie provençale." It is, beyond any doubt, the *patac* of Perpignan and Marseille. (The *patard* is really a Flemish sou.)[55] The patac is mentioned by Friar John in his conversation with Panurge after his unsatisfactory interview with Her Trippa.

As might be expected from a man who enjoyed toying exuberantly with words, Rabelais was not content with confining his numismatics to coins that actually existed. On at least three occasions he created money of his own to serve a particular literary purpose. In speaking of the funds to be utilized in the construction of the Abbaye de Thélème, for example, he mentions, in addition to such usual currency as the *escuz au soleil*, a sum composed of *escus à l'estoille poussinière*.[56] *Poussinière*, in the sixteenth century, referred, of course, to the constellation of the Pléiade whose seven stars resembled in outline a chicken. The creation of this fanciful money adds a charming levity to an otherwise solemn moment.

Another type of fantastic currency is found in Book IV. After a grand banquet given by Homenaz for Pantagruel, the latter contributes a box of *doubles escuz au sabot*[57] for the upkeep of the church. In creating his mock currency, Rabelais observes the popular practice of characterizing coins by means of the regal or reverent symbols appearing on their surfaces— "la couronne," "la croisette," "la salamandre"—but chooses a particularly lowly object as the symbol borne by the coins he donates to the holy building. A similar ironic creation is found in the scene in which Pantagruel sends Gymnaste to the island of dogs with alms consisting of "dix-huict mille beaulx petiz demys escuz à la lanterne" for distribution among its hypocritical inhabitants.[58] The coin is aptly named: the *lanterne*, the sign of the spurious money, is, in its pretense of emulating the light the *soleil*, which is the sign of the genuine écu, as hypocritical as the citizens who receive it.

These, then, are the coins mentioned in Rabelais, and they are taken from ancient, medieval, and contemporary currencies; from royal tender and those of lowlier princes and the provinces; from among pieces that were *décriés*; and from among those that existed only in the imagination of the author. In their variety and the richness of their associations, they reflect the interests, and indicate the creative abilities, of Rabelais himself.

---

1. L. Sainéan, in his *La Langue de Rabelais* (Paris, 1922), I, 190, deals briefly with the coins. He did not have, however, the advantage of the considerable work which has been done in numismatics since his volumes appeared.

2. A. R. Frey, *Dictionary of Numismatic Names* (New York, 1947), p. 224.

3. Rabelais, *Oeuvres Complètes*, texte établi et annoté par Jacques Boulenger (Paris, 1938), p. 168. Hereinafter cited as Rabelais.

4. Rabelais, p. 898.

5. Frey, *op. cit.*, p. 217; G. F. Hill, *Handbook of Greek and Roman Coins* (London, 1899), p. 47; H. Mattingly, *Coins of the Roman Empire in the British Museum* (London, 1923), I, lxx.

6. Frey, *op. cit.*, p. 235.

7. Rabelais, p. 581.

8. The editor of the Pléiade edition does not include the portion of the prologue which contains the mention of the sicle, contending that it is not the work of Rabelais and is to be found only in the edition of 1564. Sainéan places the citation, incorrectly, in Chapter XLII of Book V.

9. Frey, *op. cit.*, p. 218; *The Jewish Encyclopedia* (New York, 1905), II, 257.

10. See the author's article, "François Villon and His Monetary Bequest," *Speculum*, XXXIII (1958), 345.

11. Jean Chartier, *Chronique de Charles VII*, ed. Valley de Vouville (Paris, 1858), p. 29.

12. Frey, *op. cit.*, p. 8.

13. Rabelais, p. 439.

14. Frey, *op. cit.*, p. 208.

15. Rabelais, p. 711.

16. Sainéan, *op. cit.*, 191.

17. Frey, *op. cit.*, p. 160.

18. Rabelais, p. 171.

19. Frey, *op. cit.*, p. 72.

20. Rabelais, p. 157.

21. Frey, *op. cit.*, p. 85.

22. Rabelais, p. 267.

23. Frey, *op. cit.*, p. 238. Jean Lafaurie, *Les Monnaies des rois de France* (Paris, 1951), Vol. I, No. 632. The testons were struck in France throughout the sixteenth century.

24. Rabelais, p. 556.

25. Frey, *op. cit.*, p. 216. Frey also records the following citation from Tavernier's *Grand Seignior's Seraglio*: "The scherif otherwise called sequin or sultanin."

26. Rabelais, p. 251.

27. J. F. Bense, A *Dictionary of the Low-Dutch Element in the English Volcabulary* (Hague, 1939), p. 326; A. Dieudonné, *Manuel de numismatique française* (Paris, 1936), IV, 190.

28. Rabelais, p. 556.

29. A cross and the letters "ALF" appear on the reverse side.

30. *Diccionario de Historia de España* (Madrid, 1952), II, 359.

31. Rabelais, p. 373.

32. Sainéan, *op. cit.*, I, 194.

33. La Curne de Sainte-Palaye, *Dictionnaire historique de l'ancien langage François* (Paris, 1875), VIII, 310.

34. R. Cotgrave, A *Dictionary of the French and English Tongues* (Columbia, S. C., 1950).

35. Rabelais, p. 323.

36. Frey, *op. cit.*, p. 26; Lafaurie, *op. cit.*, No. 373. The later name was *guénar*.

37. Rabelais, p. 102; Lafaurie, *op. cit.*, Nos. 534, 536.

38. Frey, *op. cit.*, p. 75; Lafaurie, *op. cit.*, Nos. 524, 554.

39. Rabelais, p. 157.

40. Rabelais, p. 533; Lafaurie, *op. cit.*, No. 592. The escu bordelais had a poorer alloy.

41. Frey, *op. cit.*, p. 155; Lafaurie, *op. cit.*, No. 216.

42. Rabelais, p. 52.

43. Chamberlain and Rainfeld, *Coin Dictionary and Guide* (New York, 1960), p. 178; Lafaurie, *op. cit.*, No. 244. There was a *petit royal* first struck in 1290 (Lafaurie, *op. cit.*, No. 211).

44. Rabelais, p. 356.

45. Frey contends, *op. cit.*, p. 40, that the coin was first struck by Charles VIII, but Jean Chartier in his *Chronique de Charles VII* (p. 219) mentions it as one of the coins whose value was adjusted "a six deniers, lesquilz estoient a huit." It was more likely the *carolus* of the Emperor Charles V, which circulated in France as very base money. See Dieudonné, *op. cit.*, pp. 50, 211–13, 268, 297.

46. Rabelais, p. 410.

47. Frey, *op. cit.*, p. 108.

48. Rabelais, p. 578.

49. Sainéan, *op. cit.*, I, 193.

50. Rabelais, p. 117, n. 3.

51. Ste.-Palaye, *op. cit.*, VIII, 319; Dieudonné, *op. cit.*, p. 45.

52. Rabelais, p. 533.

53. Sainéan, *op. cit.*, p. 194.

54. Rabelais, p. 447, n. 5.

55. Ste.-Palaye, *op. cit.*, VIII, 221; Lafaurie, *op. cit.*, Nos. 552, 590.

56. Rabelais, p. 171.

57. Rabelais, p. 711.

58. Rabelais, p. 737.

Bibliography of
Alexander Herman Schutz

————————Kenneth R. Scholberg————————

Bibliography of A. H. Schutz

Books

Peasant Vocabulary in the Works of George Sand. ("University of Missouri Studies," Vol. II, Monograph I.) Columbia, Mo.: University of Missouri, 1927.

Poésies lyriques de Daude de Pradas. Toulouse: Edouard Privat & Cⁱᵉ, 1933.

Nos amis. New York: Farrar & Rinehart, Inc., 1940.

The Romance of Daude de Pradas, Called Dels Auzels Cassadors. Columbus, O.: Ohio State University Press, 1945.

Vernacular Books in Parisian Private Libraries of the Sixteenth Century, According to Notarial Inventories. Chapel Hill, N. C.: University of North Carolina Press, 1955.

The Sixteenth Century. (Critical Bibliography of French Literature, ed. D. C. Cabeen, Vol. II.) Syracuse, N. Y.: Syracuse University Press, 1956.

Books in Collaboration

With URBAN T. HOLMES. History of the French Language. New York: Farrar & Rinehart, Inc., 1938.

With URBAN T. HOLMES. *Source Book for the History of the French Language.* Columbus, O.: Hedrick, 1940.

With JEAN BOUTIÈRE. *Les Biographies des troubadours.* Toulouse: Edouard Privat & C¹ᵉ; Paris: Marcel Didier, 1950.

Articles

"Re- , ri- in the Divina Commedia," *Modern Philology,* XXII (1925), 210.

"The Nature of Charles Nodier's Philological Activity," *Studies in Philology,* XXIII (1926), 464.

"Catellus, caniculus," *Language,* III (1927), 6.

"Two Lexicographic Notes," *Language,* IV (1928), 31.

"Iter and Viaticum in French," *Studies in Philology,* XXVIII (1931), 513.

"A Preliminary Study of 'trobar e entendre,' An Expression in Medieval Aesthetics," *Romanic Review,* XXIII (1932), 129.

"The Group of the Dames des Roches in Sixteenth-Century Poitiers," *PMLA,* XLVIII (1933), 648.

"More on 'trobar e entendre,'" *Romanic Review,* XXVI (1935), 29.

"French 'bouse'—'fiente de vache,'" *Studies in Philology,* XXXIII (1936), 10.

"Three Provençal Terms of Falconry," *Modern Language Notes,* LI (1936), 175.

"Where Were the Provençal Vidas and Razos Written?", *Modern Philology,* XXXV (1938), 225.

"On Intermediate Linguistics," *Modern Language Journal,* XXII (1939), 489.

"Were the Vidas and Razos Read or Recited?", *Studies in Philology*, XXVI (1939), 565.

"A Note on the Localization of Daude de Pradas," *Speculum*, XV (1940), 478.

"Villon, Testament CXXXVIII," *PMLA*, LV (1940), 931.

"Auzels Cassadors, v. 2443 (tornar a ters)," *Modern Language Notes*, LVI (1941), 429.

"The Provençal Expression 'Pretz e valor,'" *Speculum*, XIX (1944), 488.

"The Name Lusignan in the Provençal Biographies," *Studies in Philology*, XLIII (1946), 1.

"Character Attributes in the Provençal Biographies," *Symposium*, I (1946), 119.

"Non-Lyric Provençal," in *A Critical Bibliography of French Literature*. ("The Medieval Period," ed. D. C. CABEEN, Vol. I.) Syracuse, N. Y.: Syracuse University Press, 1947. Enlarged edition, 1952.

"Ronsard's Sonnet XXXII and the Tradition of the Synthetic Lady," *Romance Philology*, I (1947), 125.

"Roland, v. 317," *Modern Language Notes*, LXII (1947), 456.

"The Lamentations of Matheolus and the Basic Tempo of Villon's Testament," *Studies in Philology*, XLVII (1950), 453.

"Gleanings from Parisian Private Libraries of the Early Renaissance," *Romance Philology*, V (1951), 25.

"Two Provençal Notes," *Philological Quarterly*, XXX (1951), 176.

"Vellutello's Commentary on the Trionfi d'Amore of Petrarch and Its Provençal Sources," *Italica*, XXVIII (1951), 104.

"History of the Language," in *A Critical Bibliography of French Literature*, ed. D. C. CABEEN, IV (1951), 43.

"La tradición cortesana en dos coplas de Juan Ruiz," *Nueva revista de filología hispánica*, VIII (1954), 63.

"Why Did Rabelais Satirize the Library of St. Victor?", *Modern Language Notes*, LXX (1955), 39.

"Did the Poets 'Feign' or 'Fashion'?", *Symposium*, XI (1957), 117.

"Joglar, borges, cavallier, dans les biographies provençales. Essai d'évaluation sémantique," *Mélanges de linguistique et de littérature romanes à la mémoire d'István Frank* (Saarbrücken, Universität des Saarlandes, 1957), p. 508.

"Some Provençal Words Indicating Knowledge," *Speculum*, XXXIII (1958), 508.

"Marcabru and Jehosaphat," *Romance Notes*, I (1959), 59.

"Pound as Provençalist," *Romance Notes*, III (1962), 1.

In addition, Professor Schutz has published important review articles that can be found in the following journals: *Books Abroad*, III (1929), 239; VI (1932), 448; *French Review*, XXVIII (1954–55), 87; *Language*, X (1934), 57; XI (1935), 47; XII (1936), 144; XXXIV (1958), 122; *Modern Language Journal*, XVII (1932–33), 475; *Modern Language Notes*, XL (1925), 50; LI (1936), 341, 342; LVII (1942), 316; LXVI (1951), 339; LXVIII (1953), 418; *Modern Philology*, XXVI (1928–29), 235; *Romance Philology*, III (1949–50), 204, 302; V (1951–52), 265; VII (1953–54), 92; *Romanic Review*, XLVII (1956), 43; *Speculum*, XIX (1944), 512; XXI (1946), 265; XXII (1947), 91; XXIII (1948), 339; *Word*, I (1945), 292.

www.ingramcontent.com/pod-product-compliance
Lightning Source LLC
Chambersburg PA
CBHW030131240426
43672CB00005B/102